Framing Ageing

Bloomsbury Studies in the Humanities, Ageing and Later Life

Series Editor
Kate de Medeiros

Bloomsbury Studies in the Humanities, Ageing and Later Life responds to the growing need for scholarship focused on age, identity and meaning in late life in a time of unprecedented longevity. For the first time in human history, there are more people in the world aged sixty years and over than under the age of five. In response, empirical gerontological research on how and why we age has seen exponential growth. An unintended consequence of this growth, however, has been an increasing chasm between the need to study age through generalizable data – the 'objective' – and the importance of understanding the human experience of growing old.

Bloomsbury Studies in the Humanities, Ageing and Later Life bridges this gap. The series creates a more intellectually diversified gerontology through the perspective of the humanities as well as other interpretive, non-empirical approaches that draw from humanities scholarship. Publishing monographs and edited collections, the series represents the most cutting edge research in the areas of humanistic gerontology and ageing.

Series editorial board:

Andrew Achenbaum, University of Houston, USA
Thomas Cole, University of Texas Health Science Center, USA
Chris Gilleard, University College London, UK
Ros Jennings, University of Gloucestershire, UK
Ulla Kriebernegg, University of Graz, Austria
Roberta Maierhofer, University of Graz, Austria
Wendy Martin, Brunel University, London, UK

Published titles

A Poetic Language of Ageing, edited by Oddgeir Synnes and Olga Lehmann
Age and Ageing in Contemporary Speculative and Science Fiction,
edited by Sarah Falcus and Maricel Oró-Piqueras
Ageing Masculinities, Alzheimer's and Dementia Narratives,
edited by Heike Hartung, Rüdiger Kunow and Matthew Sweney

Forthcoming titles

Ageing and Embodied Time in Modern Literature and Thought,
by Elizabeth Barry

Framing Ageing

*Interdisciplinary Perspectives for
Humanities and Social Sciences Research*

Edited by
Julia Langbein, Mary Cosgrove and Anne Fuchs

BLOOMSBURY ACADEMIC
LONDON • NEW YORK • OXFORD • NEW DELHI • SYDNEY

BLOOMSBURY ACADEMIC
Bloomsbury Publishing Plc, 50 Bedford Square, London, WC1B 3DP, UK
Bloomsbury Publishing Inc, 1359 Broadway, New York, NY 10018, USA
Bloomsbury Publishing Ireland, 29 Earlsfort Terrace, Dublin 2, D02 AY28, Ireland

BLOOMSBURY, BLOOMSBURY ACADEMIC and the Diana logo
are trademarks of Bloomsbury Publishing Plc

First published in Great Britain 2024
This paperback edition published 2026

Copyright © Julia Langbein, Mary Cosgrove and Anne Fuchs, 2024

The editors and contributors have asserted their right under the Copyright,
Designs and Patents Act, 1988, to be identified as the Authors of this work.

For legal purposes the Acknowledgements on p. xii constitute an
extension of this copyright page.

Series design by Rebecca Heselton.
Cover image: Mutation 2 (detail) by Jacob van der Beugel,
courtesy of the artist. Photograph by Gerrit Schreurs.

This work is published open access subject to a Creative Commons Attribution 4.0 licence
(CC BY 4.0, https://creativecommons.org/licenses/by/4.0/). You may re-use, distribute,
reproduce, and adapt this work in any medium, including for commercial purposes,
provided you give attribution to the copyright holder and the publisher, provide a link
to the Creative Commons licence, and indicate if changes have been made.

Bloomsbury Publishing Plc does not have any control over, or responsibility for,
any third-party websites referred to or in this book. All internet addresses given
in this book were correct at the time of going to press. The author and publisher
regret any inconvenience caused if addresses have changed or sites have ceased
to exist, but can accept no responsibility for any such changes.

A catalogue record for this book is available from the British Library.
Library of Congress Cataloging-in-Publication Data
Names: Langbein, Julia (Art historian), editor. | Cosgrove, Mary, editor. | Fuchs, Anne, editor.
Title: Framing ageing : interdisciplinary perspectives for humanities and social sciences
research / edited by Julia Langbein, Mary Cosgrove and Anne Fuchs.
Description: London ; New York : Bloomsbury Academic, 2024. |
Series: Bloomsbury studies in the humanities, ageing and later life |
Includes bibliographical references and index.
Identifiers: LCCN 2023030525 (print) | LCCN 2023030526 (ebook) |
ISBN 9781350341418 (hardback) | ISBN 9781350341456 (paperback) |
ISBN 9781350341425 (pdf) | ISBN 9781350341432 (ebook)
Subjects: LCSH: Older people. | Aging.
Classification: LCC HQ1060 .F736 2024 (print) | LCC HQ1060 (ebook) |
DDC 305.26—dc23/eng/20231019
LC record available at https://lccn.loc.gov/2023030525
LC ebook record available at https://lccn.loc.gov/2023030526

ISBN: HB: 978-1-3503-4141-8
PB: 978-1-3503-4145-6
ePDF: 978-1-3503-4142-5
eBook: 978-1-3503-4143-2

Series: Bloomsbury Studies in the Humanities, Ageing and Later Life

Typeset by Integra Software Services Pvt. Ltd.

For product safety related questions contact productsafety@bloomsbury.com.

To find out more about our authors and books visit www.bloomsbury.com
and sign up for our newsletters.

Contents

List of Illustrations		vii
Notes on Contributors		viii
Acknowledgements		xii

1	Introduction *Mary Cosgrove, Anne Fuchs and Julia Langbein*	1
2	Cultural gerontology: Recent developments and future challenges *Desmond O'Neill*	13
3	The concrete truth of healthy ageing: On the relevance and urgency of art *Robert Zwijnenberg*	23
4	The art of ageing: Finitude, vulnerability and opportunity in Hermann Kinder's *The Way of All Flesh* *Linda Shortt*	39
5	On old age and wisdom *Aleida Assmann*	53
6	Between Alice and the eagle: Dementia journeys and the final breath *Dana Walrath*	71
7	Happiness and ageing as performance and narrative in Jens Sparschuh's *Life Costs a Lot of Time* *Gillian Pye*	97
8	Gender, the politics of looking and the narration of old age: Elizabeth Strout's empathetic realism in *Olive, Again* *Anne Fuchs*	111
9	The end of love: An exploration of gender, sexuality and the double standard of ageing in later life through the fiction of Doris Lessing *Susan Pickard*	125
10	The meaning of midlife in Terézia Mora's Darius Kopp trilogy *Mary Cosgrove*	139
11	Unseen, unheard, untouched: *A view from the interior* *Ailbhe Smyth*	155
12	Views from the living room: Older people speak out on television about the Covid-19 pandemic *Helen Doherty*	167
13	Born old: Race, judgement and the limits of 'late style' *Julia Langbein*	181
14	Race, ethnicity, culture and later life: Problematic categorizations and unsatisfactory definitions *Moïse Roche, Claudia Cooper and Paul Higgs*	199

15 JR's *Wrinkles of the City* project: Representing global old age, 2008–2015 *David G. Troyansky* 215

16 Reframing LGBT+ ageing: Self, others and queer generations *Andrew King and Matthew Hall* 229

Index 242

Illustrations

1	Jacob van der Beugel, 'A Mutating Story'	24
2	Jacob van der Beugel, 'Mutation 2', 2019	24
3	Jacob van der Beugel, 'Mutation 2', 2019	25
4	Hermann Kinder, *Der Weg allen Fleisches* [*The Way of All Flesh*]	40
5	Hermann Kinder, *Der Weg allen Fleisches* [*The Way of All Flesh*]	40
6	Film stills from the documentary *Cocooned*, 2021	173
7	JR, *Wrinkles of the City*, Havana, 2012	220
8	JR, *Wrinkles of the City*, Los Angeles, 2012	222
9	JR, *Wrinkles of the City*, Shanghai, 2012	224

Contributors

Aleida Assmann is Emeritus Professor of English and Comparative Literature, University of Konstanz, Germany. She is the author of seminal books and articles on cultural memory, memory and forgetting/frames of memory that have been translated into twenty languages. Together with her husband Jan Assmann she was the recipient of the Balzan Prize in 2017 and the Peace Prize of the German book trade in 2018.

Claudia Cooper is Professor at Queen Mary University of London where she directs the Centre for Psychiatry and Mental Health. She is a consultant old age psychiatrist in East London NHS Foundation Trust memory services. She is Principal Investigator on the NIHR/ESRC APPLE-Tree programme (Active Prevention in People at risk of dementia: Lifestyle, bEhaviour change/Technology to REducE cognitive decline), investigating how lifestyle and behavioural change can prevent dementia in older people.

Mary Cosgrove is Professor in German at Trinity College Dublin where she is Director of Research in the School of Languages, Literatures and Cultural Studies. Her teaching, research and publications explore melancholia, depression and boredom in contemporary literature and culture, as well as Holocaust memory and cultural trauma. Working across the Neuro- and Medical Humanities, she has (co)curated public engagement cultural events on melancholia and depression, in Dublin and in Edinburgh. From 2016 to 2020 she was Germanic Editor of the international literary journal, *Modern Language Review*.

Helen Doherty holds a PhD in media and film education and history. She was Senior Lecturer at the Institute for Art, Design and Technology, Dublin, where she directed the MA in Broadcast Production. Her research includes the history of film education, the future of the film school and the politics of major art shows such as *Documenta*. Helen was a member of the jury for the Prix Europa Documentary Awards for television and radio in 2018/19 and chair of the jury for the Prix Europa Television Documentary award in 2020. As a committee member of the Republic of Ireland branch of the Royal Television Society, she actively promotes the cultural value of broadcast television.

Anne Fuchs is Professor of Modern German Literature and Culture and Director of the UCD Humanities Institute. She has published widely on modernist and contemporary literature, cultural memory, and time and temporality. Her latest monograph is *Precarious Times: Temporality and History in Modern German Culture* (2019). Recent co-edited volumes: with Ines Detmer, 'Ästhetische Eigenzeit in Contemporary Literature and Culture', *Oxford German Studies* (2017, vol. 46.3. and 46.4); with J. J. Long, *Time in German Literature and Culture, 1900–2015: Between Acceleration and Slowness* (2016).

Matthew Hall is a lecturer in Criminology and Sociology at the University of Surrey, UK and former Research Fellow on the NORFACE/Horizon 2020 project '*Comparing Intersectional Life Course Inequalities amongst LGBTQI+ Citizens in Four European Countries*' (CILIA-LGBTQI+). His current research covers areas from LGBTQ workplace inequalities and queer generational identities to hate crime and extremism. Matthew also currently leads an impact project exploring intergenerational exchange within LGBTQ+ communities.

Paul Higgs is Professor of the Sociology of Ageing in the UCL Faculty of Brain Sciences. His research interest is in the changing nature of contemporary later life. He edits the journal *Social Theory and Health* and has published widely in social gerontology and medical sociology. Professor Higgs is a fellow of both the UK Academy of Social Sciences and the Gerontological Society of America. In 2021 he received the British Society of Gerontology's 50th anniversary outstanding achievement award.

Andrew King is a professor of Sociology at the University of Surrey, UK and co-director of the 'Centre for Research on Ageing and Generations' (CRAG). He is an expert on LGBTQ+ ageing. His publications include *Older Lesbian, Gay and Bisexual Adults: Identities, Intersections and Institutions* (2016), *Older LGBT People: Minding the Knowledge Gaps* (2018) and *Intersections of Ageing, Gender and Sexualities: Multidisciplinary International Perspectives* (2019). Andrew currently edits the journals *Ageing and Society* and *Sociology*.

Julia Langbein is a writer and art historian specializing in nineteenth-century visual culture. She was a postdoctoral research fellow at Trinity College Dublin from 2019 to 2022 and before that held a Junior Research Fellowship at Trinity College, Oxford. She is the author of *Laugh Lines: Caricaturing Painting in Nineteenth-Century France* (2022).

Desmond (Des) O'Neill is Professor of Geriatric Medicine and scholar in cultural gerontology and medical humanities at Trinity College Dublin. He is the co-lead of Medical and Health Humanities in Trinity College Dublin, and a former chair of the Humanities, Arts and Cultural Gerontology Advisory Panel of the Gerontological Society of America.

Susan Pickard is Professor of Sociology at the University of Liverpool and Director of the Centre for Ageing and the Life Course. Her research interests lie across the intersections of age studies, medical sociology and feminist theory. Her most recent books are *Age Studies* (2016) and *Age, Gender and Sexuality through the Life Course: The Girl in Time* (2018). She is currently leading a three-year ESRC-funded project on Frailty and Ethnicity and finishing a book on Simone de Beauvoir's contribution to gender and age theory to be published in 2024.

Gillian Pye is Associate Professor in the School of Languages, Cultures and Linguistics at University College Dublin. She has published on twentieth-century German prose literature and drama, with special emphasis on theories of comedy, materiality and the built environment, pop and consumer culture, and memory and identity in global consumer capitalism. Her most recent research draws on performative concepts of happiness and well-being, engaging critically with the Western 'happiness industry' and asking in what ways and to what ends are constructs of happiness circulated and deployed in contemporary literature.

Moïse Roche is a researcher in dementia, ageing and ethnicity at University College London (UCL) in the Division of Psychiatry in UK. He is also a Senior Atlantic Fellow for Equity in Brain Health at the Global Brain Health Institute (GBHI) and a Visiting Research Fellow at Trinity College Dublin, Institute of Neuroscience and School of Psychology. His interest and involvement in the promotion of ageing well and older adults' health and well-being include advocating for diversity and inclusion in research and knowledge, ensuring that output and information are relevant and applicable to a wider audience.

Linda Shortt is Lecturer in Modern Languages and Head of German at Maynooth University. A specialist of memory studies, migration and border studies, and the theory and representation of intergenerational trauma, Shortt is the author of the monograph *German Narratives of Belonging: Writing*

Generation and Place in the Twenty-First Century (2015) and has published articles on the European refugee crisis and concepts of borders and bordering.

Ailbhe Smyth is a feminist, LGBTIQ and socialist activist. The founding head of Women's Studies at UCD, she has published widely on feminism, sexuality and politics. In Ireland Ailbhe played a leading role in the Marriage Equality referendum and was Co-Director of the *Together for Yes* abortion referendum campaign. She is a Trustee of *Age Action Ireland*, and Chair of Women's Aid. In 2019, she was included in *Time Magazine*'s '100 Most Influential People' list.

David G. Troyansky is Professor of History at Brooklyn College and the Graduate Center of the City University of New York. He is the author of *Old Age in the Old Regime: Image and Experience in Eighteenth-Century France* (1989), *Aging in World History* (2016), and *Entitlement and Complaint: Ending Careers and Reviewing Lives in Post-Revolutionary France* (2023). He is co-editing a six-volume *Cultural History of Old Age* for Bloomsbury Academic.

Dana Walrath has published award-winning works blending creative writing, comics, art and anthropology. Her publications include *Aliceheimer's*, a graphic memoir about her mother's dementia journey; *Like Water on Stone*, a verse novel about the Armenian genocide; *The Book of Genocides*, an interactive installation that uses artists books to counter genocide; and a contribution to *Menopause: A Comic Treatment*. A Fulbright Scholar and Atlantic Fellow, her illustrated essays, comics and poetry have appeared in *The Lancet, The Irish Times, Slate, Foreign Policy* and on public radio. She recently completed a libretto for *Aliceheimer's: A Chamber Opera*.

Robert Zwijnenberg is Emeritus Professor of Art and Science Interactions at Leiden University, the Netherlands. In research and publications, he focuses in particular on the unique role that contemporary art can play in the academic and public debate on the ethical, social, political, legal and cultural implications of biotechnological and biomedical innovations. Zwijnenberg explores new forms of productive collaboration between the humanities, the life sciences and the arts.

Acknowledgements

This volume is the result of a Wellcome Trust–funded project on 'Framing Ageing' (2020–2021) which created an international network of social scientists, medical practitioners, humanities scholars and artists from the US, the UK, Ireland and continental Europe. Originally planned around two academic conferences, the outbreak of the Covid-19 pandemic in 2020 radically changed our plans; instead of meeting face-to-face, we met online over two years and recorded and published our webinars on a dedicated website (see: https://framingageing.ucd.ie/). The Wellcome Trust generously funded this project and supported it throughout the pandemic. Our first thanks are extended to the Wellcome Trust.

The transition to a series of online webinars required special administrative support from the UCD Humanities Institute team; we thank Valerie Norton and Ricki Schoen who organized and provided essential technical and administrative support.

The Open Access publication of this volume was made possible by a generous publication grant from the UCD Humanities Institute. In order to make the volume accessible, all foreign language quotations have been translated into English. Unless otherwise stated all translations were made by the author of the respective chapter.

We would like to extend special thanks to Jacob van der Beugel for giving us permission to use reproductions of his art installation 'A Mutating Story' on the cover of this book as well as in Chapter 3. We also want to thank Ken Wardrop for his interview with Helen Doherty and still images from his documentary film *Cocooned*. Weissbooks Verlag gave us permission to reproduce two images from Hermann Kinder's *Der Weg allen Fleisches*.

Mary Cosgrove, Anne Fuchs, Julia Langbein,
Dublin and Paris, 27 January 2023

1

Introduction

Mary Cosgrove, Anne Fuchs and Julia Langbein

The current volume is the outcome of an interdisciplinary dialogue, funded by the Wellcome Trust and jointly organized by colleagues from University College Dublin and Trinity College Dublin, between March 2020 and December 2021. Originally designed around two in-person conferences, the Covid-19 pandemic and the ensuing period of lockdowns and travel restrictions forced the organizers to rethink and redesign the project: instead of running two conventional conferences with formal papers, we rolled out a series of webinars that were open to the public and have been preserved and made accessible in videos and podcasts.[1] What appeared at first as a major challenge in fact became an opportunity for a sustained conversation across space and time and across subject boundaries.

Framing Ageing, as the title suggests, aimed not just to bring together established and emerging scholars from the humanities, social sciences and medical sciences, but to ask those scholars to examine their own intellectual frameworks. To be sure, ageing is a biological and ontological fact resulting in death; but it is also a sociocultural process that is shaped by class, income, ethnicity, gender, geography and historical context as well as society's negotiations of these categories. What assumptions, received ideas, inherited ideologies – blind spots – might we be able, in coming together, to flush out and examine? In such an undertaking, we were hoping to find both new links between disciplines – perhaps to clear away unnecessary barriers – and also to realize where disciplinary boundaries were insurmountable, where they exist for good reason.

---

[1] Podcasts, videos and other materials are available at https://framingageing.ucd.ie/podcasts/.

Over the past thirty years the subject of old age has been a rich site for interdisciplinary scholarship, as Desmond O'Neill traces in the preface to this volume. Exemplary texts edited by, for example, Thomas Cole, David van Tassel and Robert Kastenbaum (1992), Pat Thane (2005), Julia Twigg and Wendy Martin (2015) have defined ageing studies and cultural gerontology as intersecting fields, requiring new forms of expertise and collaboration. During the same period, in some fields, the institutional requirements for funded research have prioritized interdisciplinary projects with a strong societal focus.[2] But this trend comes with major challenges. As Oughten and Bracken argue, epistemologies within established disciplines are often shared and can therefore remain implicit (2009).[3] For example, despite extremely divergent approaches to the study of history, historians share archival practices and standards of what constitutes historical fact and evidence. Interdisciplinary collaboration between the sciences, social sciences and humanities requires much more complex and explicit negotiations about research practices, methods, terminologies and contexts (Bracken and Oughten 2006). In this vein, our project participants brought to the discussion not only very different research methodologies but also differing values, interests and frames.

Of course this project itself had to be reframed in the light of Covid-19. As the pandemic unfolded, it revealed broken institutional care systems, pervasive and consequential racial and economic inequalities of ageing, and breakdowns in academic, medical and policy communication around older people. It was more than ever essential to question our own vocabularies in a dialogic process, to see where and how we might better connect. This is not a volume *about* Covid; the majority of our chapters do not take on the subject of the pandemic directly. However, the context of the unfolding pandemic influenced our thinking, and particularly led to a shared emphasis on *visibility*.

Before the Covid pandemic, cultural policymakers and scholars alike regularly described a visibility crisis of old age, a consistent erasure or repression of images of older people from public view. In 2019, a report of the AARP (the former American Association of Retired Persons) which analysed over 1,000 randomly selected marketing images in the US showed that only 15 per cent

---

[2] A good example of this trend is the EU Horizon Europe programme with its three main pillars: 1) excellent science, 2) global challenges and industrial competitiveness, 3) and innovative Europe. See: https://horizoneurope.ie (accessed 5 January 2023).
[3] An example of such implicit methodological understanding would be divergent interpretations of a work of literature: even though the interpretive frames can be very different, literary criticism shares an academic register and certain assumptions about what counts as evidence.

of media images represented people over 50, and if older people were shown at all, they were mainly portrayed in domestic settings, often in passive postures and in the company of a partner or care assistant (Hsu 2019). If the field of ageing studies has been a wonderfully progressive space for interdisciplinarity, the Covid-19 crisis made us realize how urgent the problems of old-age visibility were, how urgent the need for compelling new thinking and new ideas about ageing: socially, culturally, economically, methodologically. Indeed, the invisibility of older people in methods of contemporary data collection was cited as a direct cause of their excess deaths from Covid-19 (United Nations Executive Summary, Policy Brief 2020: 4).

Our volume, then, takes on problems of visibility, not only with a range of analyses of visual material including film, photography and fine art, but by considering how our disciplinary framing creates problems of visibility. Co-edited by an art historian and two literary scholars with a shared interest in memory, *Framing Ageing* examines the complexity of old age from a range of disciplinary angles including art history, film and visual studies, literary studies, philosophy, empirical sociology and gerontology. To reflect on ageing as a multifaceted experience the volume also includes different types of contributions: besides formal academic scholarship, there is a self-reflexive autobiographical piece by Ailbhe Smyth, the Irish feminist campaigner and political activist, who wrote about living through the Covid-19 pandemic and the detrimental effects of the lockdowns. We also include a free-standing comic by Dana Walrath, *Between Alice and the Eagle*, which shares a title with the second book, currently in progress, of her award-winning *Aliceheimer's* graphic memoir series. The first memoir, *Aliceheimer's: Alzheimer's Through the Looking Glass* (2016) uses the comic medium's imaginary, visual and verbal possibilities to immerse the reader in Walrath's experience of her mother's Alzheimer's disease and her death.

Our volume is intended to serve as a gateway to scholars in the humanities and social sciences who would like to approach the topic of ageing as students and researchers. The chapters are self-aware about the chosen approaches: disciplinary methodologies illuminate central issues from a variety of complementary perspectives without cumbersome literature reviews or unnecessary jargon. Given the disciplinary breadth, for coherence the volume takes Western societies as its primary focus. However, within that focus, chapters engage deeply with problems of race, gender and inequality.

'Successful ageing' became a socially endorsed goal from the late 1990s onwards when the idea was first introduced and later elaborated by Rowe and Kahn (1997, 1998, 2015). The concept was symptomatic of the extreme individualism promoted in neoliberal Western societies: it turned ageing into a competition of sorts with little regard to the relational and, indeed, societal dimensions of ageing that are shaped by education, income, class, gender and ethnicity. Popular publications in this domain reflect a 'can do' ethos that appeals to a self-motivating readership (Olien 2017; Robertson 2020; Dorling 2022). We do not claim to challenge ideas like 'successful ageing' (see Lamb, Robbins-Ruszowski and Corwin 2017; Berridge and Martinson 2017) for the first time, but rather, to show and critique the ideological underpinnings of such concepts, while providing a critical vocabulary that is mobile across disciplines and accessible for humanities and social sciences researchers new to the field. The field of ageing studies is complex and contested: entire volumes have been written to map the differences between 'medical humanities', 'cultural gerontology', 'critical gerontology' and so on (see O'Neill in this volume). Our concern is not to get bogged down in those debates internal to gerontology or medical humanities, but rather to welcome and inform scholars new to ageing studies from across the social sciences and the humanities.

The volume opens with O'Neill's broad survey of the relatively recent transatlantic fields of cultural gerontology and medical humanities research. O'Neill, a medical doctor who has been working in and across gerontology for decades, traces the emergence of interdisciplinary enquiry from the 1960s on, focusing on scholarly associations, committees, networks, collaborations and landmark publications. As such, this overview provides useful orientation for newcomers to the field of cultural gerontology.

Robert Zwijnenberg's chapter, 'The concrete truth of healthy ageing: On the relevance and urgency of art', asks an important, even uncomfortable question: How can humanities scholars prevent their perspective on ageing from being implicitly framed by commercialized biomedical conceptions of health and old age? Drawing on Deleuze's notion of the 'tremor', Zwijnenberg argues that allowing one's self to be shaken, confronted and shocked by art can open a zone of contemplation and consideration parallel to, but uncorrupted by, the commercial imperatives of biomedicine. Zwijnenberg uses the example of his own encounters with works by the London-based sculptor Jacob van der Beugel (b. 1978), sculptures in which medical abstractions like 'DNA' find form in organic material like clay and visibly decay with time. With attention to his own vulnerability as spectator, Zwijnenberg describes how van der Beugel's works create shocks – not merely surface surprises, but Deleuzian 'tremors' which have the power to 'violently shake a discipline' and dislodge authoritative or dominant narratives.

Continuing Zwijnenberg's theme of resistance to biomedical binaries about health and wellness, in her contribution on the literary scholar and German-language author Hermann Kinder (1944–2021), Linda Shortt discusses the author's very striking autobiographical account of severe illness and incapacitation in his later years. Kinder's *The Way of All Flesh* (2014) documents the physical and psychological experience of ageing, physical decline and vulnerability in a register that eschews both the successful ageing paradigm and the decline narrative. Shortt shows that, by adopting a laconic but always empathetic narrative style that is lined by humour, Kinder manages a 'tightrope walk between inside and outside, intimacy and distance, the mundane and the dramatic'. As he experiences extreme physical decline, the author reflects on his own ableism and against assumptions about the human body. Kinder's account is complemented by thirteen drawings that, in graphic detail, make visible the body's extreme vulnerability. By employing a grotesque style in the manner of 1920s German art, Kinder foregrounds the physical signs of decline which are normally pushed out of sight: the depiction of his amputated foot stump, of bodily excretions, internal organs and genitals, etc., challenge the societal and structural exclusion of the disabled body. Rather than promoting the decline narrative of ageing, these deliberately unflattering images accentuate what Kinder calls 'the liberating messiness' of ageing and sickness. As Shortt argues, the self inhabiting the damaged body that Kinder portrays is resilient and capable of mobilizing humour and wisdom in the face of death.

In her contribution to the volume, the literary and cultural critic Aleida Assmann, an expert on cultural memory, makes the case for reinstating the age-old concept of wisdom. Reflecting on previous work on wisdom at the University of Bielefeld in the late 1970s, she relates that when the research group attempted to rediscover wisdom as a premodern regime of knowledge they encountered methodological problems, precisely because wisdom explodes disciplinary boundaries. Wisdom is, Assmann argues, a particular type of knowledge: cross-cultural, embodied and engendered. Assmann also shows how her own understanding of wisdom was hugely enhanced by a collaboration with the lifespan psychologists Paul and Margaret Baltes, whose experimental research discovered cognitive learning capacity among older people. Wisdom thus emerges in Assmann's contribution not merely as a theme or value but as a 'mental and cultural frame'.

Dana Walrath's comic 'Between Alice and the Eagle' reframes dementia through the medium of graphic storytelling. From the perspective of the artist-anthropologist, Walrath asserts that science is not the only way to understand sickness and health. In any case, medicine is not just science for the artist-anthropologist; rather, it is a collection of beliefs and practices historically embedded in systemic inequities of race, wealth and power that continue into the present. First, Walrath's combination of visual and verbal texts allows for nonlinear, multilayered storytelling, the kind we need to capture the complexity of sickness and health, life and death, the losses and gains of dementia. Second, the interplay of the visual and verbal makes up for memory loss – comics are accessible for those with dementia, as Walrath discovered when her mother, Alice, who lived with dementia for twenty years, came to live with her. Graphic storytelling is thus empowered to support those with dementia and their caregivers. Comics in fact help us reframe dementia as a different way of being, a window onto another reality, where people living with dementia can be our teachers.[4] In this vein, Alice inspired Walrath to think of how to 'detoxify dementia' – how to imagine it, and ourselves, from a global perspective and with reference to our ancestry, in flight, through an eagle's eye. In Walrath's 'Between Alice and the Eagle', detoxifying dementia goes hand in hand with the imperative for global equity.

Gillian Pye's chapter approaches the topic of ageing from the perspective of affect studies. Debating the distinction between hedonic happiness as pleasure on the one hand and eudaemonic happiness as a meaningful life on the other, she explores the opportunities and limitations of employing narrative methodologies for well-being in old age to then outline an alternative performative approach, which is informed by Sarah Ahmed's understanding of affect as a cultural and political performance which often aligns with power structures (Ahmed 2004). The redefinition of happiness as an effective disciplinary tool provides the methodological frame for the ensuing analysis of ageing in post-unification Germany. Pye uses East German writer Jens Sparschuh's comic novel *Life Costs a Lot of Time* (2018) as a case study of a counter-narrative that not only abandons the decline and progress models of ageing but, importantly, challenges the Western idea that well-being and happiness are about the optimization of the self.

Anne Fuchs' chapter on Elizabeth Strout's novel *Olive, Again* also foregrounds the power of literary narrative to provide a counter-cultural critique of normative ageing discourses that promote 'able-ism' and self-optimization. Fuchs examines the character Olive Kitteridge's transition

---

[4] See Walrath's TEDx talk, 'Comics, Medicine and Memory'. Available at: https://www.youtube.com/watch?v=Nc67EVhuftg (accessed 6 January 2023).

from the Third to Fourth Age, and her analysis emphasizes how the theme of friendship introduces an alternative perspective on the experience of the Fourth Age. This alternative angle hinges on the deconstruction of the male gaze that renders women invisible after a certain age. In Olive, Again, women also adopt the male gaze, erasing and emasculating older men. Strout's account of ageing thus goes further than the horror and shame normally associated with the Fourth Age; while it includes difficult experiences coloured by complicated attitudes and stereotyping, the novel's perspective on the everydayness of older people, the complexity and alternativeness of their daily lives, including love, companionship and friendship, ultimately works against the abject view of the Fourth Age. The text's multi-perspectival narrative structure – Fuchs calls this 'empathetic realism' – facilitates this process of critical discernment.

Sociologist Susan Pickard, like Fuchs, finds in literary fiction specific capacities for reframing gender and ageing. Pickard takes up a series of novels by Doris Lessing in order to examine the double standard of ageing for women. Picard's chapter concerns protagonists at different life stages who were socialized in feminism and saw themselves as 'liberated' but for whom the end of love in later life presents itself as a gateway to old age. They realize that sexual liberation may in fact be a misplaced notion of freedom – yet another patriarchal myth. While it goes against mainstream sociology, tracing this phenomenon via Lessing's literary corpus makes good sense, Pickard argues: the novels capture different times, life stages and ages. Literature as a primary corpus thus enables a rich and textured understanding of the life course and the nuances of the double standard of ageing, an 'imaginative economy' that is imposed from without, to be sure, but that also works powerfully from within the individual.

Mary Cosgrove's chapter focuses on the representation of middle age in a landmark literary trilogy by the Hungarian-German author Terézia Mora. Exploring the complex depiction of midlife across the three novels, Cosgrove shows how Mora hones in on the de-institutionalization of the life course in the neoliberal economy. The trilogy interweaves the story of a white middle-aged male IT specialist, who prospered during the boom years of the 1990s and idealizes the freedom of the untethered global market, with his downfall in the aftermath of the financial crash of 2008. Even though the work tracks the downward trajectory of its protagonist across seven years, it also challenges and overturns the narrative schema of the age-decline narrative. Mora sends her character, through this phase of losses, on an extended journey of self-discovery which, over time, produces what Cosgrove terms a new form of 'careful optimism' rooted in experience, care for the other, friendship and a socially embedded resilience. Like Pickard, Fuchs and Pye, Cosgrove demonstrates the contribution of fiction to a deeper understanding of the ageing process: complex narrative forms can capture nuances of the ageing process, in particular the subjective navigation and uneven experiences of ageing in different social settings.

In her autobiographical and deeply personal chapter the Irish feminist Ailbhe Smyth offers the reader 'a view from the interior' to communicate the raw experience of isolation during the Covid-19 lockdowns. Reflecting on the absence of human touch over a prolonged period of time, Smyth highlights the hugely detrimental effects of isolation, the loss of familiar routines, the absence of visits and lack of activities as a result of enforced confinement. In Ireland the National Public Health Emergency Team (NPHET) had no members over the age of 70: NPHET exhorted people over 70 to 'cocoon', that is, not to leave their homes and have minimal or no interaction with other people, regardless of varying levels of fitness, health and circumstances. For Smyth the patronizing connotations of 'cocooning' reflects 'a dinosauric view of older people as frail, vulnerable and dependent'. In a coda written in the autumn of 2022, Smyth reflects on the TILDA report 'Altered lives in a time of crisis: The impact of Covid-19 pandemic on the lives of older adults in Ireland' (Ward, O'Mahoney and Kenny 2021), the findings of which echoed her own experience of loss and loneliness alongside stoicism and resilience. However, the remarkable coping strategies of so many older people must not eclipse the responsibility of the decision-makers who adopted a 'one-size fits all' strategy that especially failed residents of care homes. As a counter-model to the neutral tone of the clinical researcher, Smyth writes in the engaging style of a lifelong activist: in so doing she solicits an affective and intellectual response to the social dimension of ageing.

Helen Doherty's chapter on Ken Wardrop's TV documentary film *Cocooned*, which follows the lived experiences of the same 70+ group of citizens in Ireland during the pandemic, also takes issue with the term 'cocooning'. Doherty highlights how Wardrop, observing social distancing regulations, interviewed and filmed older people from outside their homes. He captured these people on camera by filming them looking out of their windows – poignant interfaces between the cocoon and the world outside. She also considers the attention Wardrop pays to different individuals' voices, showing how his careful and empathetic approach rendered audible the sharp critical perspective of this age group on government policy and their keen awareness of being both patronized and prematurely aged by cocooning. Doherty concludes that Wardrop's aesthetic approach framed older people in a way that gave them a voice and allowed them to be seen, crucially within their individual 'cocoons'. In this way, *Cocooned* demonstrates the power of public service broadcasting to be both political and empathetic: it portrays the agency of older people, not their purported passivity and helplessness.

With a focus on race, Julia Langbein's chapter takes up the issue of the invisibility of Black artists as ageing subjects in studies of 'late style' or, more recently, 'old-age creativity'. Her analysis of 'late style' shows how this supposedly neutral term smuggles in a historical bias against Black artists, rendering them invisible in studies of old-age artists. 'Late style' – an art-historical term with roots in the nineteenth century – originally evolved to move away from ideas of old-age decline toward the possibility of exceptional creativity in older age. While this may seem a worthy aim, historically and still today, the corpus of artists considered as 'late stylists' has been near-comprehensively white and male. In contrast to the exclusionary habits of most 'late style' studies, Langbein makes a case for Edward Said's concept of 'late style' as untimely and linked to the bodily, lived experience of ageing – that is, linked to differences beyond and more complex than the category of exceptional creativity.

In a similar vein but from a different disciplinary angle, Moïse Roche's, Claudia Cooper's and Paul Higgs' co-authored chapter examines how well-intentioned terminology in fact puts a limiting, blinding frame on the field of data that scholars may consider. The authors analyse the proliferation of ethnic and racial terms and acronyms in gerontological research, questioning the appropriateness of this language by highlighting the unscientific basis of the categories of race and ethnicity. The chapter tracks how such problematic ethnic labels influence research, both quantitative and qualitative, and shape its findings, producing a skewed picture of dementia in different minority groups. It also raises the issue of the exclusion of minoritized groups from any say in the conceptualization of the research conducted on them. The chapter concludes with the recommendation that the rare and always specific use of race and ethnicity should be accompanied by granular information about a subject's or group's socioeconomic background and other demographic information.

Historian David Troyansky analyses the artist JR's *Wrinkles of the City* project (2008–2015), a long-term, multi-city installation in which the artist interviewed older people, photographed them and then plastered close-cropped portraits of their faces over the walls of the fast-changing cities where they lived – including Cartagena, Havana, LA, and Shanghai. Troyansky traces through this project a parallel between bodies that are usually invisible (those of non-elite older people) and historical processes that grind away unseen, like gentrification and globalization. As Kavita Sivaramakrishnan makes clear in medical, social-scientific and policy contexts, the idea of uniform ageing derives from a particularly Western model and puts populations that don't fit its model in danger (Sivaramakrishnan 2018). Troyansky sees in *Wrinkles of the City*, with its attention to difference and specificity, a critique of an abstract vision of 'global ageing'. Troyansky, who has worked primarily as a social historian in textual and documentary archives, also reflects in this chapter on the dual impact of JR's visual interventions in the public space and the personal narrative testimonies published elsewhere. He describes *Wrinkles of the City* as a bridge between an intimate sociology of private experience and a confrontation with public memory.

In 'Reframing LGBT+ ageing: Self, others and queer generations,' Andrew King and Matthew Hall elaborate a sociological and critical idea of 'reframing' that, they argue, is particularly important to understanding LGBT+ experiences of old age. King and Hall take sociologist Erving Goffman's 1974 *Frame Analysis* as a point of departure, defining 'frames' as 'schemes of interpretation that people use in everyday life'. Drawing on poststructuralist and Queer theory, King and Hall emphasize the potential for individuals to subvert and resist dominant frames. In other words, tacit rules and norms guide but do not determine decision-making and behaviour, leaving room for individuals to 'reframe' their own experience of old age. For King and Hall, a cis-heteronormative frame pervasively shapes cultural and policy expectations of health, housing and social care, which makes 'reframing' a particularly key concept in the understanding of LGBT+ old age. King and Hall ground their analysis of 'reframing' in specific cases drawn from recent research, often revealing the deep interconnectedness of private and public frames, of the possibilities of LGBT+ ageing in relation to wider historical and generational shifts.

With King and Hall's chapter, *Framing Ageing* ends with a meditation on the very idea of framing, reflecting on ideas that have been crucial throughout the volume, including problems of visibility; the importance of 'the everyday' as a maker of meaning and source of data; narrative structure and its relation to subjective experience; the subversion of limiting biomedical models; methods for attending to difference, inequity and specificity in approaches to ageing; and possibilities of and strategies for fundamental shifts in our conception of old age, across disciplines.

Bibliography

Ahmed, Sarah (2004), *The Cultural Politics of Emotion*, Edinburgh: Edinburgh University Press.

Bracken, Louise and Elizabeth Oughten (2006), '"What do you mean?" The Importance of Language in Developing Interdisciplinary Research', *Transactions of British Geographers*, ns 31: 371–82.

Cole, T. R., D. van Tassel and R. Kastenbaum, eds (1992), *Handbook of the Humanities and Aging*, New York: Springer.

'Framing Ageing Podcasts'. Available at: https://framingageing.ucd.ie/podcasts/ (accessed 26 December 2023).

Goffman, Erwin (1974), *Frame Analysis: An Essay on the Organization of Experience*, Harmondsworth: Penguin.

Oughten, Elizabeth and Louise Bracken (2009), 'Interdisciplinary Research: Framing and Reframing', *Area*, 41(4): 385–94.

Sivaramakrishnan, K. (2018), *As the World Ages: Rethinking a Demographic Crisis*, Cambridge, MA: Harvard University Press.

Thane, Pat, ed. (2005), *The Long History of Old Age*, London: Thames & Hudson.

Twigg, Julia and Wendy Martin, eds (2015), *Routledge Handbook of Cultural Gerontology*, London: Routledge.

United Nations Executive Summary (2020), *Policy Brief: The Impact of Covid-19 on Older Persons*. Available at: https://www.un.org/development/desa/ageing/wp-content/uploads/sites/24/2020/05/COVID-Older-persons.pdf (accessed 21 November 2023).

Walrath, D. (2016), *Aliceheimer's: Alzheimer's Through the Looking Glass*, University Park: Penn State University Press.

Ward, M., P. O'Mahoney and R. A. Kenny, eds (2021), 'Altered Lives in a Time of Crisis: The Impact of the Covid-19 Pandemic on the Lives of Older Adults in Ireland', *The Irish Longitudinal Study on Ageing* (TILDA). Trinity College Dublin. Available at: https://www.doi.org/10.38018/TildaRe.2021-01

Further reading

Berridge, C. W. and M. Martinson (2017/18), 'Valuing Old Age without Leveraging Ableism', *Generations: Journal of the American Society on Ageing*, 41(1): 83–91.

Dorling, Lynne (2022), *Ageing Rewired: How to Flourish in Later Life*, Market Harborough: Matador.

Hsu, Tiffany (2019), 'Older People are Ignored and Distorted in Ageist Marketing, Report Finds', *The New York Times*, 23 September. Available at: https://www.nytimes.com/2019/09/23/business/ageism-advertising-aarp.html (accessed 28 November 2022).

Lamb, S., J. Robbins-Ruszowski and A. I. Corwin (2017), 'Introduction: Successful Ageing as a Twenty-first-Century Obsession', in S. Lamb, J. Robbins-Ruszowski and A. I. Corwin (eds), *Successful Ageing as a Contemporary Obsession – Global Perspectives*, 1–23, New Brunswick, NJ: Rutgers University Press.

Olien, Darin (2017), *Superlife: The Five Simple Fixes that Make You Healthy, Fit and Eternally Awesome*, New York: Harper Wave.

Robertson, Guy (2020), *The Ten Steps of Positive Ageing: A Handbook for Personal Change in Later Life*, London and Oxford: Green Tree.

Rowe, J. W. and R. L. Kahn (1997), 'Successful Ageing', *The Gerontologist*, 37(4): 433–40.

Rowe, J. W. and R. L. Kahn (1998), *Successful Ageing*, New York: Pantheon Books.

Rowe, J. W. and R. L. Kahn (2015), 'Successful Ageing 2.0: Conceptual Expansions for the 21st Century', *The Journals for Gerontology, Series B: Psychological Sciences and Social Sciences*, 70(4): 593–96.

2

Cultural gerontology: Recent developments and future challenges

Desmond O'Neill

What is gerontology?

Gerontology, the collection of disciplines engaged in the study of ageing, is less than a century old as a defined field, although elements of scholarly focus on ageing can be recognized over millennia across many cultures (Gruman 1957; Mulley 2012). A dynamic and rapidly evolving area of scholarship, gerontology is traditionally divided into a number of pillars: sociology of ageing, psychology, biology of ageing, and health and ageing. Health and ageing encompasses a range of disciplines, most notably geriatric medicine, psychiatry of old age (also known as geropsychiatry) and gerontological nursing.

Those disciplines directly responsible for health represent the gerontologists who are most likely to be in daily contact with older people. Therein lies a potential vulnerability in that this exposure is nearly always to those with age-related disease and disability, and may render the clinicians prone to unconsciously adopting the failure model of ageing, i.e. ageing characterized by the losses of age-related disease and disability and agnostic of the growth and positivities (Kalish 1979). For this reason I have argued that the enterprise of specialist health care for older people needs to engage with the broader fields of gerontology to keep a perspective on the wider context of ageing (O'Neill 2012).

Humanities and arts

From the earliest emergence of gerontology as a discipline, it has been recognized that perspectives on ageing from the humanities, arts and cultural gerontology enrich clinical understanding of ageing and the life course. For example, the first issue of the official journal of the Gerontological Society of America (GSA) featured a paper on ageing through the works of Shakespeare written by a professor of English literature (Draper 1946). Phrased slightly differently on either side of the Atlantic – 'humanities and ageing' in North America and 'cultural gerontology' in Europe – this humanities-inflected approach to ageing studies has attracted increasing interest. Important milestones in the field were an early survey of ageing in history and literature by Joseph T. Freeman (1979) and a two-volume study on humanistic gerontology arising from a two-year 'Human Values and Aging' project sponsored by the National Endowment for the Humanities in the US in 1978–1979 (Spicker, Woodward and Van Tassel 1978; Van Tassel 1979).

Although medical humanities activities have been a feature of medicine for a long time without being so named, at the same time scholars had begun to work in a number of related fields under the newly established rubric of 'medical humanities' in the 1960s (Rosinski 1969). The work of Thomas Cole and a broad range of co-editors has been important here, beginning with *What Does it Mean to Grow Old?: Reflections from the Humanities* (Cole and Gadow 1987), which evolved to a *Handbook of Humanities and Aging* (Cole, Van Tassel and Kastenbaum 1992). Cole's was an important addition to the three other major US handbooks of ageing, which emphasized respectively the fields of biology, psychology and the social sciences (Binstock and Shanas 1977; Birren and Warner-Schaie 1977; Finch and Hayflick 1977; Cole et al. 1992). Cole's handbook and its subsequent editions was particularly important in pioneering connections across disciplines, culminating in 2022 with *Critical Humanities and Ageing: Forging Interdisciplinary Dialogues* (Goldman, de Medeiros and Cole 2022).

In the European context, the *Routledge Handbook of Cultural Gerontology* was significant in defining the cultural gerontology and mapping its disciplinary constituents and connections (Twigg and Martin 2015). Its editors, Julia Twigg and Wendy Martin, are currently in the course of preparing a second edition. A notable element of both Cole's series and Twigg's and Martin's series of publications was a predominant emphasis on social and psychological gerontology. While in the first edition Twigg and Martin conspicuously framed the arts and humanities in contrast to the social sciences, they plan on a deeper integration of disciplinary approaches in forthcoming editions. Their aim is to provide a focal point for considering the development of a mutually beneficial relationship between cultural gerontology and medical and health humanities.

Organizational development

Within gerontology organizations, cultural gerontology has a long history of engagement. A Humanities and Arts Committee has been a part of the GSA since 1976: under recent governance changes it has been renamed the Humanities, Arts and Cultural Gerontology Advisory Panel, with a similar remit. The mission of the Advisory Panel has been to provide a focus for promotion of scholarly endeavour in humanities, arts and ageing; to engage in joint projects with other sections and special interest groups within the wider GSA community; and to continually challenge the 'gerontological imagination' (Achenbaum 2020). An example of the kinds of activities the Cultural Gerontology Advisory Panel promotes was a recent site visit during the 2022 GSA annual meeting to the Eiteljorg Museum of American-Indian art in Indianapolis. There, in collaboration with the Minorities Advisory Panel and Indigenous People Interest Group of the GSA, gerontologists were asked to think about ageing through American-Indian art.

In addition, the Advisory Panel aims to link with the welcome development of two networks in the last decade which approach cultural gerontology very much from the perspective of humanities and art scholars rather than primarily as gerontologists. These networks are the European Network in Aging Studies (ENAS), founded in 2011, and the North American Network in Aging Studies (NANAS), founded in 2013.[1]

The GSA also provides a special section in its flagship journal, *The Gerontologist*, for humanities and ageing, and this has proved a rich resource for cultural gerontology. The inclusion of humanities in other gerontological and geriatric medicine journals has become more commonplace, with the development of sections on cultural gerontology in *European Geriatric Medicine* (O'Neill 2019) and the *Journal of the American Geriatrics Society* (Clarfield and Ouslander 2021). Put simply, scholars are more likely to engage in interdisciplinary work if there are platforms to publish and promote it, and thankfully these platforms are growing in number and prominence.

---

[1] See http://www.agingstudies.eu/ and https://agingstudies.org/NANAS/ for more information (accessed 13 October 2022).

The challenges and opportunities of interdisciplinarity

However, there is room for further engagement between the broad disciplines of gerontology and the arts and humanities. Boundaries persist because of age-old perceptions and misperceptions of other disciplines, differing academic cultures, differing disciplinary incentives in academic progression, funding streams and individual costs. On this last point, for example, the costs of both society membership and attending gerontology and geriatric medicine conferences is generally substantially higher than for humanities and arts conferences – the differential is up to three times the cost between NANAS and GSA – and may not be catered for in departmental budgets and processes. Simple solutions, a special humanities-access price for admission to gerontology conferences, for example, could have major impact.

There are also difficulties in finding reviewers who are open to interdisciplinary papers and research projects, access to funding streams that cross boundaries and finding partners with sufficient simultaneous academic security and humility to allow the basic tenets of their discipline to be challenged in an interdisciplinary project. Finally, there are potentially ethical challenges in promoting doctoral and post doctoral candidates in interdisciplinary areas when employment prospects might seem more assured in the more 'standard' mono-disciplinary tracks (Callard and Fitzgerald 2015).

As against these challenges, there are substantial personal, professional, societal and academic rewards in progressing this form of interdisciplinary work in ageing. The interplay between cultural gerontology and medical or clinical gerontology has been characterized by Twigg and Martin (2015) as having fundamentally reframed our consideration of the lives of older people, refreshing the gerontological imaginary.

Conversely, arts and humanities stand to gain much from a sharper focus on ageing. Just as arts and humanities scholarship challenges the gerontological imagination (Achenbaum 2020), so too gerontology and ageing studies can stimulate the imagination of arts and humanities scholars. This has already occurred to some extent, as many of the essays in this book show. To take just one example, Linda Shortt, a scholar of modern languages, provides an analysis of the image/text hybrid works of Hermann Kinder (1944–2021) that is sharpened by a keen awareness of both the clinical and discursive matrices of the ageing male body in post-war Germany. Such an analysis not only draws on scholarship from the medical humanities but inevitably leaves the reader thinking about medical masculinity and old age in the present day. When humanities disciplines engage with gerontology, they may be even better poised to play a vital role in understanding and responding to major social changes (Benneworth 2015).

How can gerontologists, humanities scholars and social scientists find ways to overcome the barriers to joint working? One answer is to have more humanities-focused or interdisciplinary scholarly conferences, such as those hosted by NANAS and ENAS, alongside more generalist gerontology conferences. Indeed, it is probably best to have both types of conferences, one which allows in-depth focus of a specialized area, and the other engagement with the broader field. Not all members need to go to each, but a healthy degree of interaction is critical.

Insights from medical and health humanities

The fields of medical and health humanities can provide useful models for interdisciplinary working. Medical humanities[2] is a particular field of interest, given its existing synergies with health gerontology in the medical humanities literature, a relatively long period of development as an interdisciplinary field in principle, and a very significant body of literature and experience in education as well as research (O'Neill 2015). Medical humanities emerged as a formal area of study in the late 1960s largely through the pioneering work of Ed Pellegrino (Pellegrino 1974), a physician with an enquiring mind, exceptional breadth of knowledge and also a pioneer in clinical ethics (Fins 2015). His formulation that medicine was 'the most humane of the sciences, and scientific of the humanities' (Pellegrino and McElhinney 1982) reminds us that the humanities are not subjects separate from medicine, but that medicine can be considered as one form of humanistic study (O'Neill et al. 2016). Nearly all medical schools and increasing numbers of other health care disciplines promote medical humanities in their curricula while nearly all major medical journals (apart from the *BMJ*) carry elements of medical humanities in their content, with the *Lancet* notable for its 'Perspectives' section of arts and humanities every Friday.

Despite the relatively long period of development, drawing together the disciplines in joint working – multi-/inter-/trans-disciplinary – remains a work in progress, especially when it comes to publications. A bibliometric study of medical humanities literature indicates that only about one-third

---

[2] Although there is a certain degree of debate about the title of the field – medical and/or health humanities (Jones et al. 2017) – for the purpose of this chapter I will use 'medical humanities' for brevity, while not committing to either title. At Trinity College Dublin we have chosen 'medical and health humanities' as what we hope is an inclusive descriptor.

of the literature shows evidence of joint working between health and arts/humanities scholars (King et al. 2022). The majority of articles are titled in such a way as to indicate some degree of interdisciplinarity within the paper itself, although analysis of affiliations and acknowledgements suggests otherwise. The situation is even more pronounced in one of the most prominent elements of medical humanities, medical history, with only one in seven papers indicating joint working, and less than one in twelve arising from health care scholars (Duma et al. 2021).

As with cultural gerontology, while there will always be a role for single-author, mono-disciplinary contributions to the medical humanities literature, it would be preferable to encourage a range of collaborative styles to enhance the depth, range and quality of scholarship. This raises challenges for some traditional humanities fields where appointments and promotions decisions favour papers which are single-authored, even if the humanities department is involved in a cross-campus programme in medical humanities or cultural gerontology. This may pressure authors to avoid recognition of interdisciplinary work to meet promotion and re-appointment criteria. In an increasingly complex era of scholarship and promotion of interdisciplinarity, this valorization of single-authorship should be re-examined for arts and humanities departments that wish to engage in a substantive way with the medical humanities or cultural gerontology.

In addition, editors of peer-reviewed journals should encourage or promote transparency in authorship and support from other disciplines. Possible mechanisms could include brief biographies of the authors with information on scholarly experience and affiliations, encouragement of more routine and detailed use of acknowledgement sections, and more detailed descriptions of the roles and responsibilities of authors and those acknowledged for each paper. Acknowledgements (the scholar's courtesy) represent an important and under-utilized opportunity to recognize and honour collaboration between disciplines (Cronin and Overfelt 1994). Another approach would be to encourage brief commentaries from scholars in complementary fields to encourage a cross-disciplinary view, as has occurred in the most recent edition of one of the key texts (Goldman et al. 2022). Such encouragement of commentary, response, and interrogation across disciplines animated and enriched the Framing Ageing conferences that have led to the present volume. An innovative aspect of the book edited by Goldman et al. is the provision of a two-part structure that actually builds in rather than merely encouraging interdisciplinary dialogue. Each essay is followed by two short critical responses from disciplinary viewpoints that diverge from that of the essay's author, a model for future scholarship seeking meaningful interaction between fields of ageing studies.

Positive portents for future developments of cultural gerontology

Initiatives to bring scholars together as represented in this book are an important development in providing an opportunity for debate and interrogation.

But academic interdisciplinarity will depend on the structures of available research funding. A helpful example is provided by the initiative in the UK, whereby a range of funding councils came together to support ageing research across a very broad range of disciplinary perspectives. This partnership among five of the research councils resulted in the National Collaboration on Ageing Research (NCAR). Stimulating cross-disciplinary collaboration, the partnership involved scientists, funding bodies and research users to develop approaches to multi- and inter-disciplinary research, and the work conducted by the NCAR informed the New Dynamics of Ageing (NDA) Programme.[3] Over eight years, this major cross-research council programme of multi-disciplinary research spanned the social, medical, biological and engineering sciences and the arts and humanities (Hennessy and Walker 2011). Such approaches are most likely to succeed when cultural gerontologists align with all other elements of gerontology to generate a more powerful and unitary advocacy.

Conclusion

This is an exciting era of ever-increasing interest in the power of arts and humanities approaches to engage with the broader canvas of gerontology to increase our understanding of ageing. Critical to consolidation and development of cultural gerontology is the creation of initiatives which provide space, time and support to allow for an interweaving and critical interrogation of the many disciplines which potentially interact with each other. Readers of this volume

---

[3] For more on this see https://newdynamics.sites.sheffield.ac.uk/.

will be introduced into just such a space in the broad range of approaches, each influenced by the rich interdisciplinary dialogue and discussion which occurred during the series of Framing Ageing seminars.

Bibliography

Achenbaum, W. A. (2020), 'The Humanities and Arts in The Gerontological Society of America', *Gerontologist* 60(4): 591–97.

Benneworth, P. (2015), 'Tracing How Arts and Humanities Research Translates, Circulates and Consolidates in Society: How Have Scholars Been Reacting to Diverse Impact and Public Value Agendas?', *Arts and Humanities in Higher Education*, 14(1): 45–60.

Binstock, R. and E. Shanas, eds (1977), *Handbook of Aging and the Social Sciences*, New York: Van Nostrand Reinhold.

Birren, J. E. and K. Warner-Schaie, eds (1977), *Handbook of the Psychology of Aging*, New York: Van Nostrand Reinhold.

Callard, F. and D. Fitzgerald (2015), *Rethinking Interdisciplinarity across the Social Sciences and Neurosciences*, Houndmills: Palgrave MacmillanHound.

Clarfield, A. M. and J. G. Ouslander (2021), 'Ars Longa: A New Column Featuring the Humanities and Aging', *Journal of the American Geriatrics Society*, 69(1): 51–3.

Cole, T. R. and S. Gadow, eds (1987), *What Does It Mean to Grow Old? Reflections from the Humanities*, Durham, NC: Duke University Press.

Cole, T. R., D. Van Tassel and R. Kastenbaum, eds (1992), *Handbook of the Humanities and Aging*, New York: Springer.

Cronin, B. and K. Overfelt (1994), 'The Scholar's Courtesy: A Survey of Acknowledgement Behaviour', *Journal of Documentation*, 50(3): 165–96.

Draper, J. W. (1946), 'Browsing through the Ages: Shakespeare's Attitude towards Old Age', *Journal of Gerontology*, 1(1): 118–26.

Duma, D., L. Wong, D. O'Neill and B. D. Kelly (2021), 'Taking Histories: Joint Working of Disciplines in Medical History Scholarship', *Irish Journal of Medical Science*, 190(4): 1533–535.

Finch, C. and L. Hayflick, eds (1977), *Handbook of the Biology of Aging*, New York: Van Nostrand Reinhold.

Fins, J. J. (2015), 'Edmund D. Pellegrino, MD 1920-2013', *Transactions of the American Clinical and Climatological Association*, 126: cii–cix.

Freeman, J. T. (1979), *Aging, its History and Literature*, New York: Human Sciences Press.

Goldman, M., K. de Medeiros and T. R. Cole, eds (2022), *Critical Humanities and Ageing: Forging Interdisciplinary Dialogues*, London: Routledge.

Gruman, G. (1957), 'An Introduction to Literature on the History of Gerontology', *Bulletin of the History of Medicine*, 31(1): 78–83.

Hennessy, C. H. and A. Walker (2011), 'Promoting Multi-Disciplinary and Inter-Disciplinary Ageing Research in the United Kingdom', *Ageing & Society*, 31(1): 52–69.

Jones, T., M. Blackie, R. Garden and D. Wear (2017), 'The Almost Right Word: The Move from Medical to Health Humanities', *Academic Medicine*, 92(7): 932–35.

Kalish, R. A. (1979), 'The New Ageism and the Failure Models: A Polemic,' *Gerontologist*, 19: 398–402.

King, R., J. Al-Khabouri, B. Kelly and D. O'Neill (2022), 'Authorship in the Medical Humanities: Breaking Cross-field Boundaries or Maintaining Disciplinary Divides?', *Journal of Medical Humanities*, 43(1): 65–71.

Mulley, G. (2012), 'A History of Geriatrics and Gerontology', *European Geriatric Medicine*, 3(4): 225–27.

North American Network in Aging Studies. Available at: http://www.agingstudies.eu/ and https://agingstudies.org/NANAS/ for more information (accessed 13 October 2022).

O'Neill, D. (2012), 'Am I a Gerontologist or Geriatrician?', *Journal of the American Geriatrics Society*, 60(7): 1361–363.

O'Neill, D. (2015), 'Geriatric Medicine and Cultural Gerontology', *Age and Ageing*, 44(3): 353–55.

O'Neill, D. (2019), 'Geriatric Medical Humanities: Fresh Insights into Ageing and Geriatric Medicine', *European Geriatric Medicine*, 10(3): 337–38.

O'Neill, D., E. Jenkins, R. Mawhinney, E. Cosgrave, S. O'Mahony, C. Guest and H. Moss (2016), 'Rethinking the Medical in the Medical Humanities', *Medical Humanities*, 42(2): 109–14.

Pellegrino, E. D. (1974), 'Editorial: Medical Practice and the Humanities', *New England Journal of Medicine*, 290(19): 1083–85.

Pellegrino, E. D. and T. K. McElhinney (1982), *Teaching Ethics, the Humanities, and Human Values in Medical Schools: A Ten-Year Overview*, Washington: Institute on Human Values in Medicine, Society for Health and Human Values.

Rosinski, E. F. (1969), 'Human Values and Curriculum Design: A View for the Future', *Jama*, 209(9): 1346–348.

Spicker, S. F., K. M. Woodward and D. D. Van Tassel, eds (1978), *Aging and the Elderly: Humanistic Perspectives in Gerontology*, New York: Academic Press.

Twigg, J. and W. Martin, eds (2015), *Routledge Handbook of Cultural Gerontology*, London: Routledge.

Van Tassel, D. (1979), *Ageing, Death and the Completion of Being*, University Park: University of Pennsylvania Press.

3

The concrete truth of healthy ageing: On the relevance and urgency of art

Robert Zwijnenberg

Introduction

'A Mutating Story', an art installation by ceramist Jacob van der Beugel, consists of four large concrete panels (Figure 1).[1]

The surface of the panels is polished with some areas that are rough, with holes and an open-worked, grained surface. There is also a shift of colours over the surface of the panels. Scattered over the surface are areas on which rectangular blocks have been placed, on which round stones are surrounded by spots. The special quality of the work is grounded in van der Beugel's artistic practice: an obsessive handling of materials (Figures 2–3).

His work is the result of months of intensive and very heavy physical investment in firing, pouring, breaking, sanding, grinding, sawing and polishing of unruly materials such as concrete, all performed with his hands and hand tools.

In an interview in the *Financial Times*, author Hillary Mantel describes a work of art 'as a place where one takes risks every day': 'I think of it as the arena of peril rather than a place one withdraws to' (Watson 2020). If there is any truth to Mantel's description then it certainly applies to the artistic practice of Jacob van der Beugel. Making a work of art is taking a risk, especially for van der Beugel in his daily fight with unruly materials, risking his body and mind.

The risk that making a work of art can entail is mirrored in the risk the viewer might take when viewing such a work of art. That is the case in an approach to

---

[1] For more images from the 'Mutation' series, see https://jacobvanderbeugel.com/work/item/mutation-series.

Figure 1 Jacob van der Beugel, 'A Mutating Story', installation view, Museum Beelden aan Zee, 18 July 2020–25 April 2021.

Figure 2 Jacob van der Beugel, 'Mutation 2', 2019. Handmade ceramic components, concrete, aggregate and recycled aggregate, liquid rust, 300 × 175 cm. Courtesy of the artist. Courtesy of the artist. Photo credit: Gerrit Schreurs.

Figure 3 Jacob van der Beugel, 'Mutation 2', 2019. Detail. Courtesy of the artist. Photo credit: Gerrit Schreurs.

the artwork in which I, as a viewer, accept the risk of new experiences – even if they are unwanted or disturbing. It is an approach in which I demand of an artwork that it does not open up a space in which I feel safe as a spectator, a space in which I can find confirmation. Instead, it should open a space that ruthlessly challenges my ideas about art, science and my own body and life, and requires an existential exploration of my unreflected ethical notions on these matters.

The question I will try to answer in this chapter is whether works of art, such as 'A Mutating Story', can enrich my thinking about healthy ageing as a critical and unique approach which can challenge the analyses and critiques already available in the humanities. But what do we mean by 'healthy ageing'?

The World Health Organization (2020) defines healthy ageing in very general terms: 'Healthy ageing is about creating the environments and opportunities that enable people to be and do what they value throughout their lives'. The WHO mentions biomedical sciences as one of the disciplines, alongside other scientific disciplines as well as social and cultural activities that are needed in a joint approach 'to improve the lives of older people, their families and their communities' (2020). In practice, however, it is mainly the biomedical sciences and biotechnology that give substance to how healthy ageing is defined and how it can be achieved. As I will argue, the biotechnological approach to healthy ageing also raises many critical questions. Ageing is not only an individual matter but a matter of often clashing cultural, ethical, economic, social, medical and political interests. That is why society should not leave healthy ageing to the medical sciences. As citizens in a democratic society, we are equally responsible for the ethical, political and societal choices that are made regarding the meaning of healthy ageing and how we want to achieve it as a society.

For me, 'A Mutating Story' is a work of art that calls for taking such civic responsibility. I will therefore also answer the question of what kind of artworks can move me to shape and take on this responsibility. And I will answer the question of why I also turn to art and not just to philosophy and other disciplines of the humanities. The humanities offer in-depth reflections on human vulnerability and bodily integrity, on who and what we are as human beings, on identity and individuality, about the good life and a merciful death, but also about moral duties of beneficence and nonmaleficence, concepts of autonomy and health equity (see, for example, Cole, Carson and Carlin 2014). These are all things that help us to critically consider the different aspects of healthy ageing and to make choices about the direction and future of humankind and of the planet. In that respect, thinking about healthy ageing is inescapably linked to a much broader approach that is particularly elaborated in the environmental humanities: a critical thinking about our actions and existence in relation to the many urgent questions and challenges that arise in the era of rapid environmental and social change (see, for example, Hubbell and Ryan 2021). So, the question is, what can a work of art offer me that I cannot find in philosophy, or indeed in other humanities disciplines?

Biomedical sciences and healthy ageing

First, I must consider the role of biomedical sciences and biotechnology in our thinking about healthy ageing. Biotechnology approaches healthy ageing primarily as an issue of longevity. In the remainder of my chapter, I therefore equate biomedical research into healthy ageing with biotechnological research into longevity. Biomedical research on healthy ageing is consequential for society in two ways. Biomedical innovations determine to a large extent what is or is not medically possible and thus provide a compelling definition of what should be understood by healthy ageing. The medical sciences have a well-oiled publicity machine and societal credibility, not least because in recent times they have made a tremendous contribution to solving human suffering.

However, the medical view of ageing can be both convincing and presumptuous. A fine example of this is an issue of *MIT Technology Review*. Some of us, at least me, are old enough to remember the John and Yoko 'War is Over! If you want it' poster from 1969. The longevity issue of the *MIT Technology Review* replaces 'War' with 'Old Age': 'Old Age is over if you want it' (Lichfield 2019: 2). This means that old age is equated with the morally reprehensible state of war and that we have a personal responsibility for our own healthy ageing. This headline implies that 'old age' is the enemy we are at war with and that we can beat this enemy with the help of the medical sciences. The whole issue contains all kinds of articles that confirm this, with titles such as 'What if aging weren't inevitable, but a curable disease?' (Adam 2019: 14–19) and 'The anti-aging drug that's just around the corner' (Hall 2019: 22–3). There are some articles that seem to raise criticism, such as 'How old age was invented' (Coughlin 2019: 32–7), but they are mainly from a socioeconomic perspective and are not a rejection of the underlying optimistic biomedical approach and the idea that healthy ageing is a personal lifestyle choice. The longevity issue lacks a fundamental rethinking of who and what we are as humans in the light of all these medical innovations in healthy ageing.

Another reason for the hegemonic role of the medical sciences in society is that medical research into ageing has gone hand in hand with the commercialization and commodification of old age. This is undoubtedly linked to an ever-closer financial entanglement between biotech industry research and academic research, which raises the question of whether academic independence in ethical considerations can still exist. The steepening ascent of bio-entrepreneurialism continues to rub out the hazy line between university and commercial research (Stevens and Newman 2019). This explains why the rhetoric of biomedical sciences is no different from that of biotech companies in the field of healthy ageing. For example, AgeX Therapeutics declares on its website that the company 'is focused on the development and commercialization of novel therapeutics targeting human aging'.[2] Calico seeks to 'enable people to live longer and healthier lives' by applying biotechnology.[3] These statements reveal specific and essentialist conceptions of what it means to be human, about ageing and about what makes a life worth living. They share with the biomedical

---

[2] See https://www.agexinc.com/ (accessed 12 October 2022).
[3] See https://www.calicolabs.com/ (accessed 12 October 2022).

sciences a particular concept of the physical and mental development of humans and present this as established facts. The narrative of the biotech industry is creating a new medical order to which our ageing bodies must adapt. Old age and physical decay are presented as undesirable phenomena that we can combat or avert ourselves.

The prevalence of these powerful narratives raises an important question: how can we prevent that a humanities perspective on ageing is not unnoticeably fed by biomedical ideas about who and what we are as human beings, about health and old age? Again, old age is presented by these companies as the enemy we must fight. Because there is insufficient regulation, large global biotech companies with their enormous financial scope increasingly determine the ethical and legal playing field within which biotechnological and medical developments take place. We should not underestimate the combined power and impact on society of biotech industry and academic medical voices on the issue of healthy ageing. The economic and (geo)political interests in the developments of biotechnological innovations are so enormous that it is naive to assume that the humanities with all their sophisticated theories can have any substantial influence upon this force field of interests. However, this bleak conclusion is an inspiring reason for me to investigate how I can nevertheless give shape to my civic responsibility for the choices that are made.

In their book *The Techno-Human Condition*, Braden Allenby and Daniel Sarewitz argue that our technological world has become so complex that it is impossible to totally foresee or control the impact and consequences or the potential risks and dangers of technological innovations (Allenby and Sarewitz 2011). Using the example of the Fukushima Nuclear Power Plant disaster, they argue that the various circumstances that coincided and caused the disaster 'are predictable, but they are also incoherent, unintelligible and entirely unhelpful in navigating the complexities of our technological age' (109). Discussions about the dangers and benefits of genome editing show the same picture; each new technology evokes new unexpected consequences (see, for example, Doudna and Sternberg 2017). Allenby and Sarewitz remark: 'vaccines change expectations about survival and contribute to global and regional demographic challenges; cellphone technology dramatically reduces privacy and subtly transforms cognitive patterns; planes can be vectors of disease' (2011: 29). There is no reason to assume that biotechnological innovations in the field of healthy ageing or longevity cannot and will not have unexpected and far-reaching consequences of a medical, ethical, social and cultural nature. Biotechnology denies and struggles against the fact that the technological world we have created is of a confounding complexity and ambiguity that makes any thought of full controllability and social engineering ludicrous. The (bio)technological control of the body is an impossible task. Allenby and Sarewitz argue that the naive belief in social engineering and controllability should be replaced with 'the courage and wisdom to embrace contradiction, celebrate ignorance, and muddle forward' (2011: 160).

Moreover, biotechnology's conception of what constitutes a human is very narrow and denies the excesses, the messiness and the uncontrollability of the biological. It denies the fact that a human is a fragmented and contradictory being. The medical approach to ageing ignores the vague wishes and desires of individuals in everyday life, the complexities and ambiguities that define or rule our individual life, the opacity of our own needs and desires, the uncertainties and risks of life that we experience every day, which, however, give our lives weight and substance. As humanities scholars, we must ensure that in academic and public discussions about ageing, we apply our own reflective point of views about what it means to be human. This enables us to analyse and criticize the medical approach of ageing at a fundamental level, and to ensure that we do not adopt the medical approach and ideas in passing. However, we, as individuals, do not approach the world, ourselves and our health from a clearly considered (theoretical) conception of ethics and the good and right life. Our lives are rampant on all levels (physical, mental, social, political, ethical, cultural) and uncontainable. Chaos lurks within us. How can I ensure that the recognition of that chaos not only becomes part of my theoretical thinking but also of my everyday attitude and practical action in relation to issues of healthy ageing? I am convinced that I need art to be able to firmly ground this insight in the uncontainability of life in a fundamental attitude of thinking. Why and how can a work of art offer me something that I already do not know from or can find in philosophy or in the humanities at large?

Deleuze and art

I find an answer to this question in a quote from an interview with French philosopher Gilles Deleuze: 'The encounter between two disciplines doesn't take place when one begins to reflect on the other, but when one discipline realizes that it has to resolve, for itself and by its own means, a problem similar to one confronted by the other' (Deleuze 1986: n.p.). Applying this insight to art means that art should not start to reflect on biotechnology nor try to solve a problem of biotechnology. Instead, art must – for itself and within the arts themselves – solve a problem for its own sake (in French: 'résoudre pour son compte'), for the sake of art and not for the sake of biotechnology, and with its own means. So, when art deals with a problem of biotechnology, it becomes a problem of and in art.

Deleuze continues: 'One can imagine that similar problems confront [secouent] the sciences, painting, music, philosophy, literature, and cinema at different moments, on different occasions, and under different circumstances. The same tremors occur on totally different terrains' (1986: n.p.). Important in this quotation is the word 'tremor' ('secousse'). I argue that we should understand this word in its literal medico-bodily meaning, that is as an involuntary quivering movement, a convulsion, or a psychological shock. 'Secousse' derives from the verb 'secouer', which is better translated as 'shake', instead of 'confront'. It is about a tremor that shakes the sciences and that shakes the arts. If art tries to give answers to such a tremor, then, Deleuze continues, 'the risk that those answers would suggest other problems' is more than likely. Art engaging with the tremor of longevity will not provide definitive answers, but only new problems.

What Deleuze is saying here is that art should not collaborate or exchange with science in order to jointly find an answer to a tremor that is challenging that science. Rather, the artist must turn a 'science tremor' into an 'art tremor', a tremor that must be solved within the arts, for the sake of art itself and with its own artistic means. Thus, the tremor becomes a challenge to art itself; how to respond to that tremor within the arts?

In my understanding of the Deleuzian tremor, it is something that violently shakes a discipline, that disrupts the authoritative narratives, that challenges traditional ethical notions. For instance, a biotechnological innovation regarding longevity is a tremor in the Deleuzian sense within the medical domain, because it raises all kinds of unexpected medico-ethical issues as well as unexpected medical challenges. It shakes the existing authoritative or dominant narratives within the medical sciences. This is reflected in all the articles and symposium discussions within the medical field about these technologies (see, for example, *Developing an Ethical Framework for Health Ageing: Report of a WHO Meeting* 2017). In general, the medical field will always reflect on clinical pathways for new biomedical technologies; how to regulate them in such a way that patient safety and benefit is guaranteed, as well as search for medico-ethical considerations underlying biomedical research and its applications specifically to meet societal concerns (see, for example, *Second International Summit on Human Genome Editing* 2019).

If longevity technology is taken up by art as a tremor in the Deleuzian sense, then those medical-practice-based issues are obviously not central. Art should not reflect on the issues that biomedical sciences have with longevity. Longevity should become a problem of the arts themselves. Longevity should disrupt the authoritative or dominant narratives about art; it should challenge notions of what art is, or what art should look like.

Deleuze's account of art engaging with science makes clear why art can offer something that theory cannot. Of course, instead of 'art' one can use 'philosophy' in this quote, with the conclusion that longevity should become a tremor of philosophy itself, a problem to solve for its own good. However, the difference between theory and art is precisely that art can take place in a completely different medium than the medium of both philosophy and the theoretical discourse of biotechnology. The bodily and embodied experience that a work of art can make possible, evokes a different experience in the viewer than when reading a theoretical text. The ability of a work of art to evoke an experience that cannot be generated by a text is a reason for me to turn not only to philosophy but also to art when I look for an embodied attitude and civic responsibility towards the issues of healthy ageing.

Rilke and Piccinini

What is the nature and form of a work of art that can make an embodied attitude possible for me? A work of art must create a presence in the space of the beholder, that is in the ethical and aesthetic reality of the beholder, which is unexpected and inescapable, a presence that cannot be ignored. A presence that forces viewers to reflect on their own ethical and aesthetic presuppositions. A work of art must confront us with an existential choice: to answer its call or to look away. The experience of such a compelling presence is very precisely depicted in Rainer Maria Rilke's poem from 1918 'Archaïscher Torso Apollos' ('Torso of an Archaic Apollo', in Zinn 1955: 557). In this poem, Rilke looks at a sculpture from the sixth century BCE, the so-called torso of Miletus, exhibited in the Louvre, which for him has a presence that cannot be ignored. The poem ends with the sentences: 'denn da ist keine Stelle, die dich nicht sieht. Du mußt dein Leben ändern.' ('For there is no place that does not see you. You must change your life.') An art experience is essentially a one-on-one encounter between a work of art and the individual viewer, which leaves traces behind. There is an imperative, a moral appeal in the contemplation of the sculpture and in Rilke's poem: you must change your life. Once you have read this poem with as much dedication as Rilke looked at the sculpture, the moral appeal can no longer be banned from your own life: the appeal has become part of your life and pops up at unexpected moments. For those who cannot or do not want to muster this dedication, they make the choice to look away.

Although they are stylistically very different from those of Jacob van der Beugel discussed above, works by contemporary Australian artist Patricia Piccinini create a similar inescapable presence. Her work, too, presents us with a choice: commitment or looking away. Her work features, among other things, encounters between humans and non-humans. Piccinini creates monstrous living entities, that nevertheless elicit empathy or even enter into a relationship with a human, as in 'The Young Family' (2002), a nearly life-sized sculpture of a dog-human hybrid figure nursing three young pups, made of mixed media including leather, silicone and human hair.[4] Piccinini's work in this vein appears to be above all about how to shape the relationship between humans and non-human entities produced using biotechnology. Piccinini herself has stated that her work is about 'how the conceptual or ethical issues are transformed by emotional realities' (Piccinini and Fernandez Orgaz 2007). It is especially the sculptures depicting an encounter between a child and a 'monster' that put us to the test. The sculpture 'The Welcome Guest' (2011), again a life-size, realist, mixed-media sculpture made of silicone, fibreglass and human hair, presents an encounter between a happy smiling young girl and a hideous monster that seems to embrace her tenderly with razor-sharp limbs. Would we rather look away to avoid seeing an innocent girl fall prey to an evil and cunning creature? Or, do we take our emotional response as a starting point to examine our own ethical and cultural presuppositions and prejudices? 'The Welcome Guest' then confronts us with questions such as: Who and what falls within the domain of the human? What are the limits of the human? What are the limits of human physicality? Are we prepared to question those limits? We are called upon to look and behave towards living beings in a way to which we are not accustomed. We have to find an ethical attitude compatible with an aesthetic that confronts us with tangible, living entities that are beyond the realm of the known.

If we look at 'The Welcome Guest' from the perspective of the quotation from Deleuze, then this work is about the tremor of genetic modification. Piccinini turns this tremor into a problem of art itself. The disturbing power of her work

---

[4] See: https://www.artsy.net/artwork/patricia-piccinini-the-young-family-3. For other images by the artist see: http://www.patriciapiccinini.net/ (accessed 12 October 2022).

can be traced to the artistic struggle to get a grip on the tremor of genetic modification within the realm of the arts. If we consider the work merely as an illustration of the possible monstrous consequences of genetic modification, we are in fact looking away from what makes the work a work of art: the compelling aesthetic invitation to reflect on what it is to be human.

A Mutating Story

Rilke's poem and Piccinini's 'The Welcome Guest' show that a work of art requires care. Care for an art work means that you allow yourself to be stopped in your tracks by an artwork, and pay careful attention to a work of art. Wallace Heim's conception of care describes quite accurately what an attitude of care towards a work of art can mean: 'Care takes time. Caring with another might take both out of the flux of the everyday and into a realm that feels timeless. To care may be like a practice with indeterminate ends' (Heim 2022: 1).[5] Care for a work of art means that it can open a space in which life, a body, human or non-human, can be experienced in a different dimension than that of the biomedical sciences.[6] In this sense, as I argued before, contemplating a work of art in a caring approach also entails a certain risk. Risk is 'kairos', in the Greek sense, a decisive instant. What it determines is not only the future but also the past, a past behind our horizon of expectation, where it reveals an unsuspected reserve of freedom. In a caring approach the urgency and relevance of a work of art for our own lives, can unfold. The caring approach of a work of art leaves traces, can give unwanted or liberating experiences and insights. In any case, that was my experience when I stood in front of Jacob van der Beugel's 'A Mutating Story'. On van der Beugel's website we can read:

> In more recent work, Jacob's preoccupation has lain with interpreting man's attempts to rationalise the abstract: human identity in DNA samples and disease patterns in epidemiology. Jacob's output re-humanises these abstractions in an

---

[5] My notion of care in an approach to an artwork, draws also upon Donna Haraway's (2008: 84) notion of care as creating an 'ontological opening' in experimental relations that forces the one conducting the experiment to stay responsive to the suffering of the ones participating in it.

[6] It is well worth investigating to what extent the attitude of care that a work of art can solicit, could also be a productive humanities approach to ageing. Care, as a concept, is closely associated with feminist theory and was only introduced into ethics in the closing decades of the twentieth century. Instead of following universal principles, care ethics highlights the networks of relations in which ethical interaction and judgement take place. Care ethics privileges the response to the individual over generalizable standards and conceives the world as a complex network of relations rather than a collection of independent individuals acting on the basis of reason. Psychologist and feminist Carol Gilligan's *In a Different Voice* (1982) counts as the founding work of care ethics.

endeavour to depict the human condition. His original use of materials, such as ceramics and concrete, embrace their extraordinary ability to capture human traces and endeavours, in their conversion from the soft, every day and ordinary to the hard and frozen sculpted object. Artefacts designed to withstand the scrutiny and ravages of time. Jacob passionately believes in the importance of Art as a platform to discuss contemporary scientific issues.[7]

Due to the material nature and appearance of the surface of the panels, 'A Mutating Story' can easily be read as a story about the formation, development, increase, exchange and decay of cells. The panels are like a map of human tissue in transformation. Van der Beugel's stated engagement with the medical sciences may elicit such a reading, but in such interpretation the work appears almost as an illustration of a biological process. However, with Deleuze in mind, we can see that the tremor of the body's vulnerability to disease is for the artist a tremor for his own artistic practice. Van der Beugel's work cannot be regarded as an illustration or an explanation of biomedical issues; nor can it be viewed as criticism or enthusiasm for the medical sciences. With his work he does not seek to approach or collaborate with the medical sciences to help solve a problem within that domain. Van der Beugel takes up a tremor of the medical sciences, but he aims to investigate this tremor only within his work, as an art tremor, with his own artistic means and methods. The tremor of the body's vulnerability to disease, thus leads to a work that challenges our ideas about what sculpture or a ceramic work should be. This makes the work a risky challenge for the caring observer. What am I looking at? Why and how does this work relate to issues within biotechnology? Why is this an art work?

The work harbours a paradox. The four massive concrete panels that together form 'A Mutating Story' have an inescapable presence in the gallery space due to the hard material and their dimensions.

The work is immovable, it is a material obstacle in space that you have to dodge in order to continue walking. Concrete is a material that is used to build structures that withstand wind and weather as well as continuous heavy use. The concrete war bunker is an extreme example of such a construction, a deceptive safe haven for human frailty and vulnerability and for the unstable human mind and emotions (Virilio 1994). Concrete is nevertheless also susceptible to the ravages of time; 'concrete cancer' or the rusting of the reinforcement steel, is a serious problem in the construction world. As an answer to that problem,

---

[7] See https://jacobvanderbeugel.com/about (accessed 12 October 2022).

so-called 'self-healing' concrete has been developed. In self-healing concrete, calcite-precipitating bacteria repair cracks and thus extend the durability of a concrete construction.[8] The concrete panels of 'A Mutating Story' are made of self-healing concrete. 'A Mutating Story' is simultaneously indestructible, vulnerable and living material. The excess of the biological, its messiness and uncontainability, is presented to me artistically as an excess of possible meanings, which ultimately make the work impenetrable to me.

The work offers an unstable open space in which I should not seek a hold on the title or established opinions. I am on my own to choose an ethical position and to take appropriate responsibility and care for the work art. I am solely responsible for any meaning I attribute to the work. At the same time, I realize that I will ultimately be left empty-handed. Not only is 'A Mutating Story' characterized by opacity, by a confounding complexity and ambiguity, but I – as a viewer of this work – am also opaque to myself.

Rilke's appeal 'Du mußt dein Leben ändern' ultimately means that I have to get to work myself. Rilke's poem, Piccinini and van der Beugel's work let me experience on the one hand that unexpected ideas and forms of life are possible. On the other hand, these works do not give me any clear answer to the question of what the nature of such forms of life is and how I should relate to them. This feeling of empty-handedness that a work of art can evoke, can and should be the starting point for my own thinking. I see this very clearly happening, for example, with works of art from the field of bio-art that perplex us and therefore challenge us to new theoretical explorations about biological life, our own life and body. Think of the green glowing bunny of Eduardo Kac, 'GFP Bunny' from 2000, or the performance 'que le cheval vive en moi' (2011) by art orienté objet, in which the artist undergoes a transfusion of horse blood plasma, or the breastfeeding of a puppy in the performance of Maja Smrekar, 'Hybrid Family' from 2015–2016. Works of art that, due to the complex and ambiguous physical, sensory and intellectual experience they evoke, require an intellectual exercise to overcome empty-handedness.

Thus, facing the four concrete panels of 'A Mutating Story' in the gallery space, I have to find both a bodily and an intellectual attitude. The work does not give answers but challenges me – if I allow it – to theoretically explore the ambiguity and complexity of my own bodily presence in the world.

---

[8] See: https://www.tudelft.nl/en/ceg/research/stories-of-science/self-healing-of-concrete-by-bacterial-mineral-precipitation/ (accessed 14 December 2022).

The confrontation with 'A Mutating Story' calls me to a thinking that should refuse to be localized; I must not mask my own empty-handedness with existing views and theories. Rather, it should shake, vibrate, and stay multiple, leaving its identity undefinable. The nature of this reflection acknowledges that there is always something unknowable and opaque inside each artwork and each person; it does not try to formulate a centre, a core, from which everything is determined and seeks to maintain an open and subjective relationship with the world. It is thinking par excellence that can only approach what is being thought about in a very personal one-to-one relationship – in detail and from different perspectives. (Zwijnenberg 2021: 45–53). 'A Mutating Story' calls me to this attitude of thinking necessary to critically confront the biomedical essentialist attitude towards the human body and healthy ageing, and to present alternative views. The experience of 'A Mutating Story' enables me to experience the paradoxical condition of my body – transparent and opaque, vulnerable and resilient, limited and boundless.

Conclusion

Art and the humanities cannot exist without each other. The humanities cannot do without the imagination and the sensory nature of art; art is ultimately impossible without the conceptualization of the humanities to represent reality artistically. Humanities scholars who deny their own body and exclude the imagination are just as blind as artists who renounce theoretical thinking. Thinking and making art are both ethically charged activities.

As I have tried to show in this chapter, this necessary exchange between art and the humanities is a powerful nexus from which to challenge the issues surrounding healthy ageing.

John Banville, writing in *The Irish Times* about the novelist Henry James, argues that 'art gives a shape to that incoherent process of stumbling-but-not-quite-falling that constitutes our state of being in the world. We do not remember our birth, we shall not know that we are dead; all we have is the mess in between these two extremes of eternal nonexistence' (Banville 2017).

The recognition that life is 'the mess in between', that life amounts to 'stumbling-but-not-quite-falling', runs counter to the slogan 'Old age is over if you want it', which in contrast invokes a positive malleability of the human body and a moral and practical responsibility for the health of your own ageing body. I cannot do without art to firmly anchor the messiness of a life as an essential element of thinking about my ageing body.

Bibliography

Adam, David (2019), 'What if Ageing Were a Disease?', *MIT Technology Review*, 122(5): 14–18.

Allenby, B. R. and D. Sarewitz (2011), *The Techno-Human Condition*, Cambridge, MA: MIT Press.

Banville, J. (2017), 'Novels Were Never the Same after Henry James', *The Irish Times*, October 7. Available at: https://www.irishtimes.com/culture/books/john-banville-novels-were-never-the-same-after-henry-james-1.3242726 (accessed 12 October 2022).

Cole, Thomas R., Ronald A. Carson and Nathan S. Carlin (2014), *Medical Humanities: An Introduction*, Cambridge: Cambridge University Press.

Coughlin, Joseph F. (2019), 'How Old Age Was Invented', *MIT Technology Review*, 122(5): 32–7.

Deleuze, G. (1986), 'Le cerveau, c'est l'écran', *Cahiers du cinéma*, 380: 24–32, trans. M. T. Guirgis. Available at: https://www.diagonalthoughts.com/?p=2252 (accessed 21 December 2022).

Developing an Ethical Framework for Healthy Ageing: Report of a WHO Meeting (2017), Tübingen, Germany, 18 March 2017, Geneva: World Health Organization.

Doudna, J. A. and S. H. Sternberg (2017), *A Crack in Creation: Gene Editing and the Unthinkable Power to Control Evolution*, Boston: Houghton Mifflin Harcourt.

Gilligan, Carol (1982), *In a Different Voice: Psychological Theory and Women's Development*, Cambridge, MA: Harvard University Press.

Hall, Stephen S. (2019), 'Is an Anti-Ageing Drug around the Corner?', *MIT Technology Review*, 122(5): 22–3.

Haraway, Donna J. (2008), *When Species Meet*, Minneapolis and London: University of Minnesota Press.

Heim, Wallace (2022), 'The Times of Caring in a Nuclear World: Sculpture, Contamination and Stillness', *Arts*, 11(7): 1. Available at: https://doi.org/10.3390/artsll010007 (accessed 3 January 2023).

Hubbell, J. Andrew and John C. Ryan (2021), *Introduction to the Environmental Humanities*, New York: Routledge.

Lichfield, Gideon, ed. (2019), '"Old Age Is Over" – If You Want It', *MIT Technology Review*, 122(5). Available at: https://www.technologyreview.com/2019/08/21/133329/editors-letter-old-age-is-overif-you-want-it/ (accessed 30 November 2023).

Piccinini, Patricia and Laura Fernandez Orgaz (2007), 'The Naturally Artificial World', in (*Tender*) *Creatures. Exhibition Catalogue*, Araba: Artrium. Available at: http://www.patriciapiccinini.net/essays/29 (accessed 12 October 2022).

Second International Summit on Human Genome Editing: Continuing the Global Discussion (2019), Proceedings of a Workshop in Brief, Washington: The National Academies Press.

Stevens, Tina and Stuart Newman (2019), *Biotech Juggernaut: Hope, Hype, and Hidden Agendas of Entrepreneurial BioScience*, New York: Routledge.
Virilio, Paul (1994), *Bunker Archeology*, New York: Princeton Architectural Press.
Watson, R. (2020), 'Hilary Mantel: "I Think of Writing as the Arena of Peril"', *The Financial Times*, 5 December.
World Health Organization (2020), 'Healthy Ageing and Functional Ability'. Available at: https://www.who.int/news-room/questions-and-answers/item/healthy-ageing-and-functional-ability (accessed 3 January 2023).
Zinn, Ernst, ed. (1955), *Rainer Maria Rilke, Sämtliche Werke*, vol. 1, Frankfurt a. Main: Insel Verlag.
Zwijnenberg, Robert (2021), 'What Has Happened?', in Helen Westgeest and Kitty Zijlmans (eds), *Mix & Stir – New Outlooks on Contemporary Art from Global Perspectives*, 45–53, Amsterdam: Valiz.

4

The art of ageing: Finitude, vulnerability and opportunity in Hermann Kinder's *The Way of All Flesh*

Linda Shortt

Throughout his writing career the German author and literary scholar Hermann Kinder was preoccupied with age and ageing. Born in 1944, he was a member of the protest generation of 1968 which shaped West German culture and politics from the 1970s onwards. He died during the Covid-19 pandemic in 2021 after a long-term illness. In many of his literary works Kinder explores the physical and psychological dimensions of ageing, physical decline, vulnerability and mortality.[1]

This chapter focuses on *The Way of All Flesh* (2014), a text which draws on the author's own experiences with illness and ageing. One of the striking features of the text is the inclusion of thirteen hand-drawn illustrations by the author which depict the protagonist's declining body in graphic and indeed grotesque detail (see Figures 4–5). The narrative follows a complicated illness trajectory (Kinder suffered from granulomatosis with polyangiitis which led to serious impairments, including the amputation of his foot) from the beginning of symptoms through diagnosis and treatment, to adjustment and accommodation. Kinder's *The Way of All Flesh* spotlights the darker sides of ageing and deals with a wide range of difficult topics from the bodily experience of illness- and age-related disability to the challenges of living close to death. While on the one hand, this would seem

---

[1] Published in 1990, *Die Böhmischen Schwestern* rails against the agonizing societal compulsion to be happy and healthy, defending the individual's right to live an incomplete life. In *Um Leben und Tod* (1997), Kinder uses maternal illness and death as a frame for reflection on the challenges of trying to lead a meaningful and finite life. *Mein Melaten* (2006), named after a cemetery in Cologne, explores life after retirement and the micro-changes that ageing brings. Detailing how the protagonist faces up to his own diminishing significance in public life, mortality and the painful prospect of the death of loved ones, the novel ends as he collapses with a heart attack. While his death is presented as part of life, it remains nevertheless unfathomable, even as the protagonist experiences it.

Figure 4 Hermann Kinder, *Der Weg allen Fleisches* [*The Way of All Flesh*], page 100. Courtesy Weissbooks Verlag.

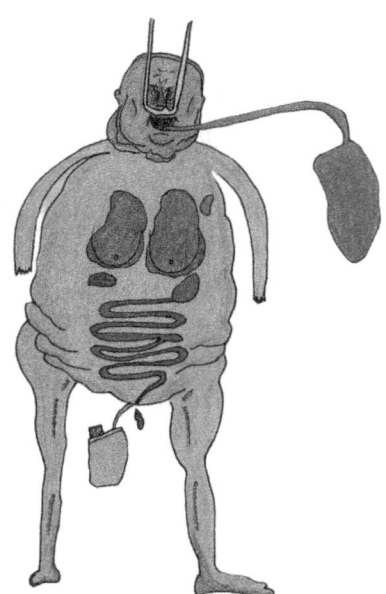

Figure 5 Hermann Kinder, *Der Weg allen Fleisches* [*The Way of All Flesh*], page 138. Courtesy Weisshaupt Verlag.

to reinforce the established 'ageing as decline' narrative, this chapter argues that Kinder's is a subversive text which actually reframes ageing and illness through the use of self-deprecating humour and graphic art.

Representing the failing body textually and graphically makes a space for reconsidering what we consider to be *normal ageing* and contributes to an awareness of the vulnerability of life, the unpredictability of health and the diversity of the ageing experience. But it also goes further. Although it depicts struggle, bodily decline and an anxiety about death as the way of all flesh, this book is remarkable in its passion for life and its Stoic refusal to allow the fear of death to ruin life. Building on Jan Baars's call for an inspirational 'art of ageing', this chapter argues that Kinder manages to eke out a way of living with finitude that is sensitive to the emotional and mental work that remaining alive and facing death require. The book reframes ageing by positioning it as a complex period in the life course which requires both resilience and acceptance.

Successful ageing vs the 'art of ageing'

As scholars of ageing studies have shown, ageing is not only synonymous with physical and mental decline; it is also a cultural script that interprets the biological realities of ageing in a certain way (Morganroth Gullette, 2004). In order to combat negative stereotypes of ageing as a period of irreversible deterioration marked by failing health and redundancy, Rowe and Kahn promoted the idea of successful ageing in the 1990s, suggesting that the right lifestyle and health choices can change how we age (Rowe and Kahn 1997, 1998, 2015). The successful ageing paradigm disassociates ageing from decline but makes individuals responsible for their ageing experience. It also suggests that this experience can be controlled and managed through careful planning. According to this logic, the decision to live an active, healthy, and productive life can postpone old age and death by extending youthfulness and physical fitness into the Fourth Age. In its efforts to reframe ageing so it is no longer a narrative of decrepitude, the successful ageing paradigm sets up an ageist and ableist framework which marginalizes those who cannot meet its standards.

Gerontological discourse distinguishes between the so-called 'Third Age' and 'Fourth Age' in the life course. The ideal of an extended life expectancy and an active Third Age as an 'era of personal fulfilment' (Laslett 1989: 4) is facilitated, as Higgs and Gilleard make clear, by shunting fears of progressive dependency, frailty and decrepitude into the negatively developed social imaginary of the Fourth Age (Gilleard and Higgs 2010; Higgs and Gilleard 2014). This deliberate exclusion of '"agedness" from the discourses of later life' (Higgs and Gilleard 2014: 12) contributes to a poverty of resources on the experience of ageing. Caught between triumphant age-defying narratives that emphasize youthfulness and narratives of hopeless decline, older people are left with what Jan Baars and Chris Phillipson call an uninspiring and 'underdeveloped vocabulary of ageing' (2013: 3) which neither reflects the full range of ageing experiences nor offers insights into living ageing meaningfully, as ageing well should not simply be equated with staying young (Baars 2012). Baars proposes to go beyond these polarized perspectives by rethinking ageing as a valuable process of learning to live a finite life (2017: 969). Building on the art of living from ancient Greek and Roman cultures, Baars tries to contribute to an inspiring culture of ageing by sketching an 'art of ageing' that ambitiously aims to encourage and support people to age well. This involves acknowledging the pleasures of a long and meaningful life *and* the sufferings and vulnerabilities that ageing may bring. Living according to this art means practising dying by being open to loss, but also being open to wonder and new opportunities (Baars 2017: 972). It involves sustaining or enlarging 'the possibilities to exercise control over certain situations' but also helping to develop 'meaningful ways of encountering situations in life that *cannot* be controlled' (Baars 2012: 244). This inclusive approach restores meaning and dignity to *all* experiences of ageing, understood as a vital part of life. The 'art of ageing' also opens up a transgenerational perspective. Ageing involves living through changes that may increase opportunities for reflection on and knowledge about what it means to be mortal. This in turn can serve wider societal needs as people are encouraged to share their real and varied experiences of ageing to inspire others to live ageing better.

Literature can play a key role in this. In his work on the body and life-writing, Thomas Couser (1997) argues that narrating illness can be a way of sharing the body with others. Reflecting on the writing individual, Couser explores this as a secular healing ritual (Couser 1997: 293). While it may not physically heal the body, narrating one's experience can help to come to terms with biographical disruption. On the other hand, writing and reading illness narratives can help us to understand what it means to inhabit a body (Couser 1997: 295). By offering 'access to lived time' (Skagen 2021: 16) and showcasing individual and sociocultural perceptions of opportunities and obstacles, as well as daily routines, fears and vulnerabilities, literature on ageing can create a space for acknowledging the variability and diversity of the ageing experience. This in turn can contribute to a 'deeper awareness of the intensity of finite lives' (Baars 2012: 223) and thus an inspiring 'perspective for ageing' (236) that takes the experiences, challenges and opportunities of ageing seriously.

Beyond words? Narrating ageing with finitude

One of the challenges of writing about illness and ageing is the problem of how to represent this experience in a way which avoids being overly pessimistic or overly positivist. In her book examining writing on illness, Kathlyn Conway develops a system for categorizing illness stories by dividing them into triumphant and untriumphant tales (2013). Similar to what Arthur Frank has called restitutive narratives (1995), triumphant stories of illness celebrate the achievement of a return to health by representing illness retrospectively as an opportunity for growth.[2] In contrast to this, untriumphant narratives reflect on the devastating aspects of walking the line between disintegration and survival (Conway 2013: 55). They show the psychological and physical damage that illness and disability can cause and offer insights into mechanisms for coping with a confrontation with bodily limits. It is easy to see how these categories could be extended to separate triumphant narratives of successful ageing on one side and more untriumphant narratives that explore the hard work involved in acknowledging and accepting limits on the other.

In *The Way of All Flesh* Kinder manages to find a way of writing about his experience of illness and ageing that avoids coming down on either side of this binary. This is partly due to the structure and style of narration. The book is divided into three distinct parts: one and three focus intensely on the personal experience of illness and are narrated coolly from a distancing third-person perspective.[3] Part two falls out of what is a rather linear narrative of physical decline. Narrated in the first person, it comprises a loose series of dream sequences, associations and potentially medication-induced hallucinations that interweave different fears, life periods and episodes to offer insights into the protagonist's internal world. Complex and multilayered, this imaginative world

---

[2] Arthur Frank (1995) identifies three main types of illness narratives restitution, chaos and quest.
[3] Perhaps in analogy of Kafka's Joseph K. from *The Trial* but also in an abbreviation of Kinder, the protagonist in *The Way of All Flesh* is called K. This short designation allows simultaneous anonymity and specificity.

is marked by writerly, professional and bodily insecurities and shame. Through quick-paced shifts between subjects, settings and scenarios that blur boundaries between past and present, these sequences show that illness and physical decline are only one part of the protagonist's story and bring together different kinds of limitations, embarrassments and shame. By changing narrative style, focus and perspective, Kinder manages a tightrope walk between inside and outside, intimacy and distance, the mundane and the dramatic. This contains the emotionality of the story, even though K.'s diagnosis is devastating.

Employing a compact and laconic style of narration, Kinder alternates between graphic descriptions of the experience of illness (35–7) and summarizing flashforwards that allude to a further deterioration in condition (24, 31). His writing style can present situations of extreme bodily vulnerability in a way which often sidelines distress – although, as argued below, this is remediated by the drawings included in the book. The text is also marked by a form of humour which is 'amusing, but not so funny' (Kinder 1995: 276), creating 'suspense, a tipping point between emotions, between horror and laughter' (Kinder 2019: 107). This can be seen, for example, in the following episode which highlights the protagonist's own internalized ageism. At the beginning of the story K. is introduced as a fit hobby cyclist: when on one of his long-distance cycling tours he encounters an older and fatter man whose body spills over the bench he is resting on, K. is overcome by disgust (10). Adamant that he will avoid such a fate, K. decides to stay fit by keeping up his exercise regime, but the onset of his illness starts to undermine his own sense of bodily integrity so that he soon inhabits a disgusting body, which resembles the old man (22). As Martha Nussbaum notes, '[a]ging is the only disgust-stigma category into which every one of us will inevitably move, if we live long enough' (Nussbaum and Levmore 2017: 109). This is also the moment when humour becomes serious and 'our laughter begins to freeze' (Iser 1976: 402).

K.'s experiences of the ageing process and his adjustment to increasing vulnerability and decline show that his initial dismissal of the ageing body was predicated on an ageist and ableist assumption that a good life can only be healthy and active. Despite its engagement with existential limits, *The Way of All Flesh* manages to present life as something worth living. This is due to K.'s interpersonal relationships and his connections to others, but also perhaps to the new opportunities for diversion and growth that he is able to uncover.[4] While those who meet him seem to already consign him to the scrapheap (121, 124),

---

[4] The book details many different stories of illness and ageing; this makes the contingency of K.'s circumstances clear.

K. holds on to life, develops coping mechanisms and concentrates on survival: 'he said to the moment: stay a while, before everything will get much worse' (122).⁵ K.'s attentive living reframes ageing by modelling a way of facing up to existential limits and finitude and 'developing meaningful ways of encountering situations in life that *cannot* be controlled' (Baars 2012: 244). It ends with K. still alive, 'always expecting the unexpected' (136).

Art and living with finitude

One of the ways to improve the experience of ageing is through an engagement with the arts. In *The Way of All Flesh* Kinder draws attention to how the everyday practices of producing and consuming culture can simultaneously offer distractions from as well as insights into the experience of finitude. The medical humanities often explore this issue from the perspective of practising arts in care settings (see, for example, Bolton 2007). In her recent book on music and healthcare, Hilary Moss adopts a broader perspective, emphasizing that consuming and participating in the arts, particularly in healthcare settings, can offer moments of companionship, self-expression, hope and beauty (2021: 1). Acting as a distraction from pain and illness, the arts can facilitate aesthetic enjoyment and create a space for dreaming (DeNora 2021) that can help the individual to transcend bodily pain. Engaging with the arts also can evoke memories and encourage reflection on difficult issues around mortality, dying, grief, fear and loss (Walter 2012: 76). They can also offer comfort.

Kinder's books on ageing are packed with references to music, literature, art and other cultural art forms. This creates a cultural arsenal that the protagonists, and also Kinder's readers, can mobilize in their own education on the art of living with finitude. K. listens repeatedly to Schubert's *Death and the Maiden* (124, 133); this aesthetic experience opens up an experiential pathway that is perhaps not accessible in the discourse on ageing. For K., interpreting and appreciating art is presented as a sedentary leisure activity that creates new vistas and fires cognitive processes, especially when physical incapacity shrinks his world. In *The Way of All Flesh*, he passes time by looking at the chaotic and unruly scenes of Pieter Breughel the Elder's *Dulle Griet* (124), in which

---

⁵ The German quote refers to Goethe's *Faust* drama in which Faust wagers that whatever kind of satisfaction Mephistopheles offers to him, he will never be satisfied: 'When I say to the moment flying; / 'Linger a while–thou art so fair!'/Then bind me in thy bonds undying,/And my final ruin I will bear!'

old mad Meg is dressed for battle, daring to plunder in front of the mouth of hell. Breughel's is a monstrous space full of disgusting creatures where Meg risks total annihilation. Collecting her booty and hoping to return unscathed, Meg is fearless. While K. enjoys the distraction of chasing interpretive leads online and thus the opportunity to co-create the work of art, the painting may hold another message for the reader as it depicts Meg's temporary triumph over death. If on the one hand, the creation of art can be linked to immortality and a desire to make something that will outlast the body, the act of engaging with culture can help to interpret individual and collective fates, facilitating a sense of agency, however mortal. Although art has been presented as a form of denial of death (Becker 1997), engaging with these paintings may help viewers to confront the topic of meaninglessness and death in a mediated and non-existential way.

Drawing bodily transformation: Ageing and the grotesque

The drawings included in Kinder's book have a different effect. While in hospital, writing and drawing helps K. to process his experiences, restoring a sense of agency that is limited by illness. Thirteen coloured pen drawings which open, close and punctuate the text are reproductions from Kinder's own autobiographical journals. They capture different stages of bodily transformation and, taken as a series, they create a visual record of increasing physical decline.[6] Marked by an economy of means, these drawings can be graphically linked to the German inter-war artists Otto Dix and George Grosz who after the First World War depicted life during the 1920s in grotesque caricatures that often accentuate the deformed body.

Kinder's drawings show everyday scenes and experiences from K.'s daily life that are largely in sync with the textual narrative. They follow the arc of K.'s illness trajectory, moving from pre-diagnosis and diagnosis through to decreasing health, medical intervention, the amputation of his foot and renewed readjustment, followed by further decline. However, they represent more than just visual translations of the written word. While the textual narrative is at pains to maintain

---

[6] In 2019, a more extensive volume of his drawings entitled *Harms Selfies* was published which includes some similar images to *The Way of All Flesh*. 'Harm' is a shortened form of Hermann. If the contemporary selfie culture aims to document presence, but also to control how one is seen, Kinder's selfies can be seen to achieve similar ends, but the means are more self-deprecating. In *The Way of all Flesh*, Kinder's drawings are left untitled. I will refer to them here by a number which reflects the order in which they appear in this book.

a factual tone and avoid sentimentality, using foreshadowing to compress events and speed up the illness story, the insertion of the drawings slows things down, revealing levels of complexity and emotion that the text deliberately masks. In the textual narrative K. attempts to be a good patient by pushing forward and not dwelling on his illness and massive bodily changes; however, the drawings probe new stages of embodiment in great detail, revealing the self's disgust and shame while also mobilizing humour. This double vision facilitates deeper insights into the complex inner world of experiencing illness – and age-related decline.

By forcing a confrontation with the ageing male body and bodily dysfunction, the drawings push at the boundaries of what is considered to be *normal ageing*. Variously depicting excretions, genitals, body orifices, saggy skin folds, inflammations and the amputated foot stump, these drawings use the grotesque to explore what it means to live with certain body configurations (Kayser 1968). They foreground a physical decline that is often culturally denied and pushed out of sight, perhaps out of a sociocultural fear of contamination or a reluctance to face up to the reality of mortality. Other pictures address the normalcy of societal and structural exclusion of the disabled body. This can be seen, for example, in a drawing which depicts K. after the amputation of his forefoot (drawing four, 45). He is seen brushing his hair in the hospital bathroom. Sitting in his wheelchair, K. can only see the very top of his head and his eyes as the hospital bathroom mirror has been positioned above the sink. The image of K.'s partial reflection, framed by the mirror, along with his wheelchair and a view of his back in the hospital gown, highlights the cultural construction of bodily visibility and invisibility. Encapsulating a brief experience of everyday exclusion, the drawing calls attention to societal acceptability of inaccessibility, emphasizing that the private is political.

A later image of K. standing in a bikini in front of an advertisement for swimwear at a bus stop in Konstanz (drawing eleven, 108) reinforces this idea of structural bodily exclusion. Here, K.'s sagging, speckled and swollen body, squeezed unfavourably into a pink bra and shorts and standing in a way which displays his bare foot stump and his surgical scars, presents the antithesis of the beautifully smooth, symmetrical and lithe body of the young woman in the advertisement. It is K.'s real body that dominates the image and demands to be observed. Although this portrayal would superficially seem to confirm a stereotype of the ugliness of ageing, Kinder's drawing employs an oppositional visual comedy to subvert this. The inappropriateness of K.'s dress raises questions about the beauty ideal and not his body.

The drawings do not represent a cool or rational medical gaze on the body, and the body depicted here is not to be envied or emulated. Instead, bodily comedy and elements of the grotesque are employed to present K. unflatteringly as an exaggerated, distorted and ugly figure. Reflecting on his sketches in a volume of self-portraits published in 2019, Kinder describes how the ugly portrait, 'located between wanting to live and having to die' (2019: 108), mobilizes a form of conciliatory humour that channels anxieties around unreliable bodies by making them amusing. Emphasizing the effect of the grotesque depiction of his altered body, Kinder calls this a 'liberating messiness' (2019: 108). Drawing ten (see Figure 4) offers an excellent example of this.[7]

In this drawing, we see K.'s post-operative and rehabilitating body hooked up to a series of weights; he cannot lift them, but they lift him. Comically dangling in the air, but with a chair underneath, K.'s suspended body highlights the limits of bodywork. Instead of empowering the body, his sporting efforts only confirm his incapacity. If sport is a way of taking control of one's health and reshaping the body to extend the life course through 'good pain', this drawing shows K.'s painful and futile attempts to be a good patient. His efforts to abet his recovery and extend his life through torturous exercise will not achieve anything. The self-deprecating style of the drawing signals simultaneous abjection and acceptance. Laughter at his own situation and his own failure are ways of putting the viewers at ease by absolving them of what Tom Shakespeare calls 'the unbearable weight of empathy which they feel obligated to carry' (1999: 50). The visual incongruity of the immovable heavy weights and K.'s precarious body creates an opportunity for humorous release. This kind of humour reframes the ageing and disabled body for the viewer by establishing a rapport that can overcome stigma and diminish the personal sense of shame and embarrassment connected to the ageing body.

In the final drawing of the series, Kinder employs the whole arsenal of the grotesque to present the body as a generator of disgust (Figure 5). The illness which has wrought destruction under the surface of the skin, has broken out onto the surface of the drawing: we see how internal body organs and fluids are leaving this fleshy sinking ship, escaping out to take up space in the public sphere. This is a representation of the crisis of the body, but also a depiction of what Kathleen Woodward refers to as the fear of the fragmenting body in ageing (1991: 182). Hovering suspended while still attached, the ambiguity of

---

[7] In *Harms Selfies*, a variation of this drawing is included as a part of a quadriptych on fitness, entitled 'Fitness 2' (2019, 80).

the organ on display – is it a stomach or is it a tongue? – challenges any notion of bodily integrity. The body shown is a body that has been medicalized. It is naked, with a catheter dangling and oxygen tubes. It appears monstrous, an impression which is reinforced by the horn-like tubes that dominate K.'s red and swollen face and the yawning dark hole of the mouth which is the entrance to the site of illness, but which appears to be laughing. Drawing on the carnivalesque and its associations with comic exaggeration and its focus on the inside out, this laughter may signal a resistance to the fear of death (Bakhtin 1984).

The drawing only depicts some organs, reflecting how the anatomy and the body are experienced and perceived, internally as well as externally. This makes the physical and the psychic body visible. For example, the greyed-out and misshapen lungs accentuate their diminished capacity in the mode of the grotesque. The surgical scars on K.'s legs and his turned-out foot draw attention to his amputated foot stump. Usually hidden in his shoe, the stump is the unseen cause of his rolling gait and off-balance stance which causes him to lean more heavily to the right. This grotesquely excessive and transgressive body exceeds its confines and sags and leaks, but it still continues to be alive and sentient. The drawing, alongside the others in the series, emphasizes the painful process of staying alive as well as the process of decline already underway. Documenting adjustments to uncontrollable change, alienation and the difficult process of acceptance, these drawings contribute to a culture of knowledge on what it means to have a body and to live a finite life.

In its reflections on finitude *The Way of All Flesh* reminds readers of the vulnerability and the limitations inherent in life which cannot be avoided or overcome. Attending to the emotional work and the resilience that facing up to the reality of ageing and particularly ageing with illness requires, the book highlights the importance of holding on to life and what makes life liveable. In this way, it opens up a new horizon that reframes ageing as a refusal to allow fear or the decline in physical capabilities to impede life. When his world shrinks due to illness, K. carefully adjusts how he lives: even though he is aware that 'you die in sections' (9), this experience of progressive disintegration is countered by moments of happiness that come in small steps (50) as he adjusts to life after the amputation. As his time runs out, he uses time differently to minimize discomfort and maximize enjoyment. This is the art of ageing facilitated by experience and reflection: it processes, assimilates, and adjusts to loss but refuses to be defined by it. Exploring a way of living that is open to death, Kinder draws on the transgressive spirit of carnival; in so doing his works contribute to what Baars calls an 'inspiring culture of ageing' (Baars 2012: 201). In turn, in its reflections on finitude, this text provides a rehearsal for the reader who witnesses this illuminating moment.

Bibliography

Bakhtin, M. M. (1984), *Rabelais and His World*, trans. Helene Iswolsky, Bloomington: Indiana University Press.

Baars, J. (2012), *Aging and the Art of Living*, Baltimore: Johns Hopkins University Press.

Baars, J. (2013), 'A Deepening Involvement in Life with Others: Towards a Philosophy of Aging', *Research on Ageing and Social Policy*, 1(1): 6–26. Available at: https://doi.org/10.4471/rasp.2013.01 (accessed 9 January 2023).

Baars, J. (2017), 'Aging: Learning to Live a Finite Life', *The Gerontologist*, 57(5): 969–96. Available at: https://doi.org/10.1093/geront/gnw089 (accessed 20 December 2022).

Baars, J. and C. Phillipson (2013), 'Introduction', in Jan Baars, Joseph Dohmen, Amanda Grenier and Chris Phillipson (eds), *Ageing, Meaning and Social Structure: Connecting Critical and Humanistic Gerontology*, 1–10, Bristol and Chicago: Policy Press.

Becker, E. (1997), *The Denial of Death*, New York: Free Press Paperbacks.

Bolton, G., ed. (2007), *Dying, Bereavement and the Healing Arts*, London and Philadelphia: Jessica Kingsley Publishers.

Conway, K. (2013), *Beyond Words: Illness and the Limits of Expression*, Albuquerque: University of New Mexico Press.

Couser, T. G. (1997), *Recovering Bodies: Illness, Disability, and Life Writing*, Madison: University of Wisconsin Press.

DeNora, T. (2012), 'Resounding the Great Divide: Theorising Music in Everyday Life at the End of Life', *Mortality*, 17(2): 92–105. Available at: https://doi.org/10.1080/13576275.2012.673375 (accessed 3 December 2022).

Frank, A. (1995), *The Wounded Storyteller: Body, Illness, Ethics*, Chicago: University of Chicago.

Gilleard, C. and Paul Higgs (2010), 'Aging without Agency: Theorizing the Fourth Age', *Aging and Mental Health*, 14(2): 121–28. Available at: https://doi-org.may.idm.oclc.org/10.1080/13607860903228762 (accessed 28 November 2022).

Hamann, C. and Siegmund Kopitzki, eds (2008), *Hermann Kinder*, Eggingen: Edition Isele.

Higgs, P. and Chris Gilleard (2014), 'Frailty, Abjection and the "Othering" of the Fourth Age', *Health Sociology Review*, 23(1): 10–19. Available at: https://doi.org/10.5172/hesr.2014.23.1.10 (accessed 10 October 2022).

Iser, W. (1976), 'Das Komische: Opposition oder Kipp-Phänomen?', in Wolfgang Preisendanz and Rainer Warning (eds), *Das Komische*, 398–401, Munich: Wilhelm Fink Verlag.
Kayser, Wolfgang (1968), *The Grotesque in Art and Literature*, trans. Ulrich Weisstein, Gloucester: P. Smith.
Kinder, H. (1990), *Die Böhmischen Schwestern*, Zurich: Haffmans.
Kinder, H. (1995), *Von gleicher Han: Aufsätze, Essays zur Gegenwartsliteratur und etwas Poetik*, Eggingen: Edition Klaus Isele.
Kinder, H. (1997), *Um Leben und Tod*, Hamburg: Rotbuch.
Kinder, H. (2006), *Mein Melaten: Der Methusalem-Roman*, Frankfurt am Main: Haffmans Verlag bei Zweitausendeins.
Kinder, H. (2014), *Der Weg allen Fleisches*, Frankfurt am Main: Weissbooks.
Kinder, H. (2019), *Harms Selfies*, Norderstedt: Books on Demand.
Laslett, P. (1989), *A Fresh Map of Life*, London: Weidenfeld & Nicolson.
Morganroth Gullette, M. (2004), *Aged by Culture*, Chicago: University of Chicago Press.
Moss, H. (2021), *Music and Creativity in Healthcare Settings: Does Music Matter?*, Abingdon: Routledge.
Nussbaum, M. C. and Saul Levmore (2017), *Aging Thoughtfully: Conversations about Retirement, Romance, Wrinkles, and Regret*, New York: Oxford University Press.
Rowe, J. W. and R. L. Kahn (1997), 'Successful Ageing', *The Gerontologist*, 37(4): 433–40.
Rowe, J. W. and R. L. Kahn (1998), *Successful Ageing*, New York: Pantheon Books.
Rowe, J. W. and R. L. Kahn (2015), 'Successful Ageing 2.0: Conceptual Expansions for the 21st Century', *The Journals for Gerontology, Series B: Psychological Sciences and Social Sciences*, 70(4): 593–96.
Shakespeare, T. (1999), 'Joking a Part', *Body & Society*, 5(4): 47–52.
Skagen, M. V. (2021), 'How Can Literary Studies Contribute to a Cultural History of Ageing', in Margery Vibe Skagen (ed.), *Cultural Histories of Ageing: Myths, Plots and Metaphors of the Senescent Self*, 1–20, New York: Routledge.
Walter, T. (2012), 'How People Who Are Dying Or Mourning Engage with the Arts', *Music and Arts in Action*, 4(1): 73–98.
Woodward, K. (1991), *Aging and its Discontents: Freud and Other Fictions*, Bloomington: Indiana University Press.

5

On old age and wisdom

Aleida Assmann

Introduction

In an interview in November 2020, the German pop musician and painter Wolfgang Niedecken (b. 1951) was asked to comment on his last album *Everything Flows*. The interviewer mentioned that this title goes back to the Greek philosopher Heraclitus and was thus connected to an ancient tradition of wisdom. He wanted to know: 'How about yourself? Have you gained the wisdom of old age?' The musician responded as follows:

> Well, I don't know about the wisdom of old age. Of course, one has picked up one or two things in life. I no longer jump on a table, instead, I walk around the block and try to reflect. Yes, that is right: everything flows. I see the world now in a much more relaxed attitude. (Radio Interview with *Zwischentöne* and Niedecken 2020)

Two years later Niedecken had a chance to return to this topic. He was now asked to comment on his song *Tenth of June*, forty years after a big peace demonstration in Bonn, the former capital of West Germany. Niedecken and his band BAP had been part of the German peace movement which opposed NATO and the nuclear rearmament during the Cold War in the Reagan era. In the context of Putin's war against Ukraine and collective Western efforts to rebuild NATO, the songwriter was asked about his pacifist commitment, and he admitted that he now had a broader and more realistic attitude to the political issue of military defence. He did not disown his earlier values but was ready to reassess them in the light of the new political context: 'One should not be stubborn and dogged. It is possible to change one's opinion. I do not need to be always right. "The times they are a-changin"' (Wiele 2022).

This interview shows that there is a tacit connection between wisdom and (old) age in the popular imagination (see 'Weisheit', Wikipedia). To become wise means to adopt a certain distance to current events and debates, and it includes the ability to respond to higher complexity and responsibility by changing one's opinions over time. Old age, however, is in itself no guarantee for acquiring wisdom. Ancient cultures promote widely varying standards of wisdom: some define it with reference to the capacity for self-criticism, others highlight pessimism, quietism or stoicism in old age. But they all converge in their negative judgement of a behaviour that extolls human vices such as greed or lying. In addition, all ancient models of wisdom reject a narcissistic ego and are averse to forms of pride and self-promotion at the expense of the common good.

Evidently, while age is no guarantee for attaining wisdom, the connection between age and wisdom deserves further analysis. According to a definition in the German dictionary of the brothers Grimm, published in the nineteenth century, the core of wisdom is set off from general knowledge and defined as 'knowledge about the meaning of life' and 'attention to the whole of life'.[1] The emphasis on 'the whole of life' is important; it can also mean: drawing on long experience, seeing the world in a broader perspective and developing a more relaxed attitude – these seem to be common markers of wisdom. I take this intuitive understanding as a starting point to reconsider the relationship between wisdom and old age: what exactly is meant by and included in the concept of wisdom? How is it framed in different cultures? Can it be defined as a specific type of knowledge?[2] How can it be investigated empirically? How is wisdom related to age and ageing, and what is its relevance today?

Wisdom as a trans-cultural topic in the humanities

The concept of wisdom lies beyond the contemporary concerns of the humanities and has remained largely outside its paradigms, discourses and discussions. And this is so even though wisdom has played a major role in many languages: in Hebrew it is 'hokma', in Arabic 'hekmet', in Greek 'sophia', and in Latin 'sapientia'.

---

[1] See *Deutsches Wörterbuch von Jacob Grimm und Wilhelm Grimm*. For the online version and entry on wisdom see: https://www.dwds.de/wb/dwb/weisheit (accessed 12 September 2022).

[2] By linking wisdom to a specific kind of knowledge, I am limiting the thematic focus of this chapter and do not cover the range of emotions related to old age and ageism. For a discussion of the social politics of the emotions with respect to old age see Kathleen Woodward (2002) who argues that anger as 'the virtual opposite of wisdom' can itself become a kind of wisdom, 'a wise anger' (187).

The term can be applied to masters of contemplation in the Far East such as Confucius and Mencius, to Western philosophers from Plato, Aristotle and the Stoics to Erasmus, but also to ancient Egyptian tomb inscriptions, the Bible, the whole archive of literary texts and inconspicuous everyday experiences. The question 'what makes humans wise?' is a central topic in popular fairy tales, where characters that are mindful of other human beings and animals are often more successful in overcoming obstacles than those who only pursue their self-interests. The search for wisdom is also a perennial quest in popular guides to a good life. But because of its semantic fuzziness and practical embeddedness in specific genres and contexts, it has rarely featured as a topic in historical, cultural or empirical research. This, however, might be changing right now; recent studies signal a new interest in the topic (Sternberg and Glück 2022; Keynes 2021). My own interest in wisdom started in the context of comparative cultural history. Together with Jan Assmann in 1979 I co-founded the research group 'archaeology of literary communication' at the newly established Centre for Interdisciplinary Studies at the University of Bielefeld. The research theme brought together an interdisciplinary group of scholars who shared the common aspiration to reinject ancient and non-Western text-cultures (like Egyptology) into the debate on contemporary phenomena and advanced theory. In 1989 Wisdom was the third topic chosen by the group (Assmann 1991); volumes on other topics followed. It was a new step in the humanities to recover this rich archive of non-European cultures and premodern traditions for the history and sociology of knowledge by investigating their different sources, institutional transmission, pathways of diversification, conflicts and competitions, as well as types of knowledge.

Yet the great interdisciplinary potential of the label 'wisdom' for scholars and specialists of different cultures created new problems. Editing a collection of essays proved to be a real challenge: how could I bring together all these materials from different disciplines and non-Western ancient cultures and establish some order and coherence in the vast field of 'wisdom texts'? One way of dealing with the diversity and complexity of wisdom was a conceptual classification of the field. The result is a 'wisdom-compass', that is a tool to navigate wisdom literature which is offered as an introduction to the volume (Assmann 1991). It is based on a distinction between four types of wisdom literature, each marked by a prominent name. In this case classification did not reduce but exposed the inherent complexity of the idea, while also providing a structured way in which it could be addressed. It was centrally important to avoid the reproduction of a fuzzy idea of wisdom that indiscriminately conflates heterogeneous sources and types of evidence. Here are my four types of wisdom, each personified by a cultural hero or fictional character:

Solomon: this name goes back to the king in the Bible and refers to a collection of proverbs in the context of ancient near Eastern wisdom literature. He personifies the wisdom of power in the sense of a deeper knowledge of what preserves peace and holds society together. This is the wisdom of the judge or ruler which is often expressed in simple rules and proverbs. Bertolt Brecht offered a compelling rendition of Solomon's wisdom in his play *The Caucasian Chalk Circle* ([1944–45] 1963): the judge Adzdak stages a competition for a child in order to identify through the contest the empathic woman as the right mother (the biological mother proves unworthy). But wisdom of this kind – with connotations of regal and biblical profundity – can also be generated in more humble circumstances. In large families children discover rules for themselves that all can agree on, leading to mutual satisfaction. One of these rules is: one sibling cuts the pie and the others are free to choose their own slice. This homegrown piece of wisdom already reflects the wise strategy of a division of power.

Prospero in Shakespeare's *The Tempest* represents the wisdom of magic or a deeper esoteric knowledge of what holds nature and the world together ([1623], 1916, 1959). This is the wisdom of the magi, the magicians, the sorcerers and the pan-sophists which are also to be found in non-Western and indigenous cultures. The role of the revered sage became a prestigious form of self-fashioning in the period of the Renaissance, when in their publications and compendia humanists collected, translated and compiled esoteric knowledge from ancient books and foreign languages. Johannes Reuchlin and Athanasius Kircher in Germany or John Dee in England are humanists in the sixteenth and seventeenth centuries who aimed at advancing 'wisdom' in the sense of a total knowledge of the world. This is picked up in Peter Greenaway's film *Prospero's Books* (1991), where Prospero is presented in intimate intercourse with his books on water, mirrors, mythologies, geometry, colours, birth, an inventory of the dead, books on the earth, on languages and universal cosmography. Some essays in the volume on wisdom deal with the figure of the sage in Russia, India and Ancient Egypt (Assmann 1991).

Polonius in Shakespeare's *Hamlet* ([1603] 1916, 1959) stands for the practical wisdom of everyday experience, neatly packaged in commonplace lessons for a good life and traditionally transmitted from the father to the son. While in the play his character represents 'the tedious fool', I use his parental guidance to his son Laertes to highlight a form of pragmatic wisdom that can also be found in ancient Egyptian conduct books and many other non-Western cultures. Before

Laertes leaves for Paris, he receives his father's blessing and a few lessons that are to guide and protect him in a world of strangers:

> My blessing with thee!
> And these few precepts in thy memory.
> Give thy thoughts no tongue,
> Nor any unproportion'd thought his act.
> Be thou familiar, but by no means vulgar.
> ... Beware
> Of entrance to a quarrel; but, being in,
> Bear't that th' opposed may beware of thee.
> Give every man thy ear, but few thy voice; ...
> Neither a borrower nor a lender be; ...
> This above all – to thine own self be true,
> And it must follow, as the night the day
> thou canst not then be false to anyone. (Act I, scene 3, 57–80)

It is interesting to note that the last precept breaks with and transcends all the previous rules of conduct because it anticipates an authentic notion of the self as a modern and unfathomable source of identity (Assmann 2004). While this notion of a 'true self' points to a protestant tradition that later boomed within a distinctly Western tradition, the essays collected under this heading deal with paternal wisdom in Mesopotamia, in Africa and in Roma communities.

Jaques in Shakespeare's *As You Like It* ([1623] 1916, 1959) represents the critical wisdom of the fool and sceptic. On Shakespeare's stage, the position of the fool is not defined by the hierarchy of court and power. He has the licence to speak out freely and remind the king of what he desires most to forget. It is the sceptical wisdom of Jaques to compare human life to the theatre:

> All the world's a stage,
> And all the men and women merely players;
> They have their exits and their entrances,
> And one man in his time plays many parts,
> His acts being seven ages. (Act II, scene 4, 139–43)

Jaques goes on to describe each of the seven acts, emphasizing the vanity of human existence, which is in itself an important tradition of wisdom literature. The last stage in the human lifespan is a dominated by 'childishness' and physical incapacity:

> Last scene of all,
> That ends this strange eventful history,

Is second childishness and mere oblivion,
Sans teeth, sans eyes, sans taste, sans everything. (Act II, scene 7, 139–66)

According to Jaques' pessimistic model, ascribing wisdom to the final stage of life would be an act of delusion and pride. He speaks in the tradition of the biblical book Ecclesiastes that unmasks the futility of human aspirations. We are dealing here with a paradox of wisdom that effaces its own existence. In this way, Socrates' famous axiom – 'I know that I don't know' – has a certain affinity with the biblical concept of 'vanity' as expressed in the Hebrew word 'hevel', meaning 'puff of wind'. Essays in this section also elaborate on the subversive role of Confucius in Chinese tradition, or the figure of the trickster in the tradition of the Oglala (Africa).

This tentative wisdom compass is certainly incomplete, because it exclusively centres on male representatives of wisdom. While it would be problematic and essentialist to single out a specific form of 'female knowledge', it does make sense to point to traditional forms of knowledge that are valued, transmitted and shared by women in particular. An example would be the female rites of initiation in indigenous societies, focusing on arts and concerns for which women are endowed with a special social and cultural responsibility, covering folk knowledge of the body and the environment. Cultural competences such as nursing and nurturing, cooking and healing are 'at the heart of ensuring the health and progress of society' (Mbewe 2021: 62). In Western history in the early modern era, the long practised and esteemed traditional wisdom of women came under pressure when male-dominated institutions like the Church or the universities took over and created a canonized body of knowledge and fortified it in exclusively male formats of legitimate transmission. The persecution of so-called 'witches' is the traumatic historical evidence of the repression and persecution of the generation and transmission of female knowledge (Honegger 1978; Rowlands 2001). Recent concepts such as 'epistemic violence' or 'epistemic injustice' have alerted us to the wider dimensions of this problem.

Wisdom as a type of knowledge

We can glean from the above that it is hard to define wisdom because this fuzzy notion spills across epochs into different sociocultural contexts. As the wisdom compass shows, its manifestations are so broad that it is even difficult to discover a certain family resemblance among its different dimensions. Bearing this in mind, the following aims to characterize wisdom more generally as a particular type of knowledge with certain distinctive features.

Firstly, wisdom is a cross-cultural phenomenon. Knowledge dealing with practical issues of a good life is highly valued in all cultures and extends beyond other forms of professional knowledge and experience. It is contained in the oldest text corpora of various cultures and has a long history of being canonized as outstanding knowledge. Wisdom as a type of knowledge is therefore historically varied and culturally polymorphous. This global esteem for wisdom is an important indication that the most diverse groups and cultures have substantial common ground for productive cross-cultural research on wisdom.

Secondly, wisdom is embodied and engendered knowledge. It is knowledge saturated with experience. In this, it clearly differs from abstract and discursive knowledge as produced by theory, science, philosophy and theology. The knowledge of wisdom cannot be built into a system because it is not abstract but concrete, which also explains its proximity to literature. There is no prescriptive pathway for attaining wisdom. Knowledge qualified as wisdom cannot be used in competitive contexts, because it bypasses binary oppositions that tend to separate and polarize communities. Unlike religion (based on the distinction of good or evil) and science (based on the distinction of true or false), it does not aim at certainty but allows for ambiguity, complexity, inclusion and indecision. Wisdom is complex but not necessarily complicated. It requires abiding with contradictions rather than resolving them.[3]

Thirdly, wisdom is habitually associated with old age. This is due to its capacity for retrospective evaluation of events in the human lifespan that is overshadowed by death. Views and judgements are often considered to be wise when they transcend rigid binary patterns of social or moral norms of right or wrong and allow for a more inclusive sense of order, complexity and balance. Wisdom in this sense articulates a broader view of the human condition, often in a wider cosmic context.

Fourth, wisdom requires a personal response. It is a common-sense concept that is not easy to theorize (Sowarka 1989). Abstract definitions do not get us very far. It is a word for a value that is generated not in observation but in interaction. What is considered a wise saying or wise behaviour is confirmed in interaction. Communication about wisdom is never objective but inherently

---

[3] In a letter to his brother in 1817, John Keats coined the phrase 'negative capability': 'I mean Negative Capability, that is, when a man is capable of being in uncertainties, mysteries, doubts, without any irritable reaching after fact and reason' (cited in Rollins 1958: 185).

interpersonal, creating immediate links of understanding and value, approval and estimation between human beings. Unlike information, political dogma or personal opinions which can be disseminated in print and social media, wisdom is not easily detachable from a person's individual authority and experience, hence it is not so easy to transmit. Lacking the support and backbone of an institution such as the court, the state, the Church or the university, wisdom thrives wherever it is individually received, recognized and acclaimed. What or who is wise is decided by those who recognize and acknowledge a person or a phrase as wise. Wisdom is not imposed as a binding command from above, but as an offer that is valued or ignored, accepted or rejected. It is fulfilled only in the response, the reception, the acceptance, the transmission.

Fifth, wisdom is practical knowledge about how to live a good life. It combines cognitive, affective and reflexive knowledge and is geared to avoiding harm and violence. Rules of wisdom are designed to reduce the ego by strengthening the sense of reciprocity, to avoid violence through a critical assessment of its consequences and to embrace sustainable solutions. Its central principle is the 'golden rule' which has global significance and universal acclaim: 'Do not do unto others what you do not want to have done unto yourself.' Here, the choice of words must be carefully observed. 'Universal acclaim' means that there is empirical evidence for the fact that a version of the golden rule has been formulated and acknowledged all over the world. It is even transmitted in the canonized texts of all monotheist religions.[4] Kant, however, replaced the popular and informal quality of the golden rule with a formula that carried a stronger normative force. His 'categorical imperative' articulates a 'universal principle' that is meant to have global application ([1785] 2019). In this shape, it has morphed into a Western concept, created by an individual philosopher and designed to be exported around the world.

Rather than providing a clear definition of what wisdom is, it is more productive to describe the circumstances under which wisdom flourishes. This is an intermediary space that is neither structured by fixed rules nor totally arbitrary and confusing. It belongs to a complex world in which order is neither clearly visible nor normatively prescribed but can be discovered and recognized. A deeper intuition of order seems to be characteristic for wise attitudes and behaviour.

---

[4] This wide-ranging acceptance is even the topic of an exceptionally rich Wikipedia article in German which equals the length of a full publication. See: https://de.wikipedia.org/wiki/Weisheit (accessed 19 September 2022).

In the ancient world, different cultures and religions were in mutual agreement about the superb quality of wisdom. In Western culture, however, the high evaluation and trace of wisdom was lost in the evolutionary process of civilization. Western philosophers like Plato, Aristotle or Kant explicitly opted out of the wisdom-tradition and created a new culture and tradition based on the principles of science, progress and universal truths. The embodied and often oral wisdom of sages fell flat in the process of modernization. As the value system of Western culture privileged youth over old age, rupture over continuation, revolution over tradition, and the future over the past, it largely lost its regard for the last phase of life as a generator of wisdom. While in traditional societies old men and old women are figures of a venerable status and old age is invested with social prestige, in Western culture old age is often associated with a demise of intellectual capacity, leading to dementia and 'second childishness', as the fool Jaques puts it in Shakespeare's *As You Like It*.

Wisdom as a topic in psychological research on ageing

In the 1960s and 1970s, psychology was dominated by an evolutionary perspective based on the hypothesis that moral development and social evolution progress together. The backbone was provided by Lawrence Kohlberg's schema consisting of six developmental stages of cognitive and moral development (Kohlberg 1976). His model was highly influential in other disciplines and eagerly picked up by sociologists and philosophers because it resonated perfectly with basic norms and principles of Western modernization theory. Kohlberg's schema constructs a linear progression from egotistic orientation towards in-group norms and finally to universalist principles. The first two stages avoid punishment and aim at reward: they constitute the 'pre-conventional level'. The next two stages engender the 'good boy' and 'good girl' attitude as well as loyalty to law and order: they constitute the 'conventional level'. The last two stages give rise to justice, the spirit of the law and universal principles of ethics: they constitute the 'post-conventional level' (Kohlberg 1976). Within these six stages, there is no place for the *unconventional* concept of wisdom. If at all, it could be applied to a highly speculative and abstract seventh stage of development that Kohlberg defined as 'post-postconventional stage', describing it vaguely as a cosmic worldview:

> In this stage, the individual shifts from seeing himself as the center of the universe to identifying with the universe and seeing himself from this perspective. What

results is that the individual senses the unity of the universe in which he is but one element. The acquisition of this non-individualistic, non-egoistic orientation signals resolution to these ontological questions. (Clayton and Birren 1980: 122)

A more flexible and empirical approach to the psychology of ageing was introduced in the research frame of 'lifespan psychology'. In 1990, Margaret and Paul Baltes published *Successful Aging – Perspectives from the Behavioral Sciences* (Baltes and Baltes 1990).[5] In his role as director of the Max Plank Research Center for Human Development in Berlin from 1980 to 2000, Paul Baltes probed the concept of wisdom for experimental gerontological research together with American and German colleagues. Due to this specific research agenda, Paul Baltes spotted my book, contacted me and became an inspiring colleague to discuss dimensions of wisdom that clearly transcended my purely historical and textual work. For me, this encounter between the humanities and natural sciences was a unique experience that developed into a respectful, serious and rewarding interdisciplinary dialogue (Assmann 1994).

Thirty years later, the collaborative project on 'framing ageing' gives me a welcome opportunity to reassess this research and dialogue in a contemporary historical, cultural and scholarly context. The term 'successful ageing' stood for a new paradigm in gerontology that broke with two mainstream ideas: that individual psychic development is a continuous mental or moral progress and that the process of ageing is an irreversible process of diminishing capacities. One of the new premises was that the period of old age needs to be integrated into the whole lifespan and that every phase of individual human development is characterized by specific challenges that come with gains and losses. In the context of the 'successful-ageing-approach', Baltes and Baltes started to empirically search for positive developments that help people in the Third Age, that is the post-retirement age group, to compensate for capacity losses and optimize their living conditions. The idea was to maximize the gains and minimize the losses. In her experimental gerontological work carried out between the 1970s and 1990s Margaret Baltes had discovered evidence for cognitive learning capacity among older people. Even decades before the neurosciences peaked around 2000, she could show that ageing is not a physically determined regressive process, but one that can be actively shaped and supported due to the remaining high plasticity of the brain in old age and 'the ability of pointed use of resources' (1993: 7).

---

[5] For a survey of different schools and theoretical approaches to wisdom, see: https://medicine.jrank.org/pages/1852/Wisdom-Explicit-theories-assessment-wisdom.html (accessed 22 September 2022).

Rediscovering wisdom

In their collaborative work on wisdom, Paul Baltes and Ursula Staudinger (1993) broadened the conceptual and methodological frame. While they recognized that humans do not grow wiser with the same irresistible logic that they grow older, they paid careful attention to the possibility reframing the last phases of the lifespan with the help of the idea of wisdom. Scholars of lifespan psychology use the term 'life-event determinants' in order to point to generic biographical challenges and age-specific horizons of possibilities, tasks and challenges (Baltes and Reese 1984). While the generic challenges of maturity are reproduction, upbringing of children and professional life – including the question of how to combine these tasks in a gender-equitable relationship – the generic challenges of old age are the waning of influence and power, the loss of skills and physical strength, together with the imminence of death, all pointing to limitations of former potential.

Baltes and Staudinger focused also on social and emotional competence and life experience. As their website states, they found that quite a number of older people 'not only master their lives successfully and have a positive impact on society, but also continue developing as personalities'.[6]

Investigating the interdependence between a person's age and their mental abilities, Baltes discovered that intelligence is not to be seen as a single, homogeneous capacity. It includes, on the one hand, the 'fluid mechanics of the mind', the sheer speed and accuracy of information processing, which grows rapidly in childhood but declines steadily from early adulthood. The other feature of intelligence, which he terms 'crystalline pragmatics', is a form of culture-bound knowledge and reflexive thinking that is based on practice.[7] This form of intelligence includes linguistic skills, specific and experiential knowledge, plus social competence – abilities that can be maintained into old age, provided that they are continuously exercised and not impaired by illnesses.

In order to carry out experimental research on wisdom, Baltes and Staudinger had to devise ingenious tests to pin down the 'performance of wisdom' as a scientific topic yielding objective results. These test set-ups included a system of 'wisdom points' that help to make wisdom more 'measurable'. In a detailed study, Gerd Scobel has carefully assessed their methodology (Scobel 2017: 149–59).

---

[6] See: http://www.margret-und-paul-baltesstiftung.de/Germanwebsite/contributionsciencegerman.htm?id=Die%20Stiftung&subid=Beitrag%20der%20Stifter%20zur%20Forschung (accessed 30 August 2022).
[7] See: https://courses.lumenlearning.com/suny-lifespandevelopment/chapter/intelligence-and-wisdom/ (accessed 19 September 2022).

This empirical research, however, was not conducted within a neo-liberal model of merit and reward. The answer to the crucial question 'what makes a person wise?' was not evaluated in terms of peak performance in old age, but rather as a creative mingling of cognitive, social and emotional knowledge in response to deeper questions concerning the complexity of human existence.

The work of Baltes shows that, fuzzy as it is, the concept of wisdom is not incompatible with serious empirical research but can open doors within cognitive psychology and its scientific methodology towards a more complete notion of what it means to be human. Allowing for more complexity in the field of study and structure of one's research can itself be considered a wise move. Wisdom is generated in dealing with difficult questions concerning planning, shaping and evaluating what is considered a good life. This complex form of knowledge is highly valuable and needed when dealing with the practical dimension of existential questions.

To further qualify this complex form of knowledge or competence, Baltes and Staudinger (2000) offer five categories for wisdom in their 'Berlin Wisdom Paradigm': 1. rich factual knowledge about life; 2. rich procedural knowledge about life; 3. lifespan contextualization; 4. relativism of values and life priorities; and 5. recognition and management of uncertainty. For both researchers, wisdom is a specific form of knowledge in which intelligence and personality interact. Wisdom is described as an 'orchestration of mind and virtue'.[8] This inclusive approach implies a clear deviation from the Kohlberg-schema with its strong focus on linear cognitive development. For Baltes and Staudinger, wisdom is something that can be generated in youth, mature age as well as in old age. For them, age does not produce a *disposition* for wisdom, but it can be a *context* in which it appears and becomes manifest. Here is a summary of the leading ideas of the Berlin Wisdom Paradigm:

> Wisdom knowledge most impressively characterizes the spiritual-personal potential of older people. Wisdom refers to knowledge of the human condition, of the interaction between virtue and knowledge in the shaping of life. Growing old alone is obviously not a sufficient condition for this to happen; only when life experience is combined with certain personality traits and styles of thinking do older people achieve above-average top performance in wisdom tasks. The same applies to certain areas of art as well as professional expertise. For example, older composers or conductors are often among the best, and expertise can also have an 'age-friendly' effect as long as the older person remains professionally active.

---

[8] This is the title of a ms. published by Paul Baltes online by the Max Planck Institute: https://library.mpib-berlin.mpg.de/ft/pb/PB_Wisdom_2004.pdf (accessed 22 September 2022).

> Another strength of old age lies in the cultivation of self-image and life satisfaction. Older people manage surprisingly well to arrange their lives in an increasingly crowded environment and with physical impairments in such a way that they maintain a positive sense of self. They regulate their subjective well-being by adjusting their expectations to reality. Thus, although many older people are objectively less physically well, they match a sense of subjective health that is similar to that of younger people. (Baltes 2003: 16)

The research paradigm of 'successful ageing' lightened up the traditional bleak picture of old age as a period of waning resources and ongoing loss. Paul Baltes introduced the concept of wisdom to paint a brighter picture, reminding humans of forgotten competences and hidden cultural treasures, an inclusive research orientation that takes on board a rich survey of cultural history (Baltes 2004) and is also reflected in newer studies on wisdom (Sternberg and Jordan 2005). The optimistic perspective of this research paradigm, however, has harsh limits. Gerontologists distinguish between two phases of old age; the 'Third Age' after youth and maturity, covering the period between 65 and 80 years of age, and the Fourth Age that follows it (Higgs and Gilleard 2015). The good news of successful ageing reaches its limits as physical and mental capacities deteriorate in this period and the whole human system begins to break down (Baltes and Mayer 1996; Baltes 2006). Although it makes sense to distinguish between these two phases, setting them off against each other doesn't seem to be a wise move either. The concept of wisdom as reconstructed by lifespan psychology is itself a curtailed version of wisdom. By emphasizing the human potential across the ages with the help of wisdom, it ignores the age-old relationship of wisdom and death.

Tentative conclusions

It is a special experience for me to reassess my own research project after thirty years. When I started to work on a trans-cultural collection of wisdom texts within the humanities, there was no context for such a project. The humanities and social sciences were shaped by modernization theory and investigated the foundations of Western culture and progress. Paul Baltes was an exception. He took my contribution to wisdom seriously, confirmed its relevance and extracted from it important ideas for his own project.

Today, the situation is different. Popular interest in wisdom and esoteric knowledge had of course never dwindled, but now, the topic of wisdom is no longer considered a curiosity for specialists. It is reappearing in various academic projects and collaborations with growing intellectual appeal and resonance.[9] There are palpable reasons for the return of wisdom, which have to do with the exhaustion of political ideologies, philosophical systems and grand narratives. Where theories, strict rules and precepts fail, wisdom flourishes in the more moderate shape of experiments, examples and advice.[10] In times of heightened crises, values like progress and permanent innovation are dwindling. There is a deep distrust of Western exceptionalism which has silenced other non-Western cultures and their often wiser and more sustainable practices. In this situation, the psychology of wisdom has a new chance to thrive. Stubborn individualism, coupled with competition, greed and short-term gratification cannot cope with the existential threat of the climate catastrophe. The ancient resource of wisdom is needed to coordinate intellect and emotions and to reconnect mind and virtue. Reference to traditions of wisdom can create a regulative idea of a good life embedded in the common good, restoring balance and embracing meaning, depth, a concern for the unity of life. Combining knowledge and practice, the tradition of wisdom involves self-reflection and the cultivation of affect, the acceptance of limited resources and the acknowledgement of mortality. A reassessment of wisdom in our world today could have important consequences. Instead of confining the perspective of wisdom to the Third Age in the individual lifespan, it should be applied to our current economic, political and cosmic crises. Wisdom is no longer valued only by gerontologists who mobilize it to raise the prestige of old age, today it is newly recovered as a neglected and yet urgently needed cultural orientation. A mental and cultural frame that values the possibility of a good life for all and embraces humility and solidarity, while adapting to limited resources and ongoing crises is much more than a recipe for successful ageing. It could be a goal for humanity joining forces to sustain life on the planet. I end this contribution with a few suggestions for how to reshape the idea of wisdom in the light of the present and future.

In the mainstream tradition of Western modernization, wisdom was conceived as a rival of the abstract, specialized and cumulative knowledge of the

---

[9] See *Metis: The Internet Portal for Wisdom Literature and Wisdom Practices* which promises to make available 'the world literature of wisdom, providing introductory texts, classics, podcasts and pictures.' See: https://phil.ethz.ch/en/research/current-research-projects/metis–the-internet-portal-for-wisdom-literature-and-wisdom-prac.html (accessed 30 August 2022). A research group at University of the Arts at Braunschweig focuses on the topic of vanitas, exploring the temporality of the ephemeral and fleeting moment, the 'hevel' or puff of wind, in the arts of the present (Benthien and von Flemming 2018).

[10] Similarly, in a recent paper I have called for a pragmatic approach to problem-solving in the domain of political decision-making, arguing for more balanced and inventive forms of deliberation, and, not to forget, more interdisciplinary collaboration (Assmann 2022).

modern sciences and was therefore ousted or marginalized. Picking up the term 'wisdom' again today would require us to rethink this history of devaluation. Wisdom is neither premodern nor postmodern but helps to counteract 'the modern drive' in Western culture and history.

Second, wisdom is a qualified form of knowledge that is not accumulated and built up through a linear process, but often it is generated through rupture, challenge and transformation. An important feature in the acquisition of wisdom is thus the unsettling of routines and a discontinuity in thinking and feeling. Wisdom, therefore, is generated in a profound shift of perspective.

Third, wisdom is a form of knowledge that focuses on the here and now of the present. But present in this sense is not 'presentism'; it is not the present moment that vanishes immediately. This form of presence, on the contrary is built on the discovery of larger patterns in the combination of flux and stability.

Fourth, wisdom as an embodied and context-dependent mode, is built on interaction with cultural frames and on interaction with other individuals. Wisdom as a form of knowledge always depends on the recognition and estimation of others. It lives in interaction and is sustained in cooperation.

Finally, wisdom is a form of knowledge that claims a broader, deeper and more inclusive view of human existence, revealing comprehensive patterns of order and balance in complexity. It transcends cognitive, moral and political binaries, including the ultimate binary between death and life. Wisdom as a mode of existence calls for moderation and balance: it is a disposition which makes it possible to endure conflicts and tension by placing them in a larger perspective.

Bibliography

Assmann, A., ed. (1991), *Weisheit*, Munich: Fink.
Assmann, A. (1994), 'Wholesome Knowledge: Concepts of Wisdom in a Cross-Cultural and Historical Perspective', *Life-Span Development and Behavior*, 12: 187–224.
Assmann, A. (2004), 'Identität und Authentizität in Shakespeares Hamlet', in Peter von Moos (ed.), *Unverwechselbarkeit: Persönliche Identität und Identifikation in der vormodernen Gesellschaft*, 411–27, Cologne: Böhlau.
Assmann, A. (2022), 'Regeln für das Navigieren im Ungewissen', in K.-R. Korte, G. Scobel and T. Yildiz (eds), *Heuristiken des politischen Entscheidens*, 91–108, Berlin: Suhrkamp.
Baltes, P. B. (2003), 'Das hohe Alter: Mehr Bürde als Würde?', *Max Planck Forschung* 2: 15–19. Available at: http://www.margret-baltes-stiftung.de/PBB-Website/MaxPlanckForschung.pdf (accessed 30 August 2022).

Baltes, P. B. (2004), 'Wisdom as Orchestration of Mind and Virtue'. Book-Manuscript, Max Planck Institute for Human Development, Berlin. Available at: https://library.mpib-berlin.mpg.de/ft/pb/PB_Wisdom_2004.pdf (accessed 31 August 2022).

Baltes, P. B. (2006), 'Facing our Limits: Human Dignity in the Very Old', *Daedalus*, 135(1): 32–9.

Baltes, P. B. and M. Baltes (1993), 'Psychological Perspectives on Successful Aging: The Model of Selective Optimization with Compensation', in P. B. Baltes and M. M. Baltes (eds), *Successful Aging: Perspectives from the Behavioral Sciences*, Cambridge University Press, Cambridge, 1–34.

Baltes, P. B. and M. Baltes (n.d.), Foundation for the Advancement of Research and Lifespan Psychology and Gerontology. Available at: http(Jahr)://www.margret-und-paul-baltes-stiftung.de/Germanwebsite/contributionsciencegerman.htm?id=Die%20Stiftung&subid=Beitrag%20der%20Stifter%20zur%20Forschung (accessed 30 August 2022).

Baltes, P. B. and H. W. Reese (1984), 'The Life-Span Perspective in Developmental Psychology', in M. H. Bornstein and A. F. Lamb (eds), *Developmental Psychology: An Advanced Textbook*, 493–531, Hillsdale, NJ: Erlbaum.

Baltes, P. B. and U. M. Staudinger (1993), 'The Search for a Psychology of Wisdom', *Current Directions in Psychological Science*, 2(3): 75–80.

Baltes, P. B. and U. M. Staudinger (2000), 'Wisdom: A Metaheuristic (Pragmatic) to Orchestrate Mind and Virtue toward Excellence', *American Psychologist*, 55(1): 122–36.

Benthien, C. and V. von Flemming, eds (2018), 'Vanitas: Reflexionen über Vergänglichkeit in Literatur, bildender Kunst und theoretischen Diskursen der Gegenwart', *Paragrana: Internationale Zeitschrift für historische Anthropologie*, 27(2): 1–316.

Brecht, B. ([1944–45], 1963), *Der kaukasische Kreidekreis*, Frankfurt: Suhrkamp.

Clayton, V. P. and J. E. Birren (1980), 'The Development of Wisdom across the Life-Span: A Re-Examination of an Ancient Topic', in P. Baltes and O. G. Brim, Jr. (eds), *Life-Span Development and Behavior*, 103–35, New York: Academic Press.

Greenaway, P. (1991), *Prospero's Books*, film adaptation of William Shakespeare's *The Tempest*, produced by D. Cunningham, Four Walls Eight Windows.

Higgs, P. and C. Gilleard (2015), *Rethinking Old Age: Theorising the Fourth Age*, London: Palgrave Macmillan.

Honegger, C. (1978), 'Die Hexen der Neuzeit: Analysen zur anderen Seite der okzidentalen Rationalisierung', in C. Honegger (ed.), *Die Hexen der Neuzeit: Studien zur Sozialgeschichte eines kulturellen Deutungsmusters*, 21–151, Frankfurt: Suhrkamp.

Kant, I. ([1785] 2019), *Groundwork of the Metaphysics of Morals*, ed. and trans. Christopher Bennett, Joe Saunders and Robert Stern, Oxford: Oxford University Press.

Keynes, W., ed. (2021), *The Oxford Handbook of Wisdom and the Bible*, Oxford: Oxford University Press.

Kohlberg, L. (1976), 'Moral Stages and Moralization: The Cognitive-Developmental Approach', in T. Lickona (ed.), *Moral Development and Behavior: Theory, Research and Social Issues*, 31–53, New York: Holt, Rinehart and Winston.

Mbewe, M. (2021), 'Problematic Museum Heritage in a Postcolonial Context: The Case of the Moto Museum Chisungu Collection', Special Issue: 'The Post/Colonial Museum', *Zeitschrift für Kulturwissenschaften*, 2: 61–75.
Metis: The Internet Portal for Wisdom Literature and Wisdom Practices. Available at: https://phil.ethz.ch/en/research/current-research-projects/metis-the-internet-portal-for-wisdom-literature-and-wisdom-prac.html (accessed 30 August 2022).
Rollins, H. E., ed. (1958), *The Letters of John Keats*, 2 vols, Cambridge: Cambridge University Press.
Rowlands, A. (2001), 'Witchcraft and Old Women in Early Modern Germany', *Past & Present*, 173: 50–89.
Scobel, G. (2017), *Weisheit: Über das, was uns fehlt*, Cologne: DuMont.
Shakespeare, W. ([1603], 1916, 1959), 'Hamlet Prince of Denmark', in W. J. Craig (ed.), *The Complete Works of William Shakespeare*, 870–907, Oxford: Oxford University Press. Available at: https://oll.libertyfund.org/title/craig-hamlet-prince-of-denmark.
Shakespeare, W. ([1623], 1916, 1959), 'As You Like It', in W. J. Craig (ed.), *The Complete Works of William Shakespeare*, 217–42, Oxford: Oxford University Press. Available at: https://oll.libertyfund.org/title/craig-as-you-like-it.
Shakespeare, W. ([1623], 1916, 1959), 'The Tempest', in W. J. Craig, (ed.), *The Complete Works of William Shakespeare*, 1–22, Oxford: Oxford University Press. Available at: https://oll.libertyfund.org/title/shakespeare-the-tempest.
Sowarka, D. (1989), 'Weisheit und weise Personen: Common-Sense-Konzepte älterer Menschen', *Zeitschrift für Entwicklungspsychologie und Pädagogische Psychologie*, 21(2): 87–109.
Sternberg, R. S. and J. Jordan, eds (2005), *A Handbook of Wisdom: Psychological Perspectives*, Cambridge: Cambridge University Press.
Sternberg, R. S. and J. Glück (2022), *The Psychology of Wisdom*, Cambridge: Cambridge University Press.
'Weisheit'. Wikipedia. Available at: https://de.wikipedia.org/wiki/Weisheit (accessed 19 September 2022).
Wiele, J. (2022), '"Was wurde aus dem Pazifismus, Herr Niedecken?"', *Frankfurter Allgemeine Zeitung*, 10 June.
Woodward, K. (2002), 'Against Wisdom: The Social Politics of Anger and Aging', *Cultural Critique*, 51: 186–218.
'Zwischentöne mit Wolfgang Niedecken' (2020), [radio interview] Deutschlandfunk, 29 November. Available at: https://www.deutschlandfunk.de/zwischentoene-mit-wolfgang-niedecken-vom-29-11-2020-musik-gekuerzt-dlf-0201cc05-100.html (accessed 22 September 2022).

6

Between Alice and the eagle: Dementia journeys and the final breath

Dana Walrath

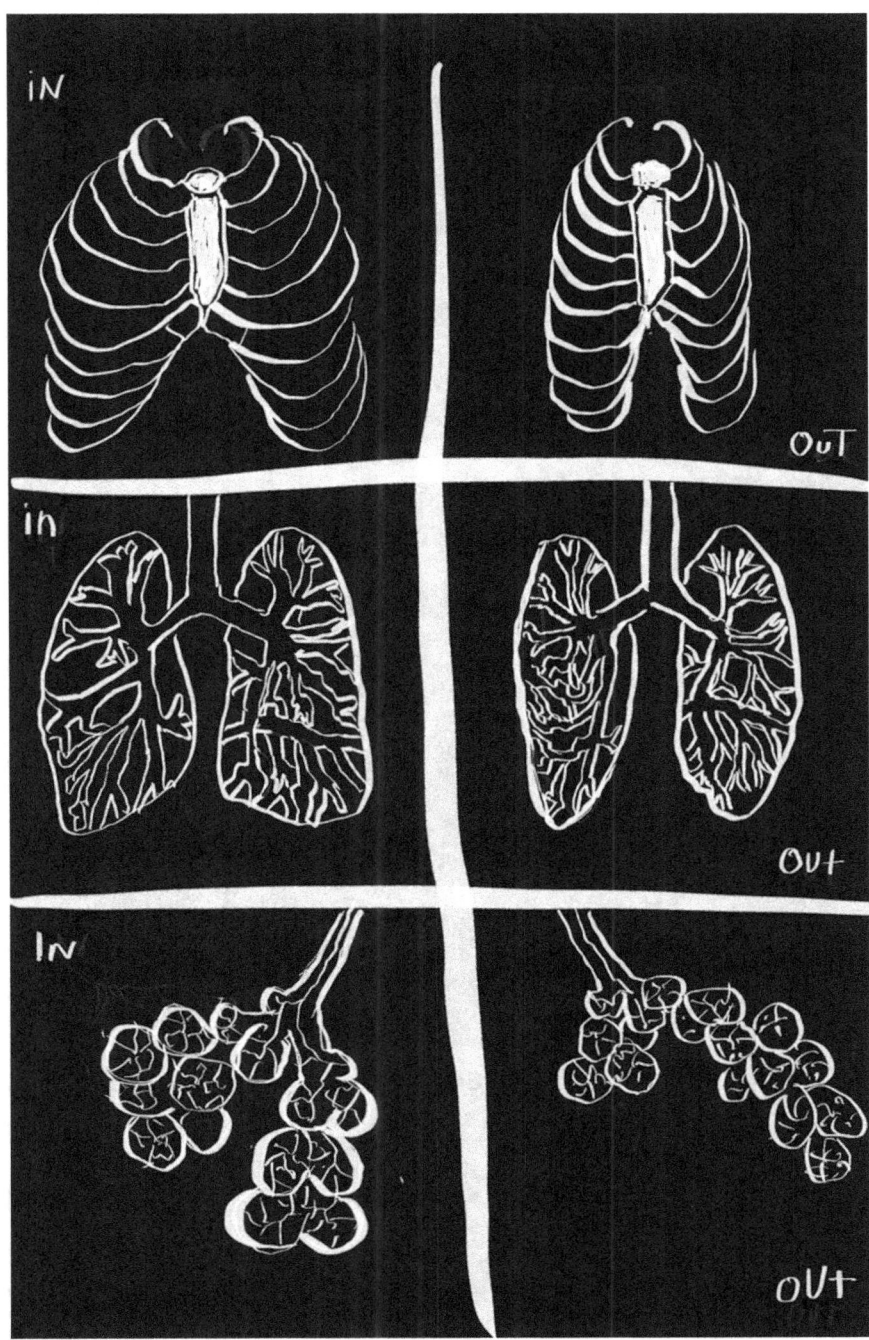

Privelege White and otherwise confers longevity thru access to the expensive biomedical interventions food, education, shelter, and safety upon which long life depends. Restoring Equal access to life and breath requires interrogating the dominant conceptions of sickness and death. These are rooted in civilization, a relatively new social form in which power and wealth pass thru the generations based on conquest, extraction and domination not just of other peoples, but of nature itself. As we interrogate we have to separate science — a magnificent method for discovering the mechanisms of the universe — from the power structures that monetize and profit from it without regard for the earth and its inhabitants. It's a tall order but we have helpers.

Between Alice and the Eagle: Dementia Journeys and the Final Breath

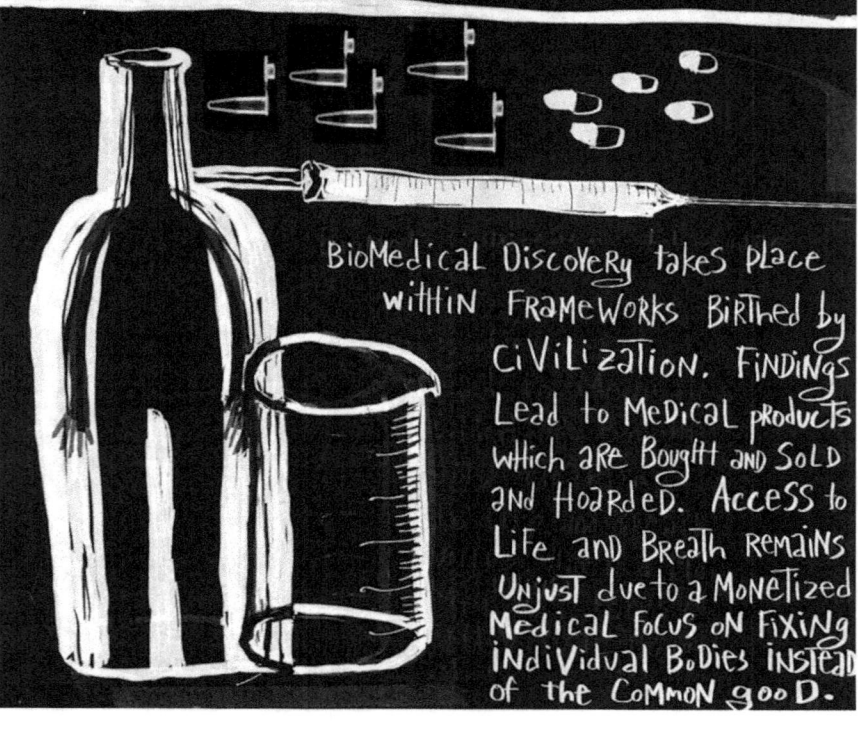

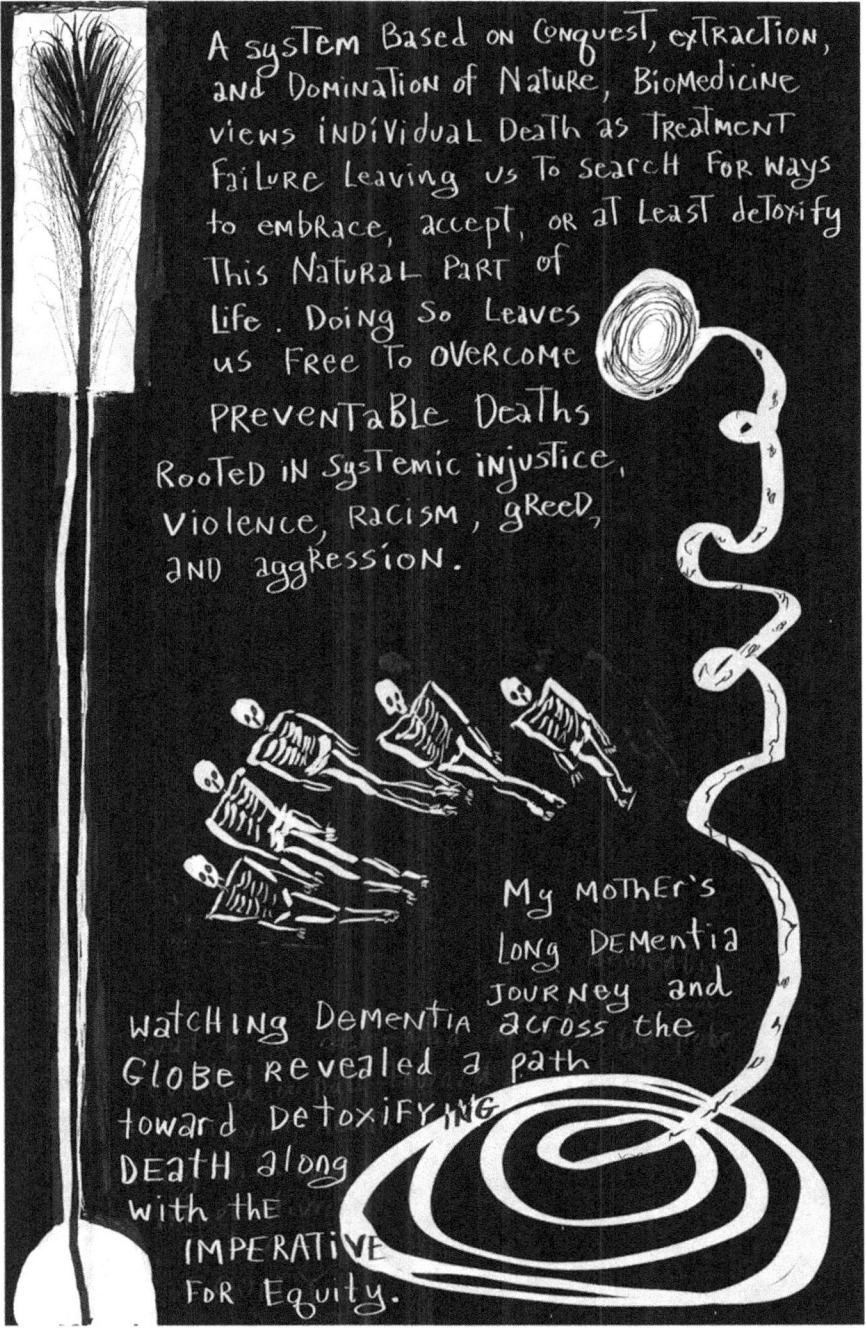

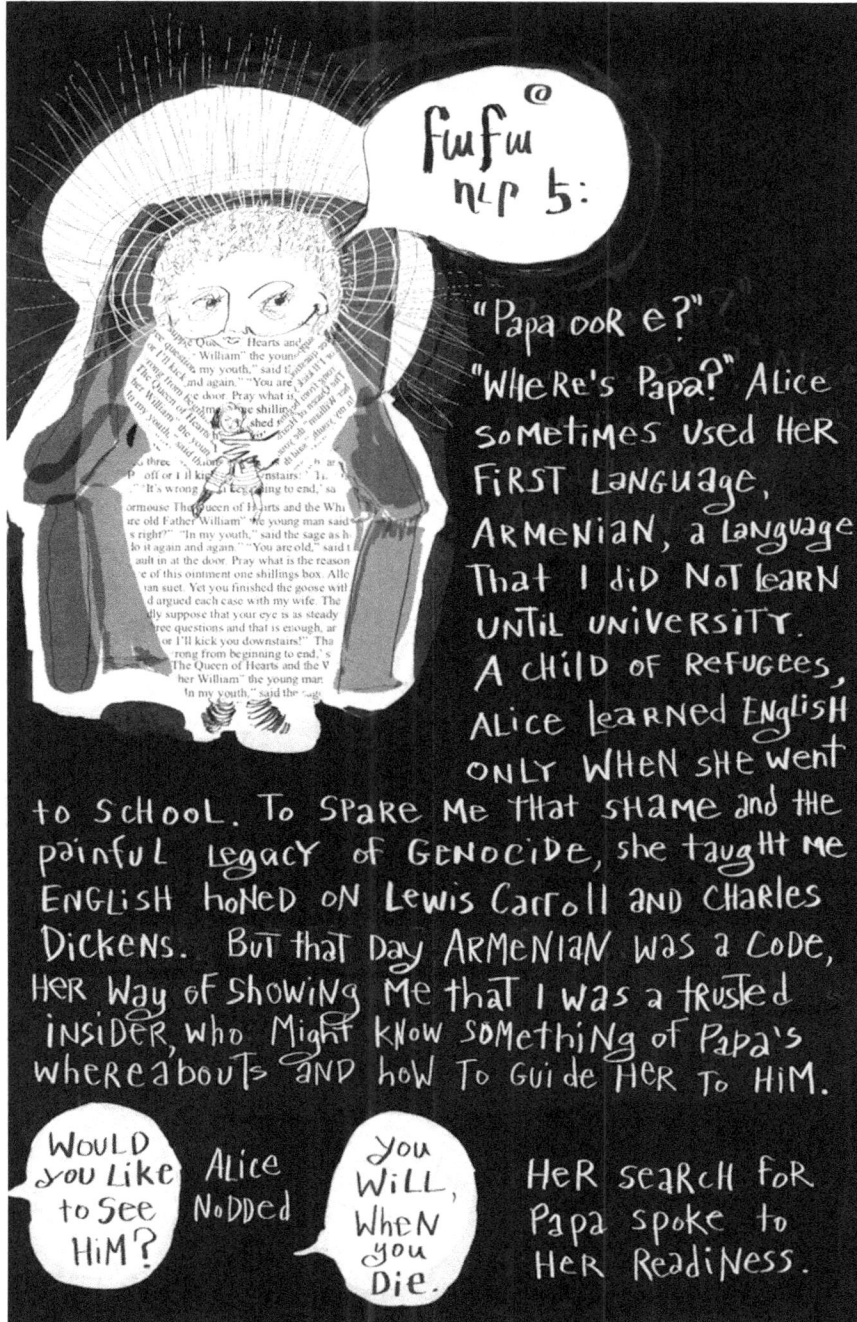

"Papa oor e?"
"Where's Papa?" Alice sometimes used her first language, Armenian, a language that I did not learn until university. A child of refugees, Alice learned English only when she went to school. To spare me that shame and the painful legacy of genocide, she taught me English honed on Lewis Carroll and Charles Dickens. But that day Armenian was a code, her way of showing me that I was a trusted insider, who might know something of Papa's whereabouts and how to guide her to him.

"Would you like to see him?" Alice nodded. "You will, when you die." Her search for Papa spoke to her readiness.

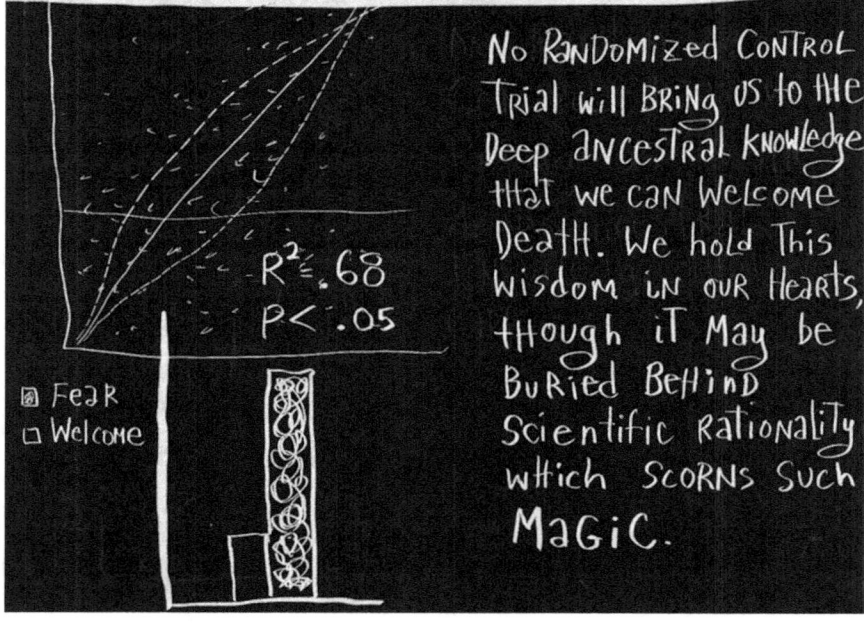

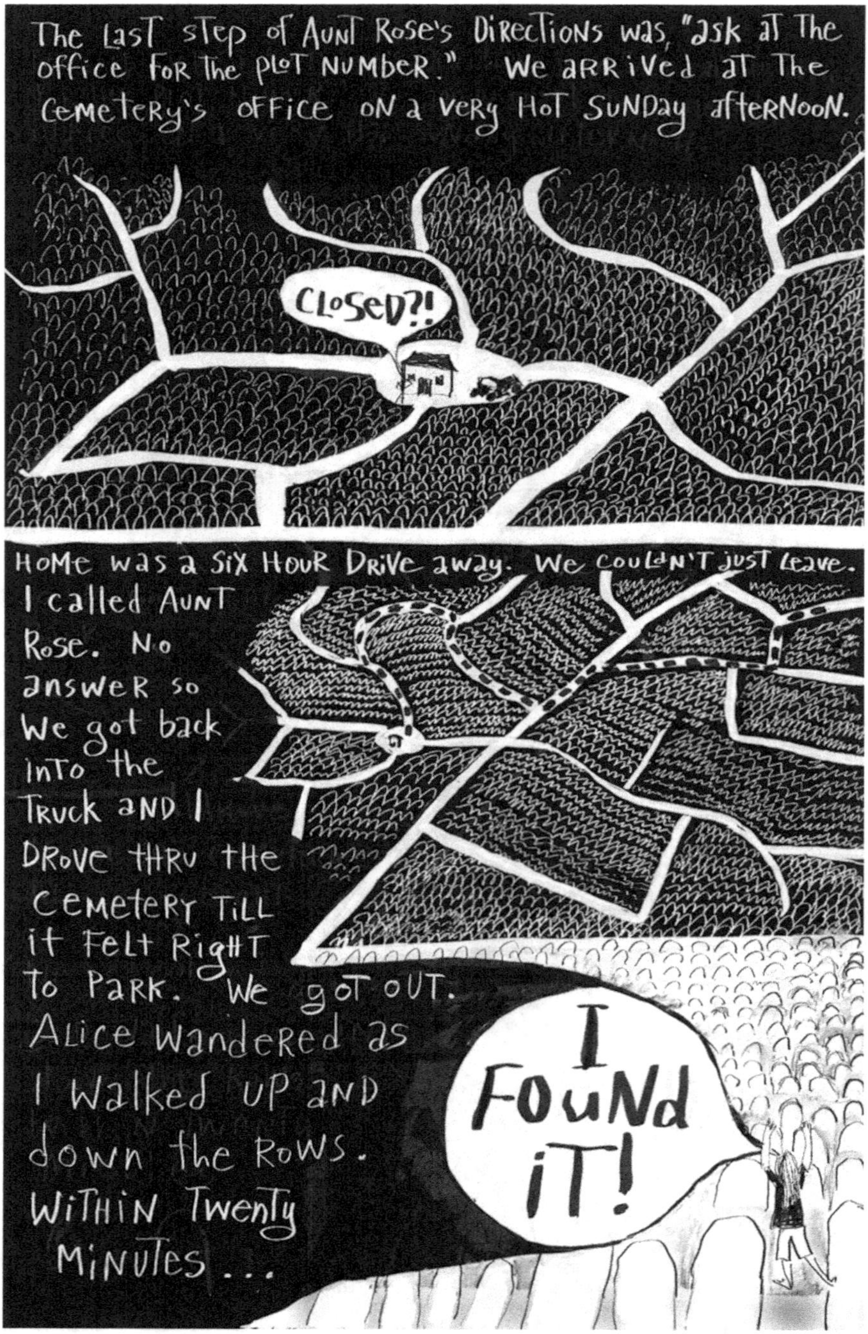

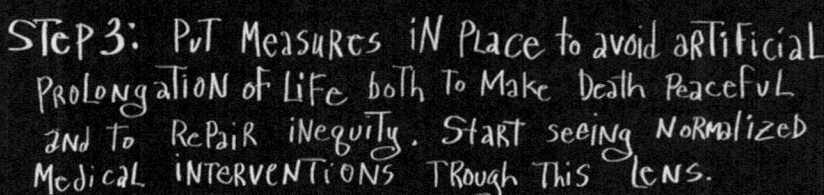

Three years before Alice died, she was kicked out of her second Memory Care Home in New York. I was told her only option was a high cost nursing home where her bodily functions could be tended and monitored. Instead she returned to a small scale, community based, Vermont Home where love and care included refusing basic medical treatments.

The care industry depends on flows of workers from poor to wealthy nations, states, and families. I saw this in Alice's care and when I studied dementia in Ireland, Armenia, and Japan.

Ireland
Russia
Poland
USA
Japan depends on workers from the Philippines.
Jamaica
Ghana
Liberia
Togo
Nigeria
Democratic Republic of Congo
Brazil

Alice's care team hailed from Nigeria, Ukraine, Jamaica, Liberia, Congo, Vermont, Ghana, Togo and more.

Ireland depends on workers from Brazil, Poland and the Philippines.

Most older Armenians live without any family in country because unemployment has forced the younger generation to Russia to find work.

We are meant to live and die in community.

Happiness and ageing as performance and narrative in Jens Sparschuh's *Life Costs a Lot of Time*

Gillian Pye

Introduction

Happiness – what it is, where to find it and how to maintain it – is a dominant theme in the contemporary world, spawning a vast, global 'happiness industry' (Davis 2015), which promises personal fulfilment to audiences navigating a world of seemingly endless choice. At national level, where optimum social outcomes are frequently identified with optimum personal happiness, governments consult happiness indices, which have become increasingly important in the development of public policy (Barrington-Leigh 2022: 66, 73). This development has been accompanied by a wealth of academic research, with the 'the rate of production of journal articles with titles or abstracts containing "happiness", "life satisfaction", "satisfaction with life", or "subjective well(-)being"' (and their equivalents in major world languages) growing 'by a factor of ten since just 2003' (Barrington-Leigh 2022: 59).[1] In recent years, this has also included an increasing number of critical perspectives, which argue against happiness agendas as a powerful neoliberal control mechanism (Ahmed 2010; Boddice 2018; Cabanas and Illouz 2019; Davis 2015; Segal 2017).

Promoting the well-being of populations with ever-increasing average life spans has ethical and practical urgency. Recent studies describe a 'u-shaped' tendency in life satisfaction and play a prominent role in public debate.

---

[1] Reflecting current usage, in which terms are frequently used interchangeably, this article will use the terms well-being, life satisfaction and happiness.

According to this perspective, a 'nadir of unhappiness' in middle age is followed by an uplift in older age, a feature which is seen to be 'remarkably consistent in most countries of the world' (Graham and Pozuelo 2017: 227). On the other hand, the 'Fourth Age' (Gilleard and Higgs 2015) poses a challenge to this: what does life satisfaction mean for the oldest old who are at increased risk of suffering debilitating ill-health and who are ever more isolated as their generational peers die out? As well as being a key component of cultural debates about what it means to be old, the issue of happiness and ageing also reveals some broad disciplinary tensions between the sceptical, theoretical perspective favoured in the humanities and the broadly more positive, practical approach of psychological-medical disciplines. If the former often reject well-being as a tool of neoliberal capitalism, the latter's concern with care mean that it nevertheless must remain an 'ethical desideratum' (Schicktanz and Schweda 2012: 160).

This chapter aims to contribute to cross-disciplinary debate by exploring how the question of well-being in old age may illuminate the role of emotions in constructing social, cultural and disciplinary boundaries. It proceeds from the recognition that 'affect ... has become a major element in the organisation of the way we live now' and that our emotions are not a 'kind of supplement only relevant as something "subjective"' but rather 'part of our effective social presence and performance' (Sharma and Tygstrup 2015: 4). Taking the example of a 2018 German novel, the discussion explores what literary texts may reveal about the narrative and performative dimensions of happiness in older age and their articulation in culturally and historically specific contexts.

Happiness and older age

The question of how to live a happy life is integral to our cultural understanding of older age, and philosophical debates have, from the earliest times, explored the relationship between embodied pleasure, longevity and a good or virtuous life. While Epicurean hedonism emphasizes the value of attaining a 'state in which the normal functioning of our natures can take place unimpaired by constraints and impervious to pains or troubles', Aristotle's account of the good life as 'eudaemonia' suggests that only a judgement about a complete life lived 'in accordance with complete excellence' and which is 'sufficiently equipped with external goods' can identify an individual as happy (Small 2007: 90–1; 53).[2] Between these two perspectives lies a slight tension: on the one hand, happiness appears as positive affect, with an emphasis on present experience. On the other, it is viewed as cognitive process, requiring a narrative perspective, therefore placing greater emphasis on positive experience through time. Today, scientific debates about happiness continue to draw on these ancient philosophical foundations by referring to 'hedonic' and 'eudaemonic' well-being. The emphasis in hedonic happiness is on pleasure, in other words an individual's perception of how good they feel. Eudaemonic happiness, on the other hand, is 'based upon how meaningful one's life feels in addition to simply how good it feels' (Bauer, McAdams and Pals 2008: 83). Frequently, these perspectives are combined in a holistic approach under the heading of 'subjective well-being' which incorporates 'cognitive appraisal of well-being (life satisfaction), positive affect and (lack of) negative affect' (Mhaske 2017: 72). In any case, narrative-based strategies, such as life-satisfaction questionnaires, continue to feature heavily in subjective well-being evaluations, begging the question of how an individual comes in the first place to appraise themselves as happy.

The two 'master' narratives – of decline and progress – that Margaret Morganroth Gullette identifies as dominant (2004: 147) in the cultural imaginary of ageing also feature centrally in discourses of happiness. As decline, old age connotes physical and mental deterioration and the foreshortening of a future perspective, both of which threaten the capacity of an individual to feel good. As progress, it connotes longevity and increased (self-)knowledge, potentially permitting a more coherent and integrated self-narrative, therefore resulting in improved life satisfaction. This latter proposition is underpinned by the insights of narrative gerontologists, who suggest that a unified life narrative is central to well-being amongst older people. Some argue that many older people may be particularly well positioned – socially, cognitively and existentially – to develop effective life narratives (Randall 2011: 30), and that narrative therapies may be

---

[2] In her detailed account of Aristotelian thinking on old age and the possibility of the good life, Helen Small points out that, in *Rhetoric*, Aristotle adopts a very negative stance on old age. However, she argues that the *Nicomachean Ethics* offers a crucial counterpoint to this perspective by asserting that 'we must wait to see how a life concludes in order to make a final judgement' (Small 2007: 63). It is important to note, too, that the translation of Aristotle's notion of 'eudaemonia' as 'happiness' is reductive. Despite this, as historian of emotions Rob Boddice (2020) notes, this 'all too easy' equation has generated a 'whole academic industry'.

useful to address depression in older patients (Steunenberg and Bohlmeijer 2011). However, adopting a critical perspective is crucial if we are to interrogate precisely which cultural and social imaginaries structure the connections between ageing, narrative and well-being. Morganroth Gullette, who advocates for a nuanced practice of age autobiography, is mindful of the balance which must be struck between the potential of narrative to open up more progressive political agendas (2004: 158) and the pressing need to avoid overemphasizing the positive in a manner which distracts attention from social disadvantage and the reality of ageism (Morganroth Gullette 2017: xvi). Other commentators point to the limitations of narrative methodologies for well-being if some, particularly the oldest old, may not be 'at all part of the story' of their lives (Freeman 2011: 5). Philosophical criticisms of narrative psychology reject the idea that coherent narrative is a necessary component of selfhood at all, let alone essential to a well-lived life. For Galen Strawson, there are 'good ways to live that are deeply non-narrative' (2004: 429). Finally, the idea that well-being is a property of the self – narratively or otherwise – is widely criticized. As Rob Boddice puts it, 'how we feel is the dynamic product of the existence of our minds and bodies in moments of time and space' (2018: 9).

Performing happiness

A performative perspective suggests a way to move beyond the binary view of happiness as either positive affect or (narrative) evaluation of life as satisfying and offers a critical standpoint on the relational and power dynamics of emotional performances. Sara Ahmed sets out a holistic view of the cultural politics of emotion in relational and performative terms, arguing that feelings do not reside in individuals, nor are they simply triggered in simple cause-and-effect relationships, but rather they 'take the "shape" of the contact we have with objects' (2004: 5). As such, emotions align us within power structures and can be mobilized to secure social hierarchies. Ahmed (2010) is particularly critical of the powerful 'intimacy' between 'measurement and prediction' which characterizes institutionalized happiness, arguing that 'the science of happiness could be described as performative: by finding happiness in certain places, it generates those places as being good' (6). In this view, happiness is a particularly powerful 'disciplinary technique' (8) because it conflates the subjective and particular with the abstract and general, reinforcing normative expectations. Ahmed argues, for example, that 'stable families' have been identified as sources of happiness (7) and this acts as a 'powerful legislative device' (43) with a tendency to consolidate traditional social structures. Moreover, displacing the social into the personal by focusing on happiness as an indicator of social progress deflects from pressing political and economic issues. Hence, despite championing happiness agendas which claim to put individual well-being at the heart of society, governments in countries such as the UK or United Arab Emirates have pursued policies which exacerbate social inequalities and undermine individual freedoms (Boddice 2018: 175; Cabanas and Illouz 2019: 44, 46).

Ahmed's (2010) concept of happiness as a disciplinary tool can reveal the ways in which it anchors normative behaviours within interpersonal relationships. In other words, part of its power is that it is mutually reinforcing: it is our 'responsibility' to be happy as this helps to ensure the happiness of others, particularly those with whom we are emotionally entangled (9). This can be especially strong within familial relationships, where kinship objects, such as photo albums with images of happy times, provide an important means by which we become aligned with certain behaviours and values (43). This provides a useful way of thinking about how feelings are constructed, controlled and embedded in intergenerational narratives that loop back into narratives of self. Furthermore, Ahmed's idea of the happiness dynamic as a 'promise' suggests a particular temporality: as a form of capital of the self, it is anticipatory and 'things become good, or acquire their value as goods, insofar as they point towards happiness' (26). At the same time, this has a retrospective component: looking back at the continuity from generation to generation suggests a 'specific image of the future' (28).

Ahmed's work provides insight into the way in which the apparently 'self-evident' (Canabas and Illouz 2019: 37) positive and universal desire for happiness may, in fact, work divisively to exacerbate inequalities and exclusion. This understanding of happiness in relational, holistic and temporal terms offers a means of expanding contemporary happiness discourses with engaged 'eudaemonic' readings (Pawelski and Moores 2013) that suggest alternative modes of doing happiness.[3] In this context, the awareness that day-to-day embodied experiences of well-being have a temporal structure and are anchored in intergenerational contexts offers a starting point for a critical exploration of happiness and age.

---

[3] For Ahmed (2010), one solution is the power implied by resisting the happiness agenda, a stance epitomized by the feminist 'killjoy'. For Segal (2017), radical, collective, joy provides the antidote to neoliberal individualist concepts of happiness.

Happiness narratives, ageing and the German perspective

With its combination of low birth rate, long average life expectancy and consequently high proportion of older citizens, Germany has been at the forefront of the pan-European trend towards ageing societies (European Commission 2021: 7). Concerns about caring for an elderly population are therefore high on the German political and cultural agenda and, as elsewhere, happiness indices inform public policy.[4] The German example illustrates how concerns about age and happiness are both posited as universal and yet are deeply inflected by cultural and historical experience. In particular, the legacy of two world wars, the division of Germany into communist East (GDR) and capitalist West (FRG), and the subsequent reunification of the country in 1990, shape the way in which ageing and intergenerational relationships are experienced. In his account of recent media representations of happiness among some of Germany's oldest old, Thomas Wilke notes that happiness discourses are impacted by a specific German memory culture (2021: 55), in which life narratives are often marked by striking discrepancies between private life, historical circumstance and media representations (56–7). Highlighting the increased interest in happiness as life experience, he registers public curiosity about how people achieve happiness in ordinary life rather than in extraordinary achievements (47).

Approaching this theme from a performative perspective illuminates happiness as intergenerational dynamic. Julia Knopp's and Hannah Fischer's 2018 TV documentary *The Rest is a Matter of Luck: On Satisfaction in Old Age* (*Der Rest ist Glückssache: Über Zufriedenheit im Alter*),[5] is an interesting case in point. Echoing Wilke's examples, the film asks how it is possible to achieve a meaningful, satisfying later life. This is a response not only to the societal challenge posed by an ageing population but also to the role of happiness as contemporary social expectation. Hence, a middle-aged interviewee, contemplating his father's impending move to a care institution, looks anxiously into the camera and wonders how one is supposed to be truly happy when there isn't much life left to live. At the same time, according to the filmmakers, many younger people yearn for the 'advantages' of older age, namely the absence of the pressure for social achievement and the ability to deal with daily challenges

---

[4] The *SKL Glücksatlas*, produced in conjunction with the University of Freiburg, has been collating and reporting on German happiness data since 2011. Available online: https://www.skl-gluecksatlas.de/index.html (accessed 15 July 2022).

[5] The original title does not easily translate into English as it contains a pun: the German word *Glück* means both 'happiness' and 'luck'.

in a more relaxed way.⁶ The operation of happiness is exposed here as mutually reinforcing and temporally complex: personal happiness is reciprocally dependent on the happiness of a significant other. Moreover, this has an impact in the present, when the pressure on younger generations to perform squeezes time and energy, and in the future when the prospect of old age threatens decline and foreclosure of the future horizon. A resolution to this anxiety is entertained in an intergenerational dialogue about the (future) possibility of happiness as cognitive mastery over the stresses and strains of life. However, in its insistence on happiness as future promise this performance upholds the divide between young and old.

Jens Sparschuh: *Life Costs a Lot of Time*

Jens Sparschuh's 2018 comic novel *Life Costs a Lot of Time* (*Das Leben kostet viel Zeit*) offers a self-reflexive view of the contemporary German interest in life narrative and happiness. The novel's middle-aged protagonist, Titus Brose, is made redundant as editor of a local newspaper and takes a job working for the *LebensLauf* (Curriculum Vitae) company. *LebensLauf* specializes in producing biographies for ordinary people, who gift them to their relatives, and the novel centres on Titus's interactions with residents of the *Altes Fährhaus* (Old Ferryhouse) care home as he interviews them and prepares their manuscripts.

From the outset, the novel emphasizes happiness as intergenerational and as historically and socially determined. Brose's memory of losing his job is illustrative of this as he recalls the moment when the newspaper, after years of agonizing decline, finally 'gasps its last breath' (2018: 41). Subsequently, the advert in the 'Jetzt-Zeit' ('Now-Time') newspaper, inviting applications to the 'young, dynamic and ambitious' team at *LebensLauf*, offers Brose an opportunity to 'give life new meaning' (53). This reveals how Brose's personal narrative is both shaped by a globalized 'economic life-course story' (Morganroth Gullette 2004: 146) that equates a dynamic CV with a good life defined by progress, but also how it is inflected by specific cultural and historical experience. Brose's life in Spandau – situated directly at the border between East and West Berlin – is disrupted by German unification, which is not only an aggravating factor in the bankruptcy of his newspaper (42) but also results in the loss of the West Berlin

---

⁶ These comments appeared on the ZDF (public TV) network website, on which the film was available to view on demand (Knopp and Fischer 2018).

he once knew, a city which disappears like 'Atlantis' (41). The combination of this historical rupture with technological change causes the figure to become aware of his age and, with characteristic melancholy irony, to question the purpose and meaning of his life. In this way, Brose's experience of historical change in unified Germany, as well as the impact of a neoliberal life-course narrative, impinges on his perception of well-being. Old age becomes visible as a metaphor for his anxiety, illustrating his preoccupation with a sense of foreclosure more usually associated with later life.

Brose's encounter with the Old Ferryhouse reveals well-being as a divisive dynamic, which undermines the potential for intergenerational solidarity. This is first indicated in the description of the care home itself, where a disparity between appearance and reality emphasizes it as a space in which well-being is performed but residents are segregated from the outside world. Inside, the walls are decorated with prints of poppy fields and windmills, evoking a natural idyll, but this is an 'artificial landscape' where the scent of lemons emanates from the cleaning fluid and is mixed with the smell of urine (57). Similarly, the exterior of the building is painted in warm tones and the pillars of the porchway suggest durability, but Brose notes that the walls emit a hollow sound and the pillars are fake (56). This image is a reference to a well-known nineteenth-century German novella *Peter Schlemihl's Miraculous Story* (*Peter Schlemihls Wundersame Geschichte*, 1813) by the writer Adalbert von Chamisso (1781–1838), the first of several references that point to this figure, who will take on a significant role in Sparschuh's novel. *Schlemihl* is the tale of a man who sells his shadow to a devil-like figure in exchange for 'Fortunatus' lucky purse' (1957: 22).[7] The novella's preoccupation with fortune, exclusion from mainstream society, and its connection to Chamisso's friend, biographer and publisher, Julius Eduard Hitzig, for whom it was written, provide a literary context to Sparschuh's reflections on narrative, well-being and old age. By referencing this very well-known text, Sparschuh brings into contact two very different historical contexts – post-unification Germany and late eighteenth-century Prussia – which nevertheless have in common a combination of abrupt political upheaval and rapid technological change. This offers a backdrop to Sparschuh's critical treatment of contemporary discourses of well-being, in which the friendship between two

---

[7] The opening paragraph of *Peter Schlemihl* describes a country house 'of red and white marble, with many pillars' (von Chamisso 1957: 15). The house belongs to Mr John, a wealthy man who eventually falls victim to the devil-like man in grey, serving as a ghastly reminder of the dangers of avarice (78).

figures of very different generations challenges a transactional, individualized and decontextualized understanding of happiness.

This critique is illustrated by a passage in the novel in which the 'biography group' at the Old Ferryhouse takes part in a reminiscence activity. Mrs Schwartze, director and group facilitator, explains that the session optimizes the residents' 'psychological resilience' (59) and, as Brose watches, she encourages participants to operate an old whisk, to smell herbs and to recall recipe ingredients. This reflects contemporary therapeutic strategies to support older people by encouraging positive memories (Steunenberg and Bohlmeijer 2011). However, Sparschuh's satirical portrayal points to a contemporary happiness culture which posits well-being as a self-evident, universal good and flattens specific personal, social and historical contexts. Moreover, despite Mrs Schwartze's use of the pronouns 'we', 'us' and 'our' (59), the scene suggests how discourses of well-being performatively reinforce the segregation between younger and older agents. Only the older participants are invited to reminisce, so when the activity evokes Brose's childhood memories there is no opportunity for him to articulate this. In fact, sharing memories other than those expected in the session is considered disruptive: when Mrs Adomeit's memory of wartime expulsion is triggered, she is very quickly silenced (77). Clear directions are given: a correct performance generates the impression of agency and confirms that the participants are functioning well – in a circular dynamic, this is shown to be both proof of as well as the means of maintaining a sense of well-being. This scene also points to the potentially coercive dimensions of intergenerational happiness as it reinforces Mrs Schwartze's sense of self-efficacy and control. This successful performance of well-being assures her own well-being by maintaining her distinction to the elderly residents, who are defined in terms of a deficiency of well-being and contained within a separate relationship to the past.

Although Brose is sincere in his efforts to help the residents to write their life stories, he is sceptical about the products of their collaborations. Capturing individual stories proves difficult as some residents lack the capacity to recall or to narrate their lives (214). Others can reconstruct their life histories but their accounts centre on stereotypical events (51) or become emptied of specific meaning with repeated telling (223). The resulting homogeneity is such that one female resident even reads someone else's biography and mistakes it for her own (15). This is compounded by the limitations of a formulaic and stereotypical use of language (205), and Brose is particularly dismayed at his colleague Schulze's clichéd prose (203–4). Moreover, the very idea of the life narrative as biographical text suggests the foreclosure of the residents' experience: the completion of the manuscript implies that, for its care-dependent subject, meaningful life is over. This serves the interests of some relatives, who use the completion of their loved-one's biography as an excuse not to have to visit them or to listen to their stories (30–1).

However, Sparschuh's novel also explores the possibility of a more ethical and holistic sense of well-being and the role of narrative within it. The friendship that develops between Brose and one resident, the former museum curator Dr Einhorn, is pivotal to this. Although separated by an age divide that places Brose on the outside and Einhorn on the inside of the care home, they have an affinity predicated on shared experiences which are culturally and historically determined. Like Brose, Einhorn has also been impacted by German unification and technological shift: in 1992 his planned Chamisso exhibition, marking the 200th anniversary of the author's flight from revolutionary France to Germany, is stymied by structural changes in the new Berlin Republic (182). Later, when the idea of the exhibition is revived, Einhorn's plans are again derailed, this time by a newly appointed curator who proposes a state-of-the-art interactive alternative (131–2). Brose is drawn to Einhorn because he recognizes this experience of exclusion from mainstream time as embodied in a performance-oriented, technologically accelerating society. Age is revealed as an experience that is not only predicated on physical health or calendar time but also on a socially and culturally constructed context. Both Brose and Einhorn, although they belong to very different generations, are prompted by the experience of unification to feel that they are somehow outdated, that their life narrative has been disrupted and they are seeking ways to address this. Like Brose, Einhorn is sceptical about personal reminiscence as a means of improving well-being and he does not want Brose to write his life history (131). Instead, he engages him in a research project concerning Chamisso. Tracing his biography, Brose learns of the author's close relationship to Julius Eduard Hitzig, a relationship which is mirrored in Brose's own friendship with Einhorn. Just as Hitzig is Chamisso's connection with the outside world, so too Brose helps Einhorn to reach a world he can no longer physically navigate.

Einhorn is particularly fascinated by the way in which Chamisso approaches the issue of time and he points to repeated instances when the author appears to prefigure subsequent real-life experiences in his texts. His 1831 poem *The Steam Horse* (*Das Dampfross*) is perhaps the most salient example, as it describes train travel before Chamisso had experienced it for himself. Moreover, in the poem the lyrical I pre-empts scientific theories of relativity by imagining that the speed of the train allows him to time travel, for example paying a visit to his mother at the moment of his birth. Einhorn's fascination with Chamisso's treatment of time is sharpened by his experiences in the care home where he witnesses, and experiences at first hand, the impact of physical decline. In the final stages of his life, Einhorn's friend Hilpert regresses to an infantile state, a curious situation in which the end of his life appears to turn back towards the beginning, reversing the life narrative. For Cynthia Port (2012), such narrative reversals may constitute a kind 'queer temporality'. She argues that 'there are significant resonances between queer subjectivity and the condition of old age', as older people are often 'figured by the cultural imagination as being outside mainstream temporalities and standing in the way of, rather than contributing to, the promise of the future' (2, 3)

Echoing Margaret Morganroth Gullette's idea of the power of the 'oldest self' to preside over the 'retrospective invention of causes' (2004: 150), that is, to take control of the process of meaning making, Einhorn believes that turning back time might offer a unique chance to provide insight into a life course. In particular, he is interested in the moment at which a life nears its end and, consequently, becomes a kind of beginning, a point when sense is made by moving backwards (316). It is with the idea of temporal flexibility in mind that Einhorn asks Brose to investigate an inconsistency in reports about Chamisso's arrival in Leipzig, from where the author embarked on a pioneering journey on one of Germany's first passenger trains. Chamisso himself stated that he travelled to Leipzig in autumn 1837, whereas Hitzig noted that he made the journey in August that year. Einhorn needs Brose's help to find evidence that will solve the puzzle, and Brose succeeds in doing this: a newspaper announcement dating Chamisso's arrival in Leipzig to 20 August 1837 proves the author's own narrative to be inconsistent.

The significance of the puzzle for Einhorn is that it points to Chamisso's ability to recreate his life narrative according to his own temporal rules, allowing him to position his arrival in Leipzig months after the fact. To Einhorn, the discovery of this inconsistency suggests the potential of a 'queer temporality' in which time is disrupted and reconfigured. Moreover, this has a bearing on the philosophical question of how eudaemonic happiness 'conceived as direction towards an inward goal' can be 'understood temporally' (Small 2007: 55). Sparschuh's novel points us away from the decontextualized, homeostatic performance of self-narration – with its anticipatory focus on the promise of happiness – that underpins a neoliberal fantasy of optimization and authenticity (Duttweiler 2016). Rather, it gestures towards a co-constructed happiness based in a self-reflexive awareness of age and life stage as fluid spaces. In its creative exploration of well-being and narrative, the novel rejects both the idea of the enclosed narrative of self as progress, and the uni-directional narrative of decline towards death. Einhorn and Brose's project emerges as an act of communicative solidarity that playfully enacts narrative control but does not ignore or contradict the reality of Einhorn's bodily decline – his physical weakness is evident, and he dies shortly after hearing of Brose's findings.

Narrative provides a malleable framework through which to imagine the end as the beginning, and the self as becoming with and through an-other. For both Einhorn and Brose, this is a mutually supportive activity based in shared connection and empathy that crosses time and generation and which mirrors their assessment of Chamisso and Hitzig whose lives must be understood in tandem (378). When Brose inherits Einhorn's suitcase full of research papers and begins to sort through them, he is transported back to the happiness he had once known as a journalist (374). By taking up the baton from his older friend, his eyes are opened to a 'whole new past' and he begins to rethink the life stories of his former clients (380). Brose's desire to re-order the stories of others is entwined with his wish to create meaning in his own life. His encounter with Einhorn and the historical figures of Chamisso and Hitzig has taught him that the way to approach this is not by beginning with 'I', but by beginning with the third person (383). This offers an ethical mode of doing life satisfaction, which is an interesting counterpoint to the popular preoccupation with measuring personal happiness. Sparschuh's novel traces a search for happiness that sets aside well-being as an optimization of the self and breaks with a linear narrative of decline or progress. It rejects the reciprocal expectations underpinning a successful, future-oriented, decontextualized well-being performance and in so doing, it pushes at the well-being barrier that separates concepts of young and old. Instead, the narrative opens a space of empathetic encounter that upholds the desire for positive feeling and attends to the need for life satisfaction across the life course but, to borrow Claire Colebrook's term, seeks to achieve this in a mode of 'expanded', that is, shared responsibility (2007: 97).

Bibliography

Ahmed, S. (2004), *The Cultural Politics of Emotion*, Edinburgh: Edinburgh University Press.

Ahmed, S. (2010), *The Promise of Happiness*, Durham, NC: Duke University Press.

Barrington-Leigh, C. (2022), 'Trends in Conception of Progress and Well-being', in J. Helliwell, R. Layard, J. D. Sachs, J. -E. De Neve, L. B. Aknin and S. Wang (eds), *World Happiness Report*, 53–74, New York: Sustainable Development Solutions Network. Available at: https://happiness-report.s3.amazonaws.com/2022/WHR+22_Ch3.pdf (accessed 14 July 2022).

Bauer, J. J., D. P. McAdams and J. L. Pals (2008), 'Narrative Identity and Eudaimonic Well-being', *Journal of Happiness Studies*, 9: 81–104.

Boddice, R. (2018), *The History of Emotions*, Manchester: Manchester University Press.

Boddice, R. (2020), 'The Happy Emotions Are Not Necessarily What They Appear', *Aeon*, 15 January. Available at: https://aeon.co/ideas/the-happy-emotions-are-not-necessarily-what-they-appear (accessed 15 July 2022).

Cabanas, E. and E. Illouz (2019), *Manufacturing Happy Citizens: How the Science and Industry of Happiness Control Our Lives*, London: Polity.

Chamisso, A. von (1957), *Peter Schlemihl*, trans. L. von Loewenstein-Wertheim, London: John Calder.

Chamisso, A. von ([1831] 1981), 'Das Dampfross', *Werke in Zwei Bänden*, vol. 1, 105–6, Leipzig: Insel Verlag.

Colebrook, C. (2007), 'Narrative Happiness and the Meaning of Life', *New Formations*, 63: 82–102.

Davis, W. (2015), *The Happiness Industry: How the Government and Big Business Sold Us Well-being*, London and New York: Verso.

Duttweiler, S. (2016), 'Alltägliche Selbstoptimierung in Neoliberalen Gesellschaften', *APuZ: Zeitschrift der Bundeszentrale für politische Bildung*, 37(38): 27–32. Available at: https://www.bpb.de/system/files/dokument_pdf/APuZ_2016-37-38_online.pdf (accessed 22 July 22).

European Commission (2021), *Demography of Europe — Statistics Visualised, 2021 Edition*. Available at: https://www.ine.es/prodyser/demografia_UE/img/pdf/Demograhy-InteractivePublication-2021_en.pdf?lang=en (accessed 15 July 2022).

Freeman, M. (2011), 'Narrative Foreclosure in Later Life: Possibilities and Limits', in G. Kenyon, E. Bohlmeijer and W. L. Randall (eds), *Storying Later Life: Issues, Investigations and Interventions in Narrative Psychology*, 3–19, Oxford: Oxford University Press.

Graham, C. and J. R. Pozuelo (2017), 'Happiness, Stress and Age: How the U-Curve Varies across People and Places', *Journal of Popular Economy*, 30: 225–64.

Higgs, P. and C. Gilleard (2015), *Rethinking Old Age: Theorising the Fourth Age*, London and New York: Palgrave Macmillan.

Knopp, J. and H. Fischer (dir.) (2018), *Der Rest ist Glückssache: Über Zufriedenheit im Alter* [TV documentary], ZDF, 4 December. Available at: https://www.zdf.de/dokumentation/37-grad/37-der-rest-ist-glueckssache-100.html (accessed 25 July 2022).

Mhaske, R. (2017), 'Happiness and Aging', *Journal of Psychosocial Research*, 12(1): 71–9.

Morganroth Gullette, M. (2004), *Aged by Culture*, Chicago: University of Chicago Press.

Morganroth Gullette, M. (2017), *Ending Ageism or How Not to Shoot Old People*, New Brunswick, NJ: Rutgers University Press.

Pawelski, J. O. and D. J. Moores, eds (2013), *The Eudaimonic Turn: Well-being in Literary Studies*, Madison, Teaneck: Fairleigh Dickinson University Press.

Port, C. (2012), 'No Future? Aging, Temporality, History, and Reverse Chronologies', *Occasion: Interdisciplinary Studies in the Humanities*, 4: 1–19. Available at: https://arcade.stanford.edu/sites/default/files/article_pdfs/OCCASION_v04_Port_053112_0.pdf (accessed 6 July 2022).

Randall, W. L. (2011), 'Memory, Metaphor and Meaning: Reading for Wisdom in the Stories of Our Lives', in G. Kenyon, E. Bohlmeijer and W. L. Randall (eds), *Storying Later Life: Issues, Investigations and Interventions in Narrative Psychology*, 20–38, Oxford: Oxford University Press.

Schicktanz, S. and M. Schweda, eds (2012), *Pro-Age oder Anti-Aging: Altern im Fokus der modernen Medizin*, Frankfurt/New York: Campus Verlag.

Segal, L. (2017), *Radical Happiness: Moments of Collective Joy*, London and New York: Verso.

Sharma, D. and F. Tygstrup (2015), *Affectivity and the Study of Culture*, Amsterdam: De Gruyter.

SKL Glücksatlas 2022. Available at: https://www.skl-gluecksatlas.de/index.html (accessed 15 July 2022).

Small, H. (2007), *The Long Life*, Oxford: Oxford University Press.

Sparschuh, J. (2018), *Das Leben kostet viel Zeit*, Cologne: Kiepenheuer & Witsch.

Steunenberg, B. and E. Bohlmeijer (2011), 'Life Review Using Autobiographical Retrieval: A Protocol for Training Depressed Residential Home Inhabitants in Recalling Specific Personal Memories', in G. Kenyon, E. Bohlmeijer and W. L. Randall (eds), *Storying Later Life: Issues, Investigations and Interventions in Narrative Psychology*, 290–306, Oxford: Oxford University Press.

Strawson, G. (2004), 'Against Narrativity', *Ratio* (new series), 17: 428–52.

Wilke, T. (2021), '"Hauptsache wir haben das Beste draus gemacht": Repräsentationen von Glückserfahrungen Hochbetagter in den Medien', *Medien und Altern: Zeitschrift für Theorie und Praxis*, 19: 45–57.

8

Gender, the politics of looking and the narration of old age: Elizabeth Strout's empathetic realism in *Olive, Again*

Anne Fuchs

Introduction

The invisibility of older women in Western society and culture has recently emerged as a prominent topic in Feminist Studies. As Kathleen Woodward argues, from the 1960s, political feminism focused on the social position of younger women, especially on issues such as reproductive rights, childcare provisions and discrimination in the workplace (Woodward 1999: xi). Academic feminism, on the other hand, was hugely influenced by Laura Mulvey's seminal essay on the male gaze which provided a psychoanalytic critique of the politics of looking in Western visual culture. Analysing representational practices in Hollywood film, Mulvey showed how women are being fetishized as passive objects in a spectacle that stages male desire. Her critique of the male gaze laid the groundwork for ensuing debates about female agency, the heteronormative conception of sexual identity, implicit racial biases and the performance of gender (Meagher 2014).

However, feminism produced its own blind spot: the gaping absence of older women in the discourse on female agency and gender politics. Even though feminism critiqued the fetishization of women, it surreptitiously affirmed the dominance of the male gaze by eclipsing the social and cultural experiences of ageing women from this discourse. In so doing feminism unwittingly colluded in the cultural fixation on youth: the recoding of the female body from a passive site of male desire to a site of resistance and agency rarely extended to the post-menopausal woman who remained subjected to an oppressive negativity and othering.[1] This gender bias only underlines the power and endurance of the socially constituted field of vision and its prejudicial effects. Woodward introduced the notion of the 'youthful structure of the look' to capture the prejudicial conventions that motivate women to pass as younger once they have reached a certain age. Defined as 'the culturally induced tendency to degrade and reduce an older person to the prejudicial category of old age', the notion of the youthful structure of the look opens up a critical perspective on the invisibility of older women (Woodward 2006: 164).

The following chapter analyzes the narration of old age in Elizabeth Strout's *Olive, Again* (2019), the sequel to *Olive Kitteridge* ([2008] 2016). The two novels track the everyday life experiences of the eponymous protagonist from middle age to old age. Both *Olive Kitteridge* and *Olive, Again* employ the narrative mode of what I will call 'empathetic realism' to break down the dualism of young and old, beauty and ugliness, virility and emasculation, agency and passivity. Strout's 'empathetic realism' employs a set of narrative devices, from the ethnographic description of the social setting, shifting points-of-view, and focalization to facilitate the deconstruction of both the male gaze and the youthful structure of the look. By providing intimate access to the characters' lived lives, these works of fiction enable readers to experience the ageing process from the inside in the mode of the 'as if' (Iser 1993: 13). On the one hand, such experiential proximity can break down social fears without denying the reality of progressive incapacitation. On the other hand, the detailed description of the protagonists' sociocultural habitat – in this case a small community on New England – delves into the pervasive normative power of the social imaginary (Taylor 2004: 23) that, as we will see later on, stigmatizes or endorses certain behaviours. In Strout's case it is precisely this interplay between the inside and outside view that brings to the fore ageing as an intersubjective experience as well as an ontological fact. However, the following analysis makes a broader point: works of fiction are 'ways of worldmaking' (Goodman 1978: 10–17) which give concrete form to the otherwise inaccessible totality of the social imaginary. They not only solicit affective and cognitive responses to the depicted world but invite critical reflection on the pivotal function of narrative in life or, to quote Jerome Bruner, of 'life as narrative' (2004).

---

[1] As art historian Griselda Pollock argues, insofar as older women exist at all in the history of art, they are 'terrifying witches, hags, (and) old bags' (Pollock 2003: 193). The eternally young woman of Western art – as exemplified by the female nude – represents and promotes the ideal of a timeless body without a future.

Strout's focus on an ageing female protagonist over a long period of time is remarkable: at the beginning of *Olive Kitteridge* the protagonist is aged 69 and by the end of the sequel, *Olive, Again,* she is 86. By tracking Olive's life across seventeen years, Strout provides the reader with an inside view of the gradual transition from active retirement into old age. Ageing is depicted as an uneven and, at times, scary process, requiring significant physical and mental adjustments. However, the novel resists the conventional decline model of ageing by exploring the protagonist's resilience and contentment in her old age.[2] Conflicting external views of her ageing protagonist in the community show that ageing is a social phenomenon regulated by explicit and implicit rules of conduct.

Ageing, the male gaze and the youthful structure of the look

Strout's two novels are characterized by an ethnographic perspective that explores the performance of community in a small town in New England: by constantly shifting the narrative perspective from the protagonist on to other characters who inhabit the same place, the third-person narrative offers dynamic views of ageing in the community. The multi-perspectival focalization tracks conflicting external perceptions of the female protagonist: Olive is perceived as a ludicrously dressed mother-in-law suffering from hot flushes, a domineering mother and wife, a formerly terrifying maths teacher, but she is also an intelligent woman with a practical mindset, perceptiveness, empathy and acumen. The local man Tom Coombs labels and dismisses her as an 'old bag' (Strout 2019: 124), but his wife Cindy, who is suffering from advanced cancer, recognizes Olive's empathy and humanity. Olive is one of the few people who are not afraid to visit Cindy and talk about her illness, loneliness and the fear of death (126–8). Free indirect style (i.e. the point-of-view focalization of a character's thoughts, emotions and perceptions in third-person narrative) provides access to Olive's changing self-perceptions over time. She is introduced as a tall and big person who is aware of

---

[2] However, the novel also rejects the successful ageing model as proposed by Rowe and Kahn in the 1990s which made ageing a project for the self-directed, Western and ultimately neoliberal self (Rowe and Kahn 1997, 1998, 2015). As Berridge and Martison (2017/18) argue, the successful ageing model exemplifies ableism, which they define as 'discrimination and prejudice against people with disabilities, based on the assumptions of inferiority, abnormality, or diminished humanity, rather than understanding disability as a dimension of difference or another way for a body and mind to be' (84).

the fact that her ankles are puffing out, her shoulders rolling up behind her neck and her wrists, and her arms have grown to a man's size (2016: 62). Even though the youthful structure of the look stigmatizes her ageing body, Olive is, on the whole, at ease with herself: for example, she observes with a degree of irony that her self-designed flowery dress at her son's wedding makes her probably look 'like a fat dozing seal wrapped in some kind of gauze bandage' (62) but at the same time she feels confident that this is much better than the 'dark grim clothes' of her son's in-laws.[3] Strout's interest lies squarely in the intersubjective and gendered constitution of aged identity and the politics of looking, which performatively produces both social visibility and invisibility.

Even though Strout's novels focus on the experiences of the eponymous character, *Olive, Again* opens with a chapter that articulates the male experience of social disempowerment. Jack Kennison, a retired Harvard professor of history and recent widower, is taking a walk in Portland. Observing the social bustle in the streets, he reflects on his isolation and social invisibility: 'he was just an old man with a sloppy belly and not anyone worth noticing' (2019: 3). His awareness of his social invisibility triggers the memory of his former self as a good-looking and authoritative Harvard professor whose students looked up at him with deference, while women would look at him with desire (4).

Jack's memory links visibility, virility and male authority; however, the rest of the chapter stages a symbolic castration scene: as Jack is pulled over by the police for speeding, the ensuing verbal exchange with the police officer turns into a competition over phallic authority. The reader perceives the scene from Jack's perspective as he is told to step out of his sports car to undergo an embarrassing body-search with his belly hanging out and his hands on the window frame (2019: 133). His flabby old body and immobility contrast sharply with the virile agility of the police officer who commands the scene. From Jack's perspective, the officer employs a well-rehearsed performance of grandstanding to stage his macho power. The rising phallic tension culminates in Jack sitting in his car seat looking at the officer's crotch which:

> … was right at Jack's eye level, and Jack thought – he *thought* but looked away quickly – that the guy might be getting a boner. There was a bulge there bigger than – Jack glanced up at the man's face, and the guy was staring down at Jack with his sunglasses on' (2019: 15)

---

[3] On fashion and ageing see Julia Twigg (2013). Her book analyses 'the systematic patterning of cultural expression with regard to dress according to an ordered and hierarchically arranged concept of age' (3).

The choreography of looking in this scene involves horizontal and vertical axes: Jack is looking horizontally at the officer's crotch before quickly turning his gaze away. The self-conscious and abrupt interruption of the gaze enacts the movement from the avowal to the disavowal of the phallus, which is at the heart of fetishism (Freud 1999).[4] In the scene under discussion, it is the officer's bulging crotch that functions as fetish for the older man who recognizes his lack of phallic power. Jack's vertical gaze upwards and the officer's look downwards at him through his sunglasses complete the symbolic spectacle of Jack's emasculation. It is of course not accidental that the scene involves Jack's sports car, the single most commodified fetish of youthful virility, potency and velocity. Culturally associated with the road movie and, in US film history, the dashing figure of James Dean, speeding in a sports car simulates thrilling freedom which, in this scene, is brought to an abrupt halt.[5]

This symbolic emasculation by means of the male gaze is repeated halfway through the novel when Jack and Olive, who are now married, are having dinner in a restaurant after an excursion to Shirley Falls, Olive's birthplace: when Jack's former lover Elaine Croft (who forced him into early retirement over a sexual harassment case even though – from Jack's perspective – she was using him for her own career advancement) walks in, the castration scene is repeated with Elaine staring down at Jack and Olive. When Jack stands up to regain his authority, he notices how her green eyes 'go from his face involuntarily down his body and back up. He sat down his belly hitting the table's edge' (2019: 158). As Elaine is clinically scanning his aged body, Jack sees himself as a spectacle and specimen of abject old age. In this re-enactment of the opening scene Elaine Croft strategically employs the male gaze to symbolically emasculate her former lover and rival. The ensuing clipped dialogue unfolds as a battle over social and academic capital. These highly charged scenes show the extent to which the social imaginary is governed by gender and youth as prime signifiers which (together with ethnicity) inform the Western grammar of looking, assigning graded degrees of social visibility in the public domain.

---

[4] On the complexity of fetishism and its function as an overdetermined signifier in cultural discourse, see Apter (1991: 1–13).
[5] On the cultural speed fantasy of modernity see Enda Duffy (2009). Duffy writes: 'As a desire clearly nurtured by capitalism, it [the desire for speed] may be the desire par excellence in Western culture that is fostered and tolerated in order to reconcile human actors to their lot as actors in a 'dynamic' capitalist economic milieu. Speed, intimately woven into a new paradigm of the modern subject's nexus of desires, becomes the new opiate and the new (after)taste of movement as power' (Duffy 2009: 35).

Strout does not merely reproduce a culturally pervasive male gaze but she displaces and 'emasculates' the male gaze in several episodes which track how the politics of looking and the youthful structure of the look coproduce social invisibility in old age. For example, Strout narrates a chapter from the point of view of Kayley Callaghan, a local girl in eighth grade who lost her father a year ago, lives with her mother and earns her pocket money as a cleaner. Kayley has just finished cleaning in the house of her older English teacher Mrs Ringrose, when, believing that she is on her own in the Ringroses' living room, she unbuttons her blouse and begins touching her breasts with her eyes closed. She is suddenly alerted to Mr Ringrose in the doorway giving her the tiniest nod: 'They watched each other, and his eyes – he wore large rimless glasses – seemed kind and oddly harmless, and so in a moment she closed her eyes and touched her breast again' (2019: 53–4). From now on, this exhibitionist-voyeuristic scene repeats itself for nine weeks with Kayley exposing herself in front of Mr Ringrose and finding a cash-filled envelope on the doormat when she leaves the house. This scene enacts the classic commodification of the female body, while also staging the economy of scopophilia by interweaving distance and desire. And yet, the focalization of this scene overturns the conventional hierarchy between male viewer and female object: by narrating these encounters from Kayley's point of view, Strout unfreezes the female actor and assigns agency to her which disrupts the phallocentric logic of scopophilia: from Kayley's perspective she is merely sharing her eroticism with Mr Ringrose whom she perceives as a kind and harmless man (2019: 59). Both Kayley and Mr Ringrose are punished in due course: Mrs Ringrose sacks Kayley and puts Mr Ringrose into an old people's home after he has been seen walking around naked in his garden.

Undoubtedly, in the age of the #MeToo movement and heightened awareness of internet-facilitated child pornography this is a risky scene which leaves open to interpretation whether or not this is an abusive relationship between the older man and the adolescent girl. All three scenes highlight the social pervasiveness and power of the male gaze, while also staging its invalidation in old age.

Empathetic realism

As already mentioned, Strout employs empathetic realism based on a multi-perspectival exploration of ageing in the community. In so doing she presents us with interwoven fictional stories which deconstruct the prevailing grammar of the look by communicating other ways of interpreting the ageing self and the other. The temporalizing capacity of narrative plays an essential role in shaping the experience of ageing: 'Time', writes Paul Ricoeur, 'becomes human to the extent that it is articulated through a narrative mode, and narrative attains its full meaning when it becomes a condition of temporal existence' (Ricoeur 1990: 52). In narration the temporal is, however, rarely experienced without spatial reference points. Mikhail Bakhtin has coined the term chronotope to describe the way in which literary texts interweave time and space in the creation of fictional worlds: 'In the literary artistic chronotope spatial and temporal indicators are fused into one carefully thought-out, concrete whole. Time, as it were, thickens, takes on flesh, becomes artistically visible; likewise, space becomes charged and responsive to the movements of time, plot and history' (Bakhtin 2008: 84). From Bakhtin's perspective, Strout's novels exemplify a modern version of the provincial novel which is defined by the unity of place: in this type of novel, it is everyday life which 'acquires thematic significance' (229). In Strout's narratives the unity of place facilitates an ethnographic perspective on ageing: the implied narrator adopts the position of the participant-observer tracking the experiences of characters who either inhabit the small town or have some tie to it. This ethnographic perspective also explains the lack of emplotment around a central conflict: the two novels explore events that make up everyday life – they are, in fact, anthropological with their focus on the inevitable passage of biographical and social time. Ordinary crises, such as Olive's son Christopher's divorce and Henry's death, foreground the unevenness and contingency of lived time. The process of ageing does not unfold in linear fashion but contains disruptive moments that puncture the present. Prominent examples are Olive's sense of guilt about having failed Henry in the latter part of their lives or Jack's painful insight that his former self was characterized by a selfish and cold persona. These episodes of alienating self-recognition not only accentuate the fragility of identity but also the everydayness of experiences which are hard to reconcile with one's self image.

Strout's empathetic realism thus highlights both the ordinariness and uniqueness of the ageing process. As the main focalizer, Olive experiences ageing as an ambivalent process which involves moments of enjoyment and freedom as well as fear. A rather witty episode of a shared experience of bodily estrangement occurs when Olive visits Jack during their courtship period: as Jack is telling Olive about his estrangement from his lesbian daughter, he is looking down at his socks 'which made Olive look down at them as well, and she was surprised to see his toe sticking out of a hole in one. His toenail needed to be cut. "God, that's unattractive," he said' (2019: 35). In the sock scene erotic titillation and sexual desire that structure the conventional courtship narrative are replaced by the perception of a small but unduly obtrusive body part. Jack's big toe sticking out of a hole in his sock functions neither as phallic signifier nor as fetish here but rather parodies the significance of the phallic signifier as dramatized in the earlier episodes. The toe episode signals a new subtle form of intimacy between Jack and Olive based on a recognition of mutual need and the desire for companionship and rapport. A repetition of the toenail scene occurs when Jack finds Olive in the bedroom with tears running down her face because she can no longer bend down to cut her toenails: 'she is too big and too old to get her feet close enough to her, and she hated, she just *hated* having her toenails so awful-looking' (2019: 151). The Freudian fetish character of feet and toenails is overwritten here by the distressing recognition of growing physical incapacity: for Olive her awful-looking toenails symbolize an existential threat to her independence. Jack – a man with considerable experience in the fetish department[6] – suggests a pedicure, from which Olive emerges with a smile on her face: 'She rubbed my calves, oh, it felt good. Massaged, that's the word. She massaged my calves. Lovely' (2019: 152). Released from heteronormative constraints, pleasure becomes a mode of unselfish caring for the other. Desire is replaced by a new choreography of intimacy:

> Jack and Olive had been together now for five years; Jack was seventy-nine and Olive seventy-eight. The first months, they had slept holding each other. Neither of them had held another person in bed all night for years. When Jack had been able to be away with Elaine, they sort of held each other at night in whatever hotel they were in, but it was not the same as what he and Olive did their first months together. Olive would put her leg over both his, she would put her head on his chest, and during the night they would shift, but always they were holding each other, and Jack thought of their large bodies, shipwrecked, thrown up upon the shore – and how they held on for dear life. (2019: 149)

Strout's empathetic realism also foregrounds those physical signs of ageing that engender disgust and shame: the uncontrolled excretion of urine and faeces which, as Paul Higgs and Chris Gilleard have shown, play a particular role in the social imagining of old age (Higgs and Gilleard 2015: 81). The same male gaze that articulated and promoted the aesthetic ideal of an eternally youthful feminine beauty, produced the reverse figure of the ugly old hag with 'folds and wrinkles, warts, larger than usual openings of the body (i.e. mouth and anus),

---

[6] The Freudian fetishes return once more when Jack remembers Elaine's beautiful feet, her high arches and ankles, and her polished, bright red toenails (2019: 161).

foul black teeth, sunk-in hollows instead of beautiful swellings, drooping breasts, stinking breath, revolting habits, and a proximity to both death and putrefaction' (Menninghaus 2003: 84). The excretion of bodily matter in particular is culturally encoded as a scandalous sign of abject corruption and shameless decay. As Higgs and Gilleard argue, to this day incontinence is abject not only 'because of its material dirtiness, but because of the implication of failed agency' (Higgs and Gilleard 2015: 89). In other words: perceived as a failure of self-care, incontinence is socially associated with intellectual impairment requiring social sanctions.

It is against this background that we can fully appreciate Strout's empathetic realism: in the chapter 'The Poet' Olive wakes up one night because she has soiled herself 'while she was asleep, and she woke immediately with the warmth of her excrement seeping from her. "Horrors," she whispered to herself' (2019: 215). Olive's shame about her accident and her attendant fear about the incremental loss of agency over her life reinforce each other, preventing her from talking to her doctor or to anyone else about it. The episode marks Olive's dread of the Fourth Age which functions as a kind of black hole in the social imaginary. While the Third Age is culturally associated with the active, fit and fulfilling post-retirement life of the well-oiled middle class, the Fourth Age 'represents a collectively imagined terminal destination in life – a location stripped of the social and cultural capital of later life which allows for the articulation of choice, autonomy and self-expression' (Higgs and Gilleard 2015: 14). The dread of the Fourth Age not only entails the fear of losing agency and the right of self-determination but also the existential anxiety of entering a black zone that marks one's social death prior to real death. And this is precisely where literary works can step in and fill the gap in the social imaginary: the representation of the experience of ageing over time embeds and integrates such fears in a shared social reality. And so it is that the soiling episode is part of the narrative exploration of Olive's growing sense of loneliness: at the beginning of the chapter Olive is having breakfast in her local diner where she accidentally runs into her former student Andrea L'Rieux who was an unremarkable high school student but has become a famed poet – in fact, a few years prior to their accidental encounter she was the US Poet Laureate. As the conversation unfolds, Olive talks about her experience of gradually losing social capital and becoming invisible in old age: "'you go through life and you think you're something … And then you see" – and Olive shrugged in the direction of the girl who had served the coffee – "that you no longer are anything. To a waitress with a *huge* hind end, you've become invisible. And it's freeing"' (2019: 204). A few months pass before Olive discovers a poem by Andrea L'Rieux in *The American Poetry Review*. Entitled 'Accosted' it contains the following lines: 'Who taught me math thirty-four years ago/ terrified me and is now terrified herself/sat before me at the breakfast counter/ white whiskered/told me I had always been lonely/no idea she was speaking of herself' (2019: 214–15). Olive is so offended by the poetic depiction of her loneliness that she drives to a remote garbage bin to dump the magazine (2019: 214). Her prime concern is that the poem has been read by other members of the Crosby community, dismantling her public façade and social standing. However, the soiling episode then makes Olive review her encounter with and attitude to Andrea L'Rieux: she admits to herself that on that day in the cafe she had only sat down across from her former student because 'she was famous. And also because she, Olive, was – Andrea was right – lonely. She, Olive Kitteridge, who would not have thought this about herself at all' (2019: 216). Strout's empathetic realism interweaves an abject bodily experience with heightened introspection and self-realization. The gradual reduction of her bodily functions is symptomatic of the broader malaise of the contraction of Olive's social life. By exploring the wider symbolic significance of the soiling episode, Strout undercuts both the protagonist's and the reader's disgust. Narrative embedding, spatio-temporal duration and chronotopic contextualization are central devices that engender empathy, thwarting the stigmatization of old age.

Narrating the Fourth Age

At the story level, Olive is progressively 'frailed', that is, categorized as being at risk, vulnerable and needing care. Even though frailty is a ubiquitous term in gerontological discourse and in care settings, it is by no means a clearly defined biomedical concept. In the words of Higgs and Gilleard, frailty reflects, 'a judgement that such people present a condition of high but poorly specified risk … (I)t represents a residual state that remains when other narratives and identities can no longer be asserted or enacted. In this sense, frailty represents ageing deprived of both narrative and "performative" agency' (Higgs and Gilleard 2015: 67). Seen from this perspective, frailty is a problematic term that defines old people through a prospective risk which requires external management and control. In line with this, Olive Kitteridge's move into the residential Maple Tree apartments home is motivated by two events that, from a gerontological and social perspective, indicate her growing frailty: after a serious heart attack, she makes a good recovery and moves back into Jack's house before a second, life-transforming event occurs – a fall on the porch of the house. When Olive steps outside to bring in the cushions before the arrival of a storm, she spots a fresh-looking cigarette butt and, alarmed at this discovery, bends down to pick it up and falls. The rain is pelting down on her as she cannot find the strength to push herself up. Strout's point-of-view description alternates between Olive's perception of her immobilized body which is exposed to the elements and her fear of dying alone. Unable to lift herself up, she experiences her body as an alienated entity that she can no longer control. Linguistic instructions to herself are meant to regain bodily mastery:

> 'Olive, get up,' she said quietly, aloud. 'Olive, get up.' She tried and tried, but she did not have the strength in her arm to push herself up. 'Get up,' she kept saying, over and over. 'Olive, get up – you damned fool. Get *up*.' The wind shifted slightly, and the rain began to come on her straight as though aimed at her. It was cold rain, and she felt the drops pelting her face, her arms, her legs. My God, she thought I am going to die out here. (2019: 258)

Even though Olive eventually does manage to get herself off the ground, the fall episode marks a shift from the capacity-based definition of being human to what one might call an anti-ableist understanding of entangled existence. In her article *Unbecoming Human* disability scholar Eunjung Kim explores the possibility of an alternative ethics that overcomes the 'exclusionary configurations of humanity' (Kim 2015: 295). Probing the very conditions attached to the notion of humanness, Kim challenges the ableist grounds for exclusion based on capability, rehabilitation and productivity. She suggests 'that unbecoming human – by embodying objecthood, surrendering agency, and practising powerlessness – may open up an anti-ableism, antiviolence queer ethics of proximity that reveals the workings of the boundary of the human' (296). For Kim '(t)he moments of object-becoming yield an opportunity – one that is perhaps counterintuitive yet potentially generative – to fashion an ethics of nonpurposive existence' (298). Strout's *Olive, Again* stages a series of highly charged moments of bodily objectification in which the protagonists surrender their agency and subject-identities.

The final part of Strout's novel relates the objective curtailment of independence in a care home where her son has placed her without her consent. But this setting also enables a nuanced exploration of other forms of agency. At first, Olive feels 'that a screen had been lowered over her, the type of thing that went over a cake on a summer picnic table to keep the flies out. In other words, she was trapped, and her vision of the world had become smaller' (2019: 267). Each morning Olive therefore drives to the local doughnut shop to buy a coffee and two doughnuts which she eats at Juniper Point, looking out across the sea. The observation of nature and seasonal change – a leitmotif throughout the two narratives – gains even greater significance as Olive struggles with settling into her new institutionalized life. A further source of connectedness is the daily news. Even though the world is in disarray – Olive is a Democrat who despises the Republicans and Trump – she keeps watching the news because it helps her to stay connected to the outside world (2019: 270). Such involvement with the exterior world is complemented by an autobiographical project: Olive asks her son Christopher to bring her an old-fashioned typewriter so that she can compose her memoirs; and she also plants a rosebush outside her small apartment. By interconnecting Olive's exterior and interior worlds, these activities reinstate scales of agency, while also challenging the one-dimensional categorization of the aged as frail and in need of surveillance.

The final chapter, 'Friend', dramatizes once more the underlying conflict between the socially stigmatizing gaze, on the one hand, and empathetic narration, on the other. A new resident has arrived who lives two doors down across the hall from Olive. When the woman enters the dining room looking around with uncertainty, Olives waves her cane at her, inviting the woman to sit and dine with her and her friends. She introduces herself as Isabelle Daignault but inside Olive's head she is 'Mousy Pants' because the woman seems to be lacking in appearance and personality. One day, however, Isabelle invites Olive to her apartment where she begins to relate her life story: 'She talked without stopping, and Olive found herself extremely interested in everything she had to say' (2019: 275). Isabelle Daignault's life story fascinates Olive precisely because it underlines both the uniqueness and everydayness of lived life: it turns out that Isabelle needed more self-reliance and courage than Olive because she was a single mother who raised her daughter while holding down a job as a secretary. The dialogic exploration of shared experiences, mutual interests and attitudes to life overcomes the stigmatizing look and transforms 'Mousy Pants' into Isabelle, Olive's friend. The final chapter functions as a kind of meta-narrative that highlights the complex interplay of the gaze and empathetic narration: Olive herself is shown to employ the youthful structure of the look by labelling Isabelle Daignault 'Mousy Pants'. However, the stigmatizing effect of the look is then overturned by autobiographical narration which performatively recovers the complexity and integrity of Isabelle's life. Both Olive Kitteridge's and Isabelle's stories contain episodes and events that, precisely because they resist narrative integration into a totalizing whole, are the basis for their friendship. In the remaining narrative the two women develop strategies of mutual support that enhance their sense of identity and self-determination.

Conclusion

Strout employs empathetic realism – defined as multi-facetted and polyphonous narration of the everyday – to deconstruct the gendered and ageist politics of looking and to foreground and challenge the pervasive social invisibility of older women. In this novel shifting narrative viewpoints between different members of the community highlight the social construction of identity. The parochial setting facilitates the intersection of social and biographical time: in the North American small town ordinary crises – to do with family, friendship, work or death – prevail. Overall, *Olive Kitteridge* adopts an ethnographic perspective that tracks how the identity of the older woman is performatively produced by means of a politics of looking which assigns social visibility and invisibility to different age groups and genders.

While *Olive, Again* maintains this interest, the sequel shifts focus onto the protagonist's difficult transition from the Third Age to the Fourth Age, an arena which, in the social imaginary, is stripped of social and cultural capital. Strout's empathetic realism is particularly skilful in narrating Olive's sense of shame when she is faced with lacking bodily control. The incontinence episode and the fall-on-the-porch scene stage the deep-seated and widely shared fear of losing agency and the right to self-determination. But Strout's novel goes beyond articulating an existential anxiety: these episodes also gesture towards an anti-ableist ethics of the relational and co-dependent self that is caring and cared for by the Other.

Strout's empathetic realism adopts an ethical anti-ableist stance: the novel tracks both Olive's loss of bodily capacity over time as well as her discovery of new kinds of agency. And so it is that in her old age Olive discovers a new sense of appreciation of life as well as the value of friendship. By focalizing the protagonist's experiences from her late 60s into her 80s, Strout overturns the ageist narrative arc of the novel which conventionally privileges youthful heroes and romantic conflicts. The ethnographic exploration of ageing in a community that ages with the protagonist foregrounds other kinds of crises which have a biographical as well as anthropological dimension. Olive's crisis of loneliness, her illness, gradual bodily decline, her regrets over missed opportunities and, finally, her fear of death underscore the brutal passage of time. And yet, Strout's empathetic realism exploits the openness of the novel as a form for the recovery of the dignity and integrity of old age in the face of death.

Bibliography

Apter, E. (1991), *Feminizing the Fetish: Psychoanalysis and Narrative Obsession in Turn-of-the-Century France*, Ithaca, NY: Cornell University Press.

Bakhtin, M. (2008), *The Dialogic Imagination*, trans. Caryl Emerson and Michael Holquist, Austin: University of Texas Press.

Berridge, C. W. and M. Martinson (2017/18), 'Valuing Old Age without Leveraging Ableism', *Generations: Journal of the American Society on Ageing*, 41(1): 83–91.

Bruner, Jerome (2004), 'Life as Narrative', *Social Research*, 71(3): 691–710.

Duffy, E. (2009), *The Speed Handbook: Velocity, Pleasure, Modernism*, Durham, NC: Duke University Press.

Freud, S. (1999), 'Fetischismus', in Anna Freud et al., *Gesammelte Werke*, vol. 14, 311–17, Frankfurt: Fischer.

Goodman, Nelson (1978), *Ways of Worldmaking*, Indianapolis and Cambridge: Hackett Publishing.

Higgs, Paul and Chris Gilleard (2015), *Rethinking Old Age: Theorising the Fourth Age*, Basingstoke: Palgrave.

Iser, Wolfgang (1993), *The Fictive and the Imaginary: Charting Literary Anthropology*, Baltimore and London: The Johns Hopkins University Press.

Kim, Eunjung (2015), 'Unbecoming Human: An Ethics of Objects', *GLQ: A Journal of Lesbian and Gay Studies*, 21(2/3): 296–320.

Meagher, M. (2014), 'Against the Invisibility of Old Age: Cindy Sherman, Suzy Lake, and Martha Wilson', *Feminist Studies*, 40(1): 101–42.

Menninghaus, W. (2003), *Disgust: Theory and History of a Strong Sensation*, trans. Howard Eiland and Joel Golb, New York: State University of New York Press.

Pollock, G. (2003), 'The Grace of Time: Narrative, Sexuality, and a Visual Encounter in the Virtual Feminist Museum', *Art History*, 26(2): 174–213.

Ricoeur, P. (1990), *Time and Narrative*, vol. 1, trans. Kathleen McLaughlin and David Pellauer, Chicago and London: The University of Chicago Press.

Rowe, J. W. and R. L. Kahn (1997), 'Successful Ageing', *The Gerontologist*, 37(4): 433–40.

Rowe, J. W. and R. L. Kahn (1998), *Successful Ageing*, New York: Pantheon Books.

Rowe, J. W. and R. L. Kahn (2015), 'Successful Ageing 2.0: Conceptual Expansions for the 21st Century', *The Journals for Gerontology, Series B: Psychological Sciences and Social Sciences* 70(4): 593–6.

Strout, E. ([2008] 2016), *Olive Kitteridge*, London and New York: Scribner.

Strout, E. (2019), *Olive, Again*, London: Viking.

Taylor, Charles (2004), *Modern Social Imaginaries*, Durham, NC: Duke University Press.

Twigg, J. (2013), *Fashion and Age: Dress, the Body and Later Life*, London: Bloomsbury.

Woodward, K. (1999), 'Introduction', in K. Woodward (ed.), *Figuring Age: Women, Bodies, Generations*, x–xxvi, Bloomington and Indianapolis: Indiana University Press.

Woodward, K. (2006), 'Performing Age, Performing Gender', *NWSA Journal*, 18(1): 162–89.

The end of love: An exploration of gender, sexuality and the double standard of ageing in later life through the fiction of Doris Lessing

Susan Pickard

Introduction

In 1972 Susan Sontag published a powerful indictment of how the cultures of ageing impact on women, generating social disadvantage as well as individual suffering and lowering their value as compared to men. One of the things she especially highlighted was the realm of sexuality and she wrote: 'Women become sexually ineligible much earlier than men do ... Thus, for most women, ageing means a humiliating process of gradual sexual disqualification' (1972: 28). This is because ideal beauty standards for women are constructed according to the standard of the young woman, scarcely out of her teens. For men, however, there are different models of attractiveness across the life course, and they can thus grow older for longer than women without losing their sexual value, or 'masculinity'. This difference, which is, moreover, instated every time a man chooses a younger female partner, constitutes 'an important arm of male privilege' (8).

Since Sontag wrote her piece fifty years ago there have been numerous societal changes but yet, as I argued in a previous piece (Pickard 2021), the double standard of ageing remains vividly and perniciously alive. Women's access to employment on an equal footing to men, the raft of legal and political changes that have occurred, as well as initiatives designed to prevent sexism and ageism, have not led to an appreciable shift either in beauty standards or, relatedly, in the emergence of a new kind of sexuality associated with older women. Indeed, Sontag's words of fifty years ago, namely, 'A woman who has won power in a competitive profession or business career is considered less, rather than more, desirable' (1972: 31) remain true today.

Importantly, the double standard of ageing is not imposed solely from without but works powerfully from within, in the 'imagination' of the woman as she considers her own body and sexuality. In this chapter, building on my above-mentioned earlier paper I look at one of the recurrent themes in this imaginative economy, found in women's life-writing and auto-fiction, in which ageing is felt to herald the end of sexual love, while, relatedly, one's disqualification from sexual relationships configures one as 'ageing'. This theme, as it impacts on an ageing woman's subjectivity, may be particularly problematic for women who have been influenced by feminism and have seen themselves as 'liberated', as for many such women sexual freedom and self-expression have been central to this condition. However, it may be that this sense of sexual freedom as a form of freedom is also misplaced and that it is, at least in part, another patriarchal myth.

To illustrate my argument, I select texts from across the corpus of the writer Doris Lessing. Lessing has written about the relationship between love, sexuality, embodiment and identity in the lives of women of all ages, as well as the end of love as a gateway to 'old age'. Her writing has influenced ordinary women as well as feminist scholars over the years and remains a resource for contemporary researchers in gender and age studies in helping think through contemporary problems and issues in women's lives. In order to truly explore the theme of the 'end of love', one needs to see how it plays out across different ages and stages of the life course. This enables a richer understanding of the double standard of ageing as emerging from configurations of both the gender and age regimes and as intersecting and multifaceted, conceptually and experientially, furthermore including both negative and positive aspects (Pickard 2022). The negative aspects illustrate what still remains to be won for women's equality; the positive requires emphasis for the purpose both of a more balanced account and in order to resist decline ideology (Morganroth Gullette 1997). Before discussing Lessing's work, however, I will first introduce some concepts pertinent to this argument by way of background, and then I will discuss my methodological stance.

Background: A review of concepts and literature: *Gender and sexuality: Becoming a female sexual being*

One both becomes a woman, and leaves womanhood behind, within the framework of the male gaze (see also Fuchs, this volume). One important and helpful way of approaching this is through Simone de Beauvoir's concept of a doubled consciousness specific to (particularly) heterosexual women, which both frames women's experience of gender and sexuality through the life course and also offers a way out of the negative imaginary constituted by the double standard of ageing.[1] Beauvoir holds that one becomes a woman, among other things, by making oneself 'prey' to the male gaze and male sexual attention. Upon puberty, she explains, the female child's subjectivity, which up to that point had scarcely been conscious of itself, becomes doubled, in which she sees her own body/self as at once the locus of her subjectivity (as it was before puberty) and simultaneously as an object reflected in the male gaze. While this self-objectification lies at the heart of her erotic experience, it sparks a friction that cannot easily be resolved whilst she is sexually active. Unlike other kinds of doubled consciousness, it is about *making oneself* an object within the male gaze: *se faire objet* is the phrase Beauvoir uses, and this implication of the reflexive case in the process of objectification is deeply significant. Philosopher Jennifer McWeeny (2016) clarifies: '*Se faire objet* is a kind of double consciousness where a woman exists [in] her body in at least two different ways at the same time. Her body is both the locus of her subjectivity and the instrument for another's desires; it is jointly that which she lives as her own and that which she lives as if it were someone else's' (159).

The paradox and ambiguity set up by this construction of feminine subjectivity – as simultaneously subject and object – causes many problems for women as social actors, especially those who take certain notional equalities for granted. This remains the case today as it did over 70 years ago when Beauvoir wrote the following words: 'It is this conflict that especially marks the situation of the emancipated woman. She refuses to confine herself to her role as female, because she will not accept mutilation; but it would also be a mutilation to repudiate her sex.' ([1949] 1997: 691) That is, both adopting this double consciousness and repudiating it carries penalties. Moreover, making oneself a sexual object lies at the base of women's sexuality; as Jessica Benjamin (1988) explains: 'the "sexy" woman ... is sexy, but as object, not as subject ... she expresses not so much *her* desire as her pleasure in being desired' (89). So what, then, is the situation when ageing intrudes?

Old age and the loss of femininity

After menopause, Beauvoir notes, women lose the ability to make themselves sexual objects which in turn, more positively, allows for this doubled consciousness to be discarded. However, the double standard of ageing, working

---

[1] Beauvoir states that Lesbians, in refusing the male gaze, have a way of avoiding the full implications of this 'second sex' position including all that relates to it such as the double consciousness and so on. Thus, whilst acknowledging that Lesbians certainly are not immune to the social aspect of the male gaze they have stronger ways of resisting this than do heterosexual women.

through tropes such as 'the end of love' (Pickard 2021), compromises the possibility of generating sexual subjectivity, so that what we see often instead is a submission to old age. In this context, being made 'old' reflects the loss of gendered value, capital and even place in the sexual regime. The double standard of ageing introduces women to the domain of ageing and old age in a way that contrasts strikingly with the experience of age-peer men in whose gaze they are now 'old' (but who elude this gaze themselves until, in many cases, much later in the life course). For women, then, the double-edged sword lies in the fact that the freedom from the oppression of the doubled consciousness is now replaced by the oppression of (old) age. In short, they go from being objects of the male gaze to being invisible within it.

Writing about the loss of opportunities for sexual relationships in later life, half a century after Beauvoir, in her own memoirs, Lynn Segal, author of an acclaimed book on sexuality (1992), reminds us that there is a difference between women refusing to take part in the heterosexual regime, through protest at its norms and exclusions, for instance, and being disqualified from doing so by age (among other things). This may be particularly difficult, she observes, for the youthful 'sexual warriors' as she calls them, who find themselves in the latter position (Segal 2017). Men can, and frequently do, rejuvenate themselves and maintain or increase their social value through later-life love affairs, especially with younger women. By contrast, accepting that one is no longer desired by a man (any man) marks a clear step change in one's identity as an older heterosexual woman: 'Relinquishing Eros, she acquiesces to old age' (Rubenstein 2001: 14). Relinquishing eros, however, is not inevitable and indeed is directly bound up with the double standard of ageing as a patriarchal ideology and thus should be resisted in the way many other 'natural' facts about women's bodies and sexualities have been resisted. One answer several prominent women writers have found is to turn to other women for love, despite being hetero- or bisexual earlier in life, and this was true for Lynn Segal, although it is not always and necessarily a panacea (see, e.g. Millett 1976).

Methodology

In this chapter I am employing the fiction and auto-fiction of Doris Lessing as a resource with which to explore theory around the double standard of ageing (in the work of both Beauvoir and Sontag). The corpus of a writer's work across the life course is particularly useful for age studies, allowing for time to be highlighted as a dimension of experience, illustrating 'progress' or self-development or freedom as something nonlinear, facilitating contrasts and comparisons across the life course and most of all understanding experiences – including sexuality and love – not as isolated events specific to particular ages or stages but as containing meaning within the context of a whole life.

By contrast to mainstream sociological approaches, which have been somewhat suspicious of employing literature as a method (Váňa 2020), feminist theorizing has more readily adopted life-writing and literature as a key resource, introducing early on as a method the tenet 'the personal is the political'. Both fiction and life-writing have been central to this method, capturing subjectivity, reflection and imagination, better than many other modes. Studies of novels of consciousness, for example (e.g. Kaplan 1975) can show how women live as embodied and feeling as well as rational beings; the balance between activity and passivity; the (mis)match between older traces in the psyche and contemporary social forms; the changing manifestation of the patriarchy and so on.

In what follows I will explore the experience of a transition to 'old' age with the shift in consciousness that underpins it, seen from within the context of a long career 'as a woman'. I will be looking at two aspects in particular: 1) the movement from *se faire objet* to a more free and unified consciousness; and 2) the processes and practices by which 'old age' is impressed upon a woman through (the end of) love and sexuality. Although both these shifts are fluid and can and do recur at different points in the life course, or unfold over a protracted period of time, in what follows I focus in particular on two key points when radical transition or rupture is taking place. I will start with the experience of old age.

Sarah Durham: Love, again?

In *Love, Again* we meet 65-year-old Sarah Durham, a woman who is self-possessed, professionally at the height of her powers, confident and content. However, her world is upended by eros, in the form of a sexual reawakening, just when she had assumed that all this was behind her. The book describes her sexually charged friendships with two younger men, 28-year-old Bill and 35-year-old Henry, and the turmoil that ensues as she re-evaluates herself as a sexual being and potential sexual partner and finds herself lacking. We never quite know as readers whether she disqualifies herself from something that otherwise may have been possible or merely correctly judges her situation as 'too old', but in any case she draws back from any involvement, forcing herself to recognize what she 'is': an older woman ineligible for sexual contact. She does this by repeatedly studying her image in the mirror and forcing herself to 'see' herself as society would see her. The mirror shows her as the Other and she stares at this and takes it in, in an act of painful self-discipline. She does so 'because the person who is doing the looking feels herself to be exactly the same (when away from the glass) as she was at twenty, thirty, forty … ' (Lessing [1996] 2007: 236). Meanwhile, the two younger men acquire young lovers and Sarah stands back, consolidating her status as an outsider to the sexual realm, and yielding in such a way to old age, the next stage in her life's journey as a woman. I will next turn to another of Lessing's writings about a similar shift of consciousness at a point twenty years earlier in a woman's life.

Kate Brown: The possibilities offered by men's eyes

In *The Summer Before the Dark* (Lessing [1973] 1975) we are presented with 45-year-old Kate Brown stepping into and out of the feminine masquerade and deciding that she wants no part in it any longer, because, although she is still able to perform it convincingly, she can no longer submit to the forms of embodied consciousness, and structural powerlessness, entailed. The clarity of vision she obtains through distancing herself from the previous twenty years of her life as wife, mother and housekeeper – the children all gone, her husband on sabbatical with a young research assistant flame, her chance to take up high-status employment for the first time since her degree, the affair with a young man that results – is something she reflects on in order to consciously age. This is positive, in general terms, as it is accompanied by a heightened feminist consciousness. That is, once she sees the construction of femininity within the gender hierarchy as 'a gigantic con-trick' and herself as a 'fatted white goose' (89) she can no longer turn herself into a sexual object. She experiments with her walk and her appearance and decides to let her grey roots grow through. The result for her is a combination of jarring and empowering, and it is interesting here to compare the same events at different points in a woman's life course to highlight the kind of empowerment we are talking about. I will focus below on a wolf-whistling incident and its effect on Martha Quest (the protagonist in

Lessing's *Children of Violence* series, aged, in this book, in her early 20s) and then on how the same sort of incident affects Kate Brown at 45.

In *A Proper Marriage*, Martha, a young mother, encounters a group of young men as she is walking home who whistle at her. She is intimidated by this and also 'furious with herself because of that self-consciousness' (Lessing [1954] 1966: 359). As she crosses to the opposite pavement and quickly turns off into the street before her own in order to give them the slip, she 'was pervaded with a disgust for herself, life, everything, so strong it was like a nausea' (359). This scene is the culmination of many examples of how the first adolescent and then youthful Martha learns to make herself a pleasing object of the male gaze. As an adolescent, for example, entering adult society she learns how to make herself a feminine object in terms of gestures and actions on the dancefloor as well as off it. The experience is of being 'revealed to herself, and to others, as something quite new, but deeply herself' (157), she notes, reflecting on a very feminine dress she chooses to wear to the club. Sometimes she is repelled by these performances – both in herself and others – and at other times she is charmed by them. However, while she is aware of the disjunction between the veneer and the reality she lacks, at this point, the resources, self-knowledge and strength to challenge the system.

For middle-aged Kate, by contrast, an encounter with wolf-whistling builders gives her the opportunity to cast off the 'second sex' subject position and reject the 'possibilities offered by men's eyes' (Lessing [1973] 1975: 176). By way of experiment, she walks in front of them with self-consciously feminine mannerisms and the appearance of sexiness ('a storm of whistles' ensues) and then with her grey roots showing and no artifice: behold, she is invisible. The way this works outrages her: 'She was trembling with rage: it was a rage, it seemed to her, that she has been suppressing for a lifetime. And it was a front for a worse [sic], a misery that she did not want to answer, for it was saying again and again: This is what you have been doing for years and years and years' (207).

That refusing to perform the part of object is a choice, not pre-determined, at this point is highlighted by Lessing via the appearance of another midlife woman in the shop where Kate waits behind her at the till. Seeing how she pathetically tries to flirt and be feminine, a position contrasting with her tired face, dry and coloured hair, Kate follows her down the street and notices how she looks in the shop windows at clothes suitable for very young women and how she 'looked long into every approaching face, to see how she was being noticed' ([1973] 1975: 177).

Kate Brown's scrutiny in the mirror comes without an overwhelming sense of loss, however; there is dismay certainly at the way she was fooled by the gender system, in which she willingly partook, shock at being invisible initially, and some nervousness as well as curiosity and optimism about what will come next. Yet, on balance, despite the sensation that she is travelling into 'the dark' of her life, she wants, most of all, to divest herself of this powerlessness. So she experiments with throwing on and off the male gaze; she dresses in fitted dresses and becomes a woman again and then abandons it. She moves from mourning to rejoicing and back again, is intoxicated but also fearful of this freedom, feeling herself, when set free from the constraint of this gaze, to be 'light floating, without ballast' but also confused and numb ([1973] 1975: 170). Yet throughout this journey of discovery, she is clear that she needs to reinvent herself. One might say that the choice being still open to her for now – feminine sexuality and attractiveness versus invisibility – makes her choice of invisibility, on balance, empowering.

At this point I will return to Sarah Durham, the protagonist of *Love, Again*, to explore the somewhat more painful and less empowering experience of transformation she experiences.

The end of love

For 65-year-old Sarah the mirror is not so much a tool of self-discovery as one of tormented re-education through which she learns to see herself as old, through the eyes of others (with the corresponding diminishment of value and opportunity that this involves). She recognizes at the outset that she would not have felt herself to be old, had she not been judging her sexual currency in relation to men. She reflects: 'I could have lived comfortably with something like a light dimming, or a fire dying down almost unnoticed, and arrived at being really old, hardly feeling the transition.' She adds: 'And I suppose I can expect soon to be cured of this affliction when I will look back and laugh' (Lessing [1996] 2007: 137). It is her status as a woman in love that plunges her into this conundrum. That she feels *this state* to be an affliction, rather than the sexless/sex-free state that preceded it, remains true throughout, as she notes: 'And yet, if it really is so terrible, so painful, that sitting here I feel like a miserable old ghost at a feast, why is it that for two decades, more, I lived content with a deprivation I only now feel is intolerable?' (137). The answer to her question lies in the structure of consciousness, as highlighted by Beauvoir, associated with the performance of femininity beneath the male gaze which means she judges herself now according to principles she had happily discarded since her last love affair ended at the age of 45. Now, once again, through her attraction to two younger men, she adopts that particular doubled consciousness involving *making herself an object* and at once this renders her intensely vulnerable to the male gaze and to the double standard of ageing it encapsulates.

What is demonstrated in *Love, Again* is the fact that the end of sexual objectification (both from the imposition of the male gaze and from within, via *se faire objet*) does not smoothly give rise to female sexual agency. The novel shows that it may open up a space, variously, for focus, (professional) self-development, stimulating friendships and the like, as in Sarah's case. What it does not automatically generate is sexual agency, desire or pleasure authored within the female psyche and without the need to configure oneself as a sexual object within the male gaze. What, the novel asks, is female sexuality without this? Sarah herself has no answer. Over the twenty years since her last relationship, Sarah reflects that she has 'sometimes masturbated, but not because she longed for a particular partner. She had perfected the little activity so that it was briefly accomplished, a relief from tension but without pleasure' ([1996] 2007: 139). Indeed, imagining herself as a sexual object has been integral to her own sexual pleasure, as she now recognizes: 'the narcissism which is so much part of eroticism now could not be fed by thoughts of how she was – was now: images of her own charms could not fuel eroticism as, she only now understood, they once had, when she had been almost as much intoxicated with herself as with the male body that loved hers' (139). This passage suggests how the double consciousness, self as object, and in the case of women, self as youthful object, is intrinsic to the configuration of both (female) sexual desire as well as of women's sexual value.

A key difference between the use of the mirror in Kate Brown's experience, as compared to Sarah Durham's, is that for the former, she looks in the mirror to see how *she* has performed – made herself an object of men's gazes – and then gauges the effect on men of dropping this performance. By contrast, Sarah has no agency here: she looks into the mirror mournfully to see how others perceive her. She is 'practising' seeing herself as the aged Other, responding and shaping her self-perception to the youthful outsider's gaze.

By the end of the novel, she has been 'cured' of her infatuation and for a few weeks she is in low spirits; the culmination of this process is that she has grown old, adopting the appearance and posture of an older woman, which includes refusing to play the role allotted to woman within the patriarchal sexual regime.

Subverting the double standard of ageing?

What are the ways in which Sarah Durham and women in her position may resist this loss associated with the double standard when (unlike Kate Brown) it is not necessarily their choice to turn their back on sexuality? We can, if we dig deep, find several suggestions in Lessing's work. Firstly, there is a reminder that, despite the association of sexual love with self-discovery and an almost mystical connection with others and with life itself, sexuality has been invested with too much value in women's lives and that it has nearly always ultimately disappointed. In the first novel in the *Children of Violence* series when the eponymous Martha Quest first has sex Lessing writes of the intense meaning with which she invests this: 'Martha, final heir to the long romantic tradition of love, demanded nothing less than the quintessence of all experience, all love, all beauty, should explode suddenly in a drenching, saturating moment of illumination' (Lessing [1952] 1966: 202). Although this failed to live up to young Martha's dreams, her real sexual awakening comes later, as described in the fourth novel (Lessing [1965] 1993) of the series, *Landlocked*. Across a number of evocative and moving passages, Lessing shows the reader both what sexual fulfilment can feel like, and also how transient it is. For Martha and her lover, Thomas: 'They felt as if they might never see each other again after this afternoon, and that while they touched each other, kissed, they held in that moment everything the other was, had been, ever could be' ([1965] 1993: 128). Yet, in the fifth volume of the series, *The Four Gated City* (1969), Martha acknowledges that she has always, in reality, been alone, the possibilities offered by men's eyes popping or deflating like balloons, including in the case of her great love, Thomas. Lessing's work, indeed, chimes with a cornerstone of Beauvoir's philosophy: namely the danger of sexuality to women and the importance of their being financially independent and involved in meaningful projects of their own.

Sarah Durham relishes the sensuality of being alive itself: 'She was finding herself in moments of quiet enjoyment, drawing vitality as she had all her life from small physical pleasures, like the feel of a naked sole on wood, the warmth of sunlight on bare skin, the smell of coffee or of earth, the faint scent of frost on a stone' ([1996] 2007: 330). This celebration, however, is all but forgotten in the awareness of what has been lost – namely youth. And yet, there are other times in a woman's life – as Lessing's writing also demonstrates – when the feeling of being outside the male gaze is a rare and precious thing and which suggests more pleasurable possibilities that can also be enjoyed by the older body. One example is from late in Martha Quest's pregnancy, as depicted in *A Proper*

Marriage. Feeling trapped by their lumbering bodies, while their husbands are out having endless 'boys' nights', Martha and her pregnant friend Alice drive out in torrential summer rain and then decide to walk in it. Removing her clothes, Martha jumps into a rain pool filled with muddy water in the long grass of the veld. It is a moment of freedom and self-communing. Sunk in the water, she feels the child move, her stomach stretching and contracting around it, and it is a glorious feeling: naked, unselfconscious and briefly free. Alice, off by herself, does much the same. When they return separately to the car, 'there was no doubt they were both free and comfortable in their minds, their bodies felt relaxed and tired; they did not care now that their men preferred other company to theirs' ([1954] 1966: 179). Similarly, when she contemplates her body, marred by stretch marks and other imperfections of pregnancy, Martha feels that it is unimportant. Looking ahead to a more permanent loss of youthful beauty, she reflects: 'It crossed her mind that perhaps, when it came to being old – at thirty or even sooner ... when it came to that moment of renunciation, perhaps she would feel no more than this amused ironical appreciation?' (180).

Conclusion

This chapter has explored the intersection of sexuality and ageing in women's lives through the discourse of the double standard of ageing. Whilst heterosexual women adopt a doubled consciousness of a very particular sort, which involves them being both subject and object, this constrains many aspects of their lives (which I have not had time to detail here, but see Pickard [2020]), including sexual agency. When they can no longer make themselves prey, this opens up opportunities for empowerment and freedom from the male gaze. It does not, however, enable women to enter the sexual regime with genuine sexual agency, and indeed the message from Lessing's work is that any gains that come with freedom also come with the cost of being 'aged'. Even so, Lessing shows, it is possible that this is still more empowering for them than (hetero) sexuality is.

The conclusion of this reading of Lessing through the lens of Beauvoir and Sontag, is of the need for women to work on the deepest structures of consciousness in order to free themselves from the 'passive' or 'object' position which provides the grounds for the double standard of ageing to take root psychosocially in the first place. Beauvoir's philosophical framework suggests more advantages relating to this. The first is that of the emergence of female sexual subjectivity, born of a new configuration of women and men as equal sexual subjects. The second is of (older) women's embracing a post-sexual empowerment. This will clearly be less appealing to many younger feminists, but here again we may possibly draw from Lessing's own insights. Indeed contemporary feminists suggest her writing is both still pertinent and resonates with their own experience. For example, Lara Feigel published a narrative study of Lessing in 2018 in which she drew inspiration from Lessing's work on sexual freedom. She begins the study with comments on Anna Wulf, Lessing's (1962) character in *The Golden Notebook,* to the effect that the questions bothering Anna were also bothering her. These include 'how as a woman to reconcile your need to be desired by men with your wish for sexual equality; how to have the freedom of independence while also allowing yourself the freedom to go outside yourself through love' (2018: 5). The course of her own autobiographically infused journey through Lessing's life and work leads Feigel to the disappointing realization that great sex renders the so-called 'free woman' even less free (133). However, when it comes to describing Lessing's discovery of the freedom of liberation from sexuality itself, in midlife, Feigel is horrified. Her verdict is: 'She had just gone through the menopause and was frightened that soon she would be undesirable ... she wanted to pre-empt this by cutting herself off from men' (11). This kind of freedom, in the form of release from the heterosexual regime leading perhaps finally to an 'amused ironical appreciation of her body' is not something Feigel can, or wishes to, understand. Again such 'mysteries' can be opened up to broader understanding, possibly even rendered attractive to younger women, through such conceptual frameworks as the one Beauvoir has provided for us, in her account of what it is to become, and un-become, a woman.

Bibliography

Beauvoir, S. de ([1970] 1996), *The Coming of Age*, New York: Norton.
Beauvoir, S. de ([1949] 1997), *The Second Sex*, New York: Vintage.
Benjamin, J. (1988), *The Bonds of Love*, New York: Pantheon.
Feigel, L. (2018), *Free Woman: Life, Liberation and Doris Lessing*, London: Bloomsbury.
Kaplan, S. J. (1975), *Feminine Consciousness in the Modern British Novel*, Champaign: University of Illinois Press.
Lessing, D. ([1952] 1996), *Martha Quest*, London: Granada.
Lessing, D. ([1954] 1966), *A Proper Marriage*, London: Paladin Grafton.
Lessing, D. (1962), *The Golden Notebook*, London: Michael Joseph.
Lessing, D. ([1965] 1993), *Landlocked*, London: Flamingo.

Lessing, D. (1969), *The Four Gated City*, London: MacGibbon and Kee.
Lessing, D. ([1973] 1975), *The Summer before the Dark*, Harmondsworth: Penguin.
Lessing, D. ([1996] 2007), *Love, Again*, London: Harper Perennial.
McWeeny, J. (2016), 'Varieties of Consciousness under Oppression: False Consciousness, Bad Faith, Double Consciousness and se faire objet', in S. W. Gurley and G. Pfeifer (eds), *Phenomenology and the Political*, 149–63, Lanham, MD: Rowman & Littlefield.
Millett, K. (1976), *Sita*, New York: Farrar, Straus and Giroux.
Morganroth Gullette, M. (1997), *Declining to Decline: Cultural Combat and the Politics of the Midlife*, Charlottesville: University of Virginia Press.
Pickard, S. (2020), 'Waiting Like a Girl: The Temporal Constitution of Femininity as a Factor in Gender Inequality', *British Journal of Sociology*, 71(2): 314–27.
Pickard, S. (2021), 'Last Love: The "Double Standard of Ageing" and Women's Experience of Gender and Sexuality at Mid-life', *Journal of Aging Studies*, 60(4). Available at: doi:10.1016/j.jaging.2021.100989.
Pickard, S. (2022), 'Exploring Ageism as a Structure of Consciousness across the Female Life Course through the Work of Simone de Beauvoir', *Gerontologist*, 20(20): 1–8. Available at: https://doi.org/10.1093/geront/gnac123 (accessed 15 August 2022).
Rubenstein, R. (2001), 'Feminism, Eros, and the Coming of Age', *Frontiers: A Journal of Women Studies*, 22(2): 1–19.
Segal, L. (1994), *Straight Sex: The Politics of Pleasure*, London: Routledge.
Segal, L. (2017), *Making Trouble: Life and Politics*, London: Verso.
Sontag, S. (1972), 'The Double Standard of Ageing', *The Saturday Review*, 23, September: 29–38.
Váňa, J. (2020), 'More than Just a Product: Strengthening Literature in Sociological Analysis', *Sociology Compass*, 14(6): e12789. Available at: https://doi.org/10.1111/soc4.12789 (accessed 1 February 2022).

10

The meaning of midlife in Terézia Mora's Darius Kopp trilogy

Mary Cosgrove

Introduction

This chapter presents a landmark literary work by Terézia Mora (b. 1971), a much-celebrated Hungarian-German author who migrated to Berlin in 1990 and writes in the German language. She is the recipient of Germany's top literary awards, including the German Book Prize (2013) and the George Büchner Prize (2018), and she also translates Hungarian works into German (Siblewski and Korte 2018). The *oeuvre* in question here is the Darius Kopp trilogy which comprises *The Only Man on the Continent* (2009), *The Monster* (2013) and *On the Rope* (2019).[1] The trilogy is compelling in the context of this volume because it stages a classic midlife crisis in the life of its upwardly mobile and white male protagonist across seven years, while also exploring the transformative potential of midlife. Its scathing critique of the neoliberal ideology of successful ageing – and the neoliberal socioeconomic system more broadly – emerges through the trials and tribulations of the main protagonist Darius Kopp and, to a lesser extent, his Hungarian wife Flora. In the tale of Kopp's downwards social mobility Mora politicizes the midlife employee as an epochal figure whose experiences expose contemporary capitalism as a radical disruptor of the affluent German (Western) life course and the institutions that once stabilized it. The trilogy tells the story of the global financial crash and its devastating aftermath, commencing in the run-up to the collapse of Lehman Brothers in September 2008 and concluding in early 2014. A former GDR citizen who in the early 1990s transitioned seamlessly from dictatorship to fun-filled employment in the global IT sector, the middle-aged

---

[1] The trilogy has not yet been translated into English; all translations are my own.

Kopp refracts this historical phase, surfing its highs and surviving its lows. He is 43 when we first meet him; when we bid him farewell, he has just turned 50.

While the current chapter is written from a literary studies angle, which prioritizes the narrative and aesthetic features of the literary text, its analysis of these features is methodologically shaped by an interdisciplinary, age-focused perspective that borrows insights from sociology and social psychology to identify what kind of midlife narrative the trilogy as a whole articulates. Such cross-fertilization of sociological and literary-aesthetic approaches is most productive for reading Mora's trilogy through an ageing studies lens (Váňa 2020). The trilogy's time span allows for plausible character development across a distinct life phase full of change, and the multi-perspectival narrative style (Mora 2014: 83) permits a nuanced representation of ageing as both subjective and culturally determined.

Ambiguity characterizes Mora's picture of Kopp's journey through midlife; indeed, she can be aligned with a centuries-old, sociocultural practice of constructing as deeply ambiguous ageing and old age in Western historical and intellectual discourses (Ehmer 2008). The trilogy employs a failing midlife character to channel the challenges of a relentlessly accelerating world on the brink of epochal collapse. Parsing seminal ageing studies scholar Margaret Morganroth Gullette ([1988] 2000, 1997, 2004), we might well ask if Mora weaponizes midlife as decline in order to critique contemporary capitalism, whose demise has been proclaimed since the crash of 2008 (see, for example, Piketty 2014; Streeck 2017; Tooze 2018). Because her poetics of midlife are ultimately ambiguous and open-ended, however, I argue that Mora's narrative goes beyond the theme of decline. While she certainly narrates midlife as a foggy, bewildering life stage fraught with risk and uncertainty, the trilogy also presents midlife experiences as potentially transformative in a modest yet meaningful way. The works' complicated narrative aesthetics help convey this nuanced angle on ageing. Before turning to the novels in more detail, however, it is useful to consider how we might define midlife. The next section identifies some insights from sociological and psychological research as well as from literary and cultural studies which are relevant for the subsequent analysis.

Midlife as narrative

Midlife is defined not only in biological terms by 'canonical patterns of aging' that persist across demographic differences (Finch 2001: 82), but critically also by powerful sociocultural signifiers that shape public discourse on and individual interpretation of midlife. On this point, menopause as both an example of biological change and an expression of what Morganroth Gullette describes as an overdetermined cultural narrative of female midlife disaster comes to mind: 'menopause as the magic marker of decline', as she puts it (1997: 99). The concept of the midlife crisis is another example of a master narrative; soon after psychoanalyst Elliot Jacques coined the phrase in the 1950s, it caught on, quickly travelling beyond academia to wider popular culture (Jacques 1965). Moreover, Elliot not only drew on his clinical experience but was also inspired by great, predominantly male artists. 'Classic sufferers' of the midlife crisis were therefore 'white, professional, and male' (Druckerman 2018). In other words, as a sociocultural narrative, midlife is gendered and heteronormative (Jackson 2020).

Cultural and individual understanding of the duration of midlife varies; in this vein, Staudinger and Bluck suggest that 'while the time from age 40 to 60 seems to comprise middle age, the boundaries are open to interpretation' (2001: 5). Critically for the present chapter they observe that '[i]nterpretation may be affected by one's own current age, as well as the historical period' (2001: 5). Thus while individual chronological age comes into play when trying to define middle age, identifying the self within the midlife span involves the subjective judgement of individuals which is typically in dialogue with 'the expected, or normative, societal timing of major events and transitions' (2001: 9) during the course of midlife and in the wider culture. Living through these changes, individuals:

> ... are aware not only of the social clocks that operate in various areas of their lives, but they are also aware of their own timing and readily describe themselves as 'early', 'late', or 'on time' with regard to family and occupational events. (Neugarten, Moore and Lowe 1968: 23)

Events and transitions normally associated with middle age include, for midlifers who are parents, children becoming young adults and leaving the home, which might herald a new beginning with less responsibility, more money and more time to explore new opportunities, such as travel or working less. Equally this change could cause empty-nest syndrome, depression and a search for new meaning. Caring for ageing parents also comes into play, as do potential changes in working life: while midlifers tend to occupy senior positions, they are expensive to employ. Their careers may not only plateau but go into reverse (Lachman 2001: xvii–xxvi).

How society and individuals semantically frame chronological age thus plays a role in the production of midlife. For Morganroth Gullette this meaning-making invariably presents midlife as a phase of 'age inferiority' (1997: 160). She argues that capitalist society of the twentieth and early twenty-first centuries ideologically privileges youth over age and that we are most powerfully 'aged by culture' as a result (3). Media driven by advertising revenue and market forces press the standard sequencing of chronological age into a master narrative of decline which is not sufficiently interrogated (Morganroth Gullette 2004: 9). Portentously attuned to the incorrigible progress of our individual chronological age, our watchful eyes are thus primed and timed to scan our bodies for signs of physical change which we read as decline. Indeed, this self-appraisal can in theory commence decades in advance of any evident physical changes, for '[t]he middle years, that mysterious land of loss, is like a foreign country without a definite border. It keeps shifting' (Morganroth Gullette 1997: 160). In this vein 'fear of midlife aging appears *before* any signs appear – long before – to keep us on guard, examining ourselves closely. But viewed from a different angle, fear of aging is what *produces* the signs' (1997: 160).

Against this tendency towards 'age inferiority', Morganroth Gullette makes the case for a new literary genre – the midlife-progress narrative. She dates its emergence to the 1970s and proposes that it overturns a good century of midlife narrative as decline ([1988] 2000: 7–9). The decline narrative features characters haunted by ageing, decaying bodies, inner demons, terrible blows dealt them by fate – in short midlifers as surrogate adults in the victim position (14). Usually decline plots are ironic and take lack of self-knowledge as a given (20). Systematic disillusionment is a major theme (12), as exemplified by the decline of Dick Diver in F. Scott Fitzgerald's novel *Tender is the Night* (1934) and the 'elderly' 50-year-old William Whittlestaff, in Anthony Trollope's *An Old Man's Love* (1884). Morganroth Gullette observes that these kinds of stories often end on images and sensations of inner helplessness (tears, outbursts, scenes of madness, death). They imply that we can never recover and naturalize a kind of panic about time and self as static, pre-determined and therefore developmentally limited.[2]

By contrast, the midlife-progress narrative separates middle age from decline; for Morganroth Gullette this is its main ethical function ([1988] 2000: 8). In the progress narrative characters have resilience and strength (8). It thus puts forward an alternative understanding of ageing, underpinned by the psychodynamic

---

[2] Famous examples from nineteenth-century European literature include Frederic Moreau in Gustav Flaubert's *A Sentimental Education*, Thomas Buddenbrook in Thomas Mann's *Buddenbrooks: Decline of a Family*. Female protagonists of midlife decline are also prominent, perhaps the most obvious examples are the adulteresses Emma Bovary in Flaubert's *Madame Bovary* or the titular anti-heroines of Tolstoy's *Anna Karenina* and Theodor Fontane's *Effi Briest*. For more on this, see Morganroth Gullette ([1988] 2000: 24). For early-twentieth-century examples, see T. Fitzon (2018), 'In der Mitte des Lebens: Zeiterfahrung im "Altersnarrativ" um 1900', *Zeitschrift für Germanistik*, 22 (2): 306–17.

view that people can continue to grow over the life course – middle age is not some end point of an earlier development but a dynamic stage in the life course (15–18). It keeps open what Morganroth Gullette calls 'the condition of possibility', the view that we may at any point change our self-understanding and story (8).[3]

In its modesty this view of the journey through midlife differs somewhat from the neoliberal ideology of successful ageing which emphasizes the pursuit of life adventures and experiences of self-discovery (Shimoni 2018: 39). It is relevant for the Kopp trilogy which reveals a complex picture of midlife against the backdrop of a technologically accelerating, yet economically stagnating neoliberal world. Through her protagonist Kopp, Mora traces the changing structure of the life course, which in late modernity is beginning to shift from the institutionalized chronology of youth-adulthood-old age to something more fluid and less predictable (Kohli 1997: 23–4; Rosa 2005: 34). Kopp's midlife story can be read in just this way, as the de-standardization and de-institutionalization of the upwardly mobile life course that he believed himself to be on. During the seven years of the narrative, his career, marriage and finances implode, all more or less at the same time. He is thus adrift and unmoored – almost a vagabond – for much of the trilogy. Kopp's experience chimes with Oliver Nachtwey's (2018) recent work on the German middle class in economic decline with attendant risks such as downwards social mobility – a reversal of strong economic growth in the post-war period. *The Only Man* provides us with a snapshot of this very decline, exposing the yawning gap between Kopp's experience and understanding thereof. It also conveys how a chronological sense of time and the individual's ability to plan their life's progress along this axis are beginning to fall apart. From this angle, the first novel of the trilogy can be viewed as a midlife decline narrative. By contrast, *The Monster* and *On the Rope* suggest that midlife is a 'condition of possibility', a space of potential and difference beyond the binary of decline and progress.

Darius in decline: *The Only Man on the Continent*

From the start, *The Only Man* flags Kopp's story as one of accelerated midlife and therefore speedy decline – in bodily and behavioural terms, both of which imply the wider socioeconomic context in which his story takes place. The

---

[3] She borrows this phrase from Frederic Jameson (1975), 'Magical Narratives: Romance as Genre', *New Literary History*, 7(1): 135–63, here 158.

opening pages hone in on his physical appearance as he awakens with a steaming hangover after a night of hard partying; we learn that he is a corpulent man with a protruding belly and a pair of 'men's tits', but that 'she [Flora, MC] says she loves me as I am' (Mora 2009: 7). In his attempt to reassure himself that his wife loves him, we can see that Kopp views his ageing midlife body as abject. The same unease comes to the fore as he catches sight of himself in the bathroom mirror:

> The round-cheeked, snub-nosed blond lad in his early forties there, that's me. My hair is already thinning, a bit too long again and sticking out all over the place ... but you hardly notice that because, first of all, the mirror is small, and second, his big, smiling blue eyes (crow's feet already there from a young age!) are a focal point that detracts all attention from the rest: double chin, stubble, the first grey hairs in his sideburns. (Mora 2009: 8)

This passage is narrated in the mode of free indirect speech which without formal warning shifts perspective from the third-person omniscient narrator to the character's inner perspective. Mora uses this mode to ironize the Kopp figure, the sudden switches back and forth from internal to external perspectives highlighting his limitations and complicity with the 'youthening' (Morganroth Gullette 1997: 241) values of neoliberal capitalist culture. While Kopp himself is a white male IT professional, the split mobile perspective reveals the extent to which his self-appraisal is in thrall to the culturally dominant patriarchal, ageist gaze – an expansion of the male gaze that stigmatizes ageing women – which would situate him as a man in decline. Efforts to observe and emphasize his youthfulness are eclipsed by the patriarchal gaze three times in this passage alone: both regimes of looking coincide in Kopp. Mora thus reveals his long-standing anxiety about ageing. The excerpt suggests that over the years he has frequently checked his appearance in the mirror (a motif that prevails throughout the trilogy) for signs of ageing, and that already in his youth he was in the habit of interpreting physical changes as ageing and decline. The reference to crow's feet in parenthesis followed by an exclamation mark betrays a nervous attention to physical markers of the passage of time, a retrospective insight into the past fear of ageing that continues seamlessly in the moment of retrospection. In other words, Kopp has always been afraid of ageing and the future (decline and ultimately death) and continues to be so. There is irony in the tension between his effort rhetorically to downplay physical 'evidence' of midlife, even as his gaze inventories this evidence. He simultaneously sees and looks past the marks of change on his face. Through this contradictory narrative perspective – marked via sudden shifts in personal pronouns – Kopp is articulated as a tragi-comical character who reads physical change negatively, tries to ignore it but ultimately only half represses it. This snapshot of midlife is ambiguous and returns periodically throughout the novel; it is also symbolically entangled with the overall worsening financial situation. In this instalment of the trilogy, economic trouble and physical decay are powerful metaphors of decline that reinforce one another.

Kopp's behaviour is instructive in this regard, betraying his nervousness about ageing and his growing sense that a financial crash is imminent. During the month of August, he boozes, gobbles and slurps his way through Berlin's strand bars with his best friend Juri, barely working by day and rarely sleeping at night. Indeed, Kopp, the sole representative in Berlin for a US global IT security conglomerate with responsibilities across eastern Europe, is unofficially on strike against his employer due to the pressure he is under from his aggressive London-based boss to chase clients for payment. Desperately trying to prolong the post-Cold War party decade of the 1990s, and thereby the optimism of his 20s, Kopp tries not to see that across the global economy liquidity is drying up. By the end of the week, which coincides with the end of the novel, he has lost his job. Although he does not know it, this is the start of the demise of his professional career as an IT security engineer and sales manager. For the rest of the trilogy, Kopp's employment becomes even more precarious and downwardly mobile in social and income terms. The events of *The Only Man* thus mark a rupture with lasting consequences that is difficult to separate from the global financial crisis. Flora's devastating suicide of spring 2009 then ushers in a phase of trauma and complete catastrophe in relationship, financial and professional terms.

Mora's portrayal of this phase operates through a narrative aesthetics that, along with the above-mentioned multi-perspectivity, points to disruptions in the institutionalized life course that orders modern life (Bäcker and Kistler 2020). Despite nominal adherence to linear temporality, time is disorder in this novel, a terrifying force that speeds up or slows down at will. The novel narrates the piecemeal seriality of the banal quotidian, exposing the near irrelevance for people living and working in fast capitalism of naturalized, supposedly stabilizing temporal structures. Its seven chapters are respectively (dis)organized around a weekday that is further subdivided into 'The Day' and 'The Night'. Kopp's efforts to do his job take place within these indistinguishable chunks of time. Work is an impossible task, as he is either pressed for time and running late or listlessly wondering how to fill the empty hours. This constant temporal disorientation speaks powerfully to Hartmut Rosa's concept of desynchronization (2005: 46–7). The latter describes how in the context of technology-driven acceleration typical for continually modernizing societies it becomes very difficult for individuals to integrate coherently the different temporal horizons that govern their lives: the day-to-day, lifetime and epochal horizons (Rosa 2005: 30–2). *The Only Man* narrates the collapse of lifetime and epochal horizons which in turn reflects the de-institutionalization of the life course, as the chronological life trajectory cedes to what remains: the temporally out-of-synch chaos of Kopp's day-to-day. The precarity of his position with the US conglomerate conveys this chaos. Not only must he coordinate his working life across three time zones, which means that working life and leisure time frequently collapse into each other; we also learn that he is a self-employed consultant who must pay his own social security and taxes. As mentioned at the outset, Mora politicizes the figure of the midlife worker in the context of the de-institutionalization of the life course and the relative absence of the state as a stabilizing force in individual lives, and she does this by making Kopp an 'entrepreneurial self' who is responsible for – yet incapable of – running all aspects of his life (he is sacked at the end of the novel). She thus suggests that formerly secure jobs are waning and that, in a youth-obsessed, fast-capitalist and ageist culture, this precarization is now impacting middle-aged, established professionals. In this way, her novel profiles how changes in the employment system wrought by globalization and the concomitant flexibilization of employment systems are impacting the life course of the individual, and that even a relatively stable economy such as Germany's is not immune from these epochal trends (Bäcker and Kistler 2020; Mahne, Wolff, Simonson and Tesch-Römer 2017: 14). For former GDR citizen Darius Kopp, the great life disruption occurs not in 1989 with the collapse of the East Bloc, but with the crisis of neoliberal capitalism, that is: during his midlife.

The condition of possibility? *The Monster* and *On the Rope*

The general question is whether rupture or disruption makes possible a new departure in an individual's life, signifying the condition of possibility rather than the pessimism of decline. The following two novels do both: *The Monster* narrates rupture and trauma but also survival. *On the Rope* continues this story of resilience and regeneration.

A scene featuring a mirror marks the start of *The Monster*, and it is interesting to note how it differs from the one discussed above. Kopp at this point has been living with Juri for a few months after his flat flooded; before that, he had been out of work for the best part of a year and had not left his flat during that time. It is summer 2010, and Flora has been dead since May 2009. Kopp observes his reflection as '[a] cross between a blond, snub-nosed lad in his mid-40s and a reptile. Tear sacs and jowls. I look drunk. Which I am' (Mora 2013: 9). While the youthful reference persists, here the image is far less ambiguous: Kopp is in deep mourning after Flora's death and has more or less given up on life. His powers of denial have weakened, and he sees himself principally as a wrecked midlife soak with only a mournful echo of his boyish self in the background. He is down on his luck so much that Juri and other friends are keeping a roof over his head and using their networks to try and get him a job which is 'only temporary to be sure, as a computer-something-or-other … no career, but better than nothing at all' (Mora 2013: 21). In other words, the narrative continues in the mode of midlife decline – personal, financial and professional.

A sense of the implosion of the individual life course comes across in a job-interview scene which emphasizes the downwards social mobility in midlife of highly skilled, white-collar professionals:

> The job is of course of a temporary nature, badly paid and – as can be deduced from Darius Kopp's professional CV – professionally at a low level, but Kopp says he doesn't mind. I'm just reorienting myself after a career break. What had he done during said 'break'? (2013: 24)

As the above suggests, the interview goes badly; not only is the job a step downwards for Kopp, both financially and in terms of career status, but the interviewers are deeply suspicious of anyone who has not worked for a time, irrespective of that person's skills and experience. When trying to re-enter the workforce, Kopp must contend with 'middle-ageism' (Morganroth Gullette 2004: 79–97) and with bad pay and poor working conditions. Mora thus illuminates from a midlife perspective a number of significant problems faced by workers who are deemed older: age-based discrimination and devaluation of professional experience and training, also scarcity and precarity of work (Hensel 2022; Heywood and Jirjahn 2016).

Kopp gets into a fight on the way home and is arrested by the police; however, he cannot stop sobbing and is seen by a psychiatrist at the station. When released without charge, he decides to leave Berlin without telling anyone, driving off towards Hungary with the aim of finding a resting place for Flora's ashes. While he continues to mourn his deceased wife throughout this extended road trip that takes him across eastern and southern Europe, the novel also focuses on another major theme of midlife: marriage failure (Fitzon 2012). Flora had already moved out of the marital home in *The Only Man*, but Kopp felt confident that he would be able to win her back. In its very layout *The Monster* refutes this aim. It is structured as two separate stories that run in parallel on the same page: Kopp's story – leaving Berlin, the road trip, his thoughts and memories – occupies the upper half of the page, while Flora's intermittently appears on the lower half. Where her story is absent, the lower half of the page remains blank. Additionally, throughout the novel a line separates the upper from the lower parts of the page. Mora thereby structures this book around a typographic imprint of marital discord, mutual misunderstanding and mis- or non-communication that ended in death. She drives this home through the theme of regret: Flora's story is the part-translation from Hungarian of various obscure notes and journals she wrote which Kopp finds on a laptop after her suicide. Belatedly he tries to understand her, but he must live with the torment of knowing that he did not do this while she was alive and suffering (her story testifies to a lifetime of severe and chronic depression which Kopp knew of but underestimated).

If Kopp is portrayed ironically as a tragi-comical decline midlifer in *The Only Man*, the account of his belated realization of the extent of Flora's pain is far more empathetic in *The Monster*. In other words, the second novel allows for character development and regeneration which were not so apparent in the first. Despite the veritable imprint of marriage failure, irrevocable loss and grief, we cannot speak of the systematic, disillusionment that Morganroth Gullette mentions in her conceptualization of midlife decline narratives ([1988] 2000: 12). Instead, this novel explores midlife resilience. Arguably these traits are already evident in Kopp's defiant decision to drop out of the unsustainable 'upwardly mobile' life course set out in *The Only Man*, skip town and dedicate himself to Flora's memory by commissioning the translation of her journals. In so doing, he begins to take himself seriously – he understands that he is trying to start and sustain a necessary yet impossible conversation with his dead wife. This is essential mourning work and explains why Mora conceives of this novel as a journey inwards (2014: 140): Kopp's conversation is with himself, and it is productive in helping him process his grief.

While *The Monster* fundamentally narrates trauma and the grieving process, Mora also gestures optimistically towards Kopp's future in a scene of resilience. Kopp is walking in a Bulgarian forest and ends up on the wrong bank of a stream; his problem is how to cross back over to the right side. In the end he strips off and wades through the freezing rapids:

> ... he got dirty but in the end he was content and proud as he hadn't been since ... (well, when actually) who knows. He shouted joyously at the forest, the rocks, I crossed the river ... look at the crosser, look! Look, Flora.' (2013: 410)

The scene is full of midlife-progress symbolism: crossing from the wrong side of the river to the right side, metaphorically he chooses recovery over trauma, rupture and despair.

Kopp's resilience also manifests in his thoughts about his working life in IT. From a distance, he begins to analyse how this sector operates. Towards the end of *The Monster*, he reflects that of the eight companies he has worked for across his career, he left (or was let go by) six of them because they were about to go broke:

> ... but that's not interesting, rather what's interesting is that all of those companies were still around, only not a single person I know from earlier works there anymore. Initially it looks like the company is going under with the whole kit and caboodle, but then it doesn't go under, just the rabble is replaced as if the whole thing was their fault. (2013: 486–7)

This is a significant insight for such a formerly myopic character, suggesting that he has seen through the global IT sector and recognizes its systemic ageism. It is an important moment in the character's development and shapes what is to come in *On the Rope* – an openness to alternative ways of living and working beyond the upwardly mobile, 'cool' white-collar ambitions that drove him in *The Only Man*.

This openness is premised on the character's growing understanding over time that kinship and friendship relations are key to his future in what he assumes will be an extended life into old age. The precursor to this realization is Flora's death and Kopp's radical act of dropping out of the career trajectory in *The Monster*, becoming a 'Loser', as he describes himself in *On the Rope* (2019: 236). This self-description aligns with the ageist, patriarchal gaze he levels at himself in the previous two novels: it betrays his complicity with the can-do, ableist culture of the neoliberal, entrepreneurial male self. It also implies that midlife is for losers: men without jobs and virility. However, this complicity begins to wane in *On the Rope*, as Kopp admits how much he enjoyed dropping out (Mora 2019: 186), integrates into new networks of social relations, including romantic attachments, and finds his way back to older ones.

At the start of *On the Rope* Kopp has been in Sicily for one year, having arrived there at the end of his epic car journey. We learn that he is the handy man in a guest house run by a woman with whom he has had a relationship that is now breaking up. He covers his bed and board by taking care of the property. He also works in a local pizzeria and drives tourists around the island for a local company. He has started over, then, adapted to the place he ended up in and opened up to a new way of life, including a sexual relationship with a different woman. He has had no contact with family and friends in Berlin for two years, until one day his sister turns up on holiday. After that awkward re-encounter – she simply goes home, but now with the knowledge of where he is – things begin to change; her daughter – Kopp's teenage niece, Lore – appears in Sicily one day without warning and moves in with him. Over time he realizes that she is pregnant. He has moved out of the guest house and is now living in a ramshackle town house which he shares with Metin, an immigrant from North Africa around the same age as Lore who also works in the pizzeria. Kopp adopts a fatherly role towards the young people who gradually become close. Indeed, when Kopp finally returns to Berlin with Lore so that she can give birth there, Metin formally declares paternity, even though he is not the father.

Through the above-sketched kinship and friendship connections, Mora outlines a type of mutually supportive relationality that can emerge in precarious spaces beyond formal employment networks, state-run social security systems and the nuclear family. It involves new and old friends, some family and immigrant others who, in Mora's account, are all thrown together on the periphery of Europe in what Anna Lowenhaupt Tsing would describe as an assemblage, an 'evanescent' and 'open-ended entanglement of ways of being' beyond a social order that might not allow for such spontaneity (2015: 81, 83). For Tsing assemblages form in 'peri-capitalist' spaces, which she describes as 'sites for salvage inside and outside capitalism' (63). In *On the Rope* Sicily is a peri-capitalist site that depends for its existence on encounters and relations. For example, here work is a black-market and word-of-mouth affair, as is living space. When Lore is unwell, Kopp somehow manages through connections and outside the Italian hospital system to access care for her, even though he has no health insurance (2019: 93–4). In Berlin the same lack of security prevails; it affects not only Kopp but also his friends (2019: 227). In this way, Mora thematizes coming demographic instability in German society and its implications for social security, as Kopp's generation is poised to create a 'mountain of pensioners' in the near future that will require a 'mountain of workers' to pay for them (Mahne et al. 2017: 14). It is thus not surprising that Kopp's eyes are attuned in public places to older people and their carers, homeless people and the unemployed when he returns to Berlin (Mora 2019: 179, 304). However, Mora counterbalances images of destitution with instances of friendship and mutual support, expressed in the restoration of old friendships when Kopp returns to Berlin. He reconnects with his estranged friends from three years previously, finds a job in a pizzeria and even begins to reconsider an attempt to resume his past career. Most interesting about this change is how it is rooted in Kopp's considered embrace of midlife precarity which is characterized by his genuine recognition of his own value and experience, rather than by careerist ambitions. Towards the end of the novel he proclaims:

> I went on the journey I needed to go on and found out that I was always happiest in my job as a Wi-Fi weirdo in Berlin. That's what suits me best and what I'm most competent in … I've just turned 50, the age in which a person ~~for the last time~~ can start over professionally … I have another 17, or who knows … up to 20 marvellous years ahead of me in the career world and I'm approaching them full of vim and vigour. I've seen the world, I'm now a man who knows what he wants. (2019: 356)

These words are said at an interview, across a table from the much younger – 'but luckily not better dressed' – interviewers (2019: 356). The strikethrough words 'for the last time' reveal Kopp's edit of his thought processes before they are verbalized. While Mora's inclusion of the strikethrough creates the impression that Kopp is still in thrall to the wider cultural discourse on midlife as decline, silencing these words typographically indicates that his sense of midlife as a last-chance turning point in life overall is waning. Instead, he recasts it as a phase in which new experiences – such as restarting a former career on a new footing and in a new context – are possible. And indeed, the interview ends on a cautiously positive note. More to the point, while he would prefer to work in the sector for which he is best qualified and has the most experience, Kopp himself does not attach too much importance to achieving this aim: '… it's ok if I have to keep on making pizza', he reflects after the interview (2019: 357–8). It does not pay terribly well, but he derives great satisfaction from the manual ritual that making pizza entails. He is open to alternative ways of starting over and he is also realistic, a great contrast to the character-in-denial of *The Only Man*. For underpinning this equanimity is the wisdom of experience, gleaned during his years on the road and in Sicily: Kopp understands profoundly that work in the IT sector is (and always was) just as, if not more, precarious than work in a pizzeria. What matters now are relationships and networks of support. The closing pages of the novel capture Kopp and one of his good friends, Rolf, who suffers from MS and is wheelchair-bound, talking about midlife and starting over:

> Actually we could always do something together, said Rolf.
> Hm?
> I have a brain, and you have legs. We could go out on our own.
> …
> We're 50, said Rolf. Anything is possible for us. (2019: 358)

This scene demonstrates how Mora's storytelling over a seven-year period moves away from Kopp's 'cruel optimism' in the first novel – his dogged chasing of the slick white-collar hi-tech lifestyle that is no longer viable for him and many others (Berlant 2011). *On the Rope* instead culminates in what I would call a careful optimism rooted in inter – and intragenerational familial and friendship relationships that illuminate the resilience of the middle-aged main protagonist. He has certainly suffered great losses and gained self-knowledge at a very high price; however, this is not the victim figure of a decline narrative, a self-sabotaging 'cruel optimist' in Lauren Berlant's sense. Rather, Kopp has arrived at an inner contentment after years of crisis, trauma, grief and recovery; along the way he has modified his outlook on midlife and getting older.

Most interesting about the ending of the trilogy is the profound message that midlife as a condition of possibility for positive change and even happiness is not the outcome of stable social systems that support safe passage through midlife into older age and beyond. Instead Kopp's story tells us that a 'good enough'[4] midlife is premised arbitrarily on individual levels of resilience, the strength of private networks and spontaneous assemblages. Kopp's midlife-progress narrative thus produces a mixed picture. On one hand, his ability to reinvent himself is part of a counter-cultural narrative that defies midlife stories as inevitable decline. That is surely a positive development. On the other, the qualities of autonomy, creativity and improvization that Kopp demonstrates as he suffers a midlife crisis are, Mora's narrative suggests, the very qualities that individuals and groups will need to develop in the context of demographic change and changes in the structure of the life course wrought by wider political and socioeconomic trends.

Bibliography

Bäcker, G. and E. Kistler (2020), 'Destandardisierung des Lebenslaufs?', *Bundeszentrale für politische Bildung*, 30 January. Available at: https://www.bpb.de/themen/soziale-lage/rentenpolitik/291710/destandardisierung-des-lebenslaufs/ (accessed 7 September 2022).

Berlant, L. (2011), *Cruel Optimism*, Durham, NC: Duke University Press.

---

[4] I am borrowing this expression from Anne Fuchs who coined it in her paper: 'After "cruel optimism": From the "good life" to the "good enough life" in Terézia Mora's *Auf dem Seil*', Humanities Institute, University College Dublin, 10 March 2022.

Druckerman, P. (2018), 'How the Midlife Crisis Came to Be', *The Atlantic*, 29 May. Available at: https://www.theatlantic.com/family/archive/2018/05/the-invention-of-the-midlife-crisis/561203/ (accessed 7 September 2022).

Ehmer, J. (2008), 'Das Alter in Geschichte und Geschichtswissenschaft', in U. M. Staudinger and H. Häfner (eds), *Was ist Alter(n)? Neue Antworten auf eine scheinbar einfache Frage*, 149–72, Berlin and Heidelberg: Springer.

Finch, C. E. (2001), 'Toward a Biology of Middle Age', in Margie E. Lachman (ed.), *Handbook of Midlife Development*, 77–108, New York and Toronto: John Wiley & Sons.

Fitzon, T. (2012), 'In der Mitte des Lebens: Zeiterfahrung im "Altersnarrativ" um 1900', *Zeitschrift für Germanistik*, 22(2): 306–17.

Hensel, K. (2022), 'Die Verteilungskampf zwischen alt und jung', *Deutschlandfunk Kultur*, 24 May. Available at: https://www.deutschlandfunkkultur.de/altersdiskriminierung-102.html (accessed 7 September 2022).

Heywood, J. S. and U. Jirjahn (2016), 'The Hiring and Employment of Older Workers in Germany: A Comparative Perspective', *Journal for Labour Market Research*, 49(4): 349–66.

Jackson, M. (2020), 'Life Begins at 40: The Demographic and Cultural Roots of the Midlife Crisis', in *Notes & Records*, 74(2020): 345–64.

Jacques, E. (1965), 'Death and the Mid-life Crisis', *International Journal of Psychoanalysis*, 46(4): 502–14.

Kohli, M. ([1985] 1997), 'Die Institutionalisierung des Lebenslaufs: Historische Befunde und theoretische Argumente (1985)', in Jürgen Friedrich, Karl Ulrich Mayer and Wolfgang Schluchter (eds), *Soziologische Theorie und Empirie*, 1–29, Bonn: Westdeutscher Verlag.

Kohli, M. (2007), 'The Institutionalisation of the Life Course: Looking Back to Look Ahead', *Research in Human Development*, 4(2007): 253–71.

Lachman, M. E. (2001), 'Introduction', in M. E. Lachman (ed.), *Handbook of Midlife Development*, xvii–xxvi, New York: John Wiley & Sons.

Lowenhaupt Tsing, A. (2015), *The Mushroom at the End Of the World: On the Possibility of Life in Capitalist Ruins*, Princeton, NJ and Oxford: Princeton University Press.

Mahne, K., J. K. Wolff, J. Simonson and C. Tesch-Römer (2017), 'Altern im Wandel: Zwei Jahrzehnte Deutscher Alterssurvey', in K. Mahne, K. Wolff, J. Simonson and C. Tesch-Römer (eds), *Altern im Wandel: Zwei Jahrzehnte Deutscher Alterssurvey (DEAS)*, 11–27, Berlin: Springer. Available at: https://library.oapen.org/bitstream/handle/20.500.12657/27858/1002146.pdf?sequence=1&isAllowed=y (accessed 27 January 2023).

Mora, Terézia (2009), *Der einzige Mann auf dem Kontinent*, Munich: Luchterhand.

Mora, Terézia (2013), *Das Ungeheuer*, Munich: Luchterhand.

Mora, Terézia (2014), *Nicht sterben: Frankfurter Poetik-Vorlesungen*, Munich: Luchterhand.

Mora, Terézia (2019), *Auf dem Seil*, Munich: Luchterhand.

Morganroth Gullette, M. ([1988] 2000), *Safe at Last in the Middle Years: The Invention of the Midlife Progress Novel*, Berkeley: University of California Press.

Morganroth Gullette, M. (1997), *Declining to Decline: Cultural Combat and the Politics of the Midlife*, Charlottesville and London: University of Virginia Press.

Morganroth Gullette, M. (2004), *Aged by Culture*, Chicago and London: University of Chicago Press.

Nachtwey, O. (2018), *Germany's Hidden Crisis: Social Decline in the Heart of Europe*, trans. D. Fernbach and L. Balhorn, London and New York: Verso.

Neugarten, B. L., J. W. Moore and J. C. Lowe (1968), 'Age Norms, Age Constraints, and Adult Socialization', in B. L. Neugarten (ed.), *Middle Age and Aging*, 22–8, Chicago and London: University of Chicago Press.

Piketty, T. (2014), *Capital in the Twenty-First Century*, trans. A. Goldhammer, Cambridge, MA: Harvard University Press.

Rosa, H. (2005), *Beschleunigung: Die Veränderung der Zeitstrukturen in der Moderne*, Frankfurt am Main: Suhrkamp.

Shimoni, S. (2018), '"Third Age" under Neoliberalism: From Risky Subjects to Human Capital', *Journal of Aging Studies*, 47: 39–48.

Siblewski, Klaus and Hermann Korte, eds (2018), *Text + Kritik 221: Terézia Mora*, Munich: edition text + kritik.

Staudinger, U. M. and S. Bluck (2001), 'A View on Midlife Development from Life-span Theory', in Margie E. Lachman (ed.), *Handbook of Midlife Development*, 3–39, New York and Toronto: John Wiley & Sons.

Streeck, W. (2017), *Buying Time: The Delayed Crisis of Democratic Capitalism*, trans. P. Camiller and D. Fernbach, 2nd edn, London and New York: Verso.

Tooze, A. (2018), *Crashed: How a Decade of Financial Crises Changed the World*, London: Allen Lane.

Váňa, J. (2020), 'More Than Just a Product: Strengthening Literature in Sociological Analysis', *Sociology Compass*, 14(6): e12789. Available at: https://doi.org/10.1111/soc4.12789 (accessed 27 January 2022).

Unseen, unheard, untouched:
A view from the interior

Ailbhe Smyth

1. Early summer 2020

Isolation is a continuing experience for me, so this is personal and raw.

Isolating

It's ninety-three days and counting since I've felt a hand in mine, at my back or on my shoulder. All that time without feeling warm breath, the smell of a small child's hot, damp skin, the embrace of someone I love, linking arms with a friend, the generous contiguity of the pre-pandemic world.

During the first weeks of confinement, I found myself wondering if for those of us who live alone, and we are many (at least a quarter of over-65s live alone, rising sharply for those in their 80s and 90s), the absence of human touch is not the hardest deprivation of all. We are such tactile creatures. My friends said, 'isn't it great we have Zoom, what a difference the internet makes, we can meet for a chat.' And we do.

> But it's not the same.
> Virtual touch is the ultimate oxymoron, leaving me with an ineffable longing,
>   an ache, a need.

> *Sometimes, like a child, I pinch myself to prove I still feel something.*

Mind you, it's better than the silent void to which 'the over-seventies' in Ireland have been condemned. We are incommunicado. Over half of older adults in Ireland have never been online, a shocking lockout.

We are unseen, unheard, untouched. Untouchable?

Beneath the numbers lies an unfathomable depth of loneliness. Calls of distress to organizations for older people shoot up. Visits to nursing and care homes are forbidden. Grandparents are denied the joy and solace of their grandchildren. In hospitals, deathbed farewells are made via Facebook or Zoom. For a time, attendance at funeral services is prohibited and relatives stand in graveyards 2 metres apart as they bury their dead. The cruellest cut of all.

The full 'collateral' impact of Covid-19 on older people has not yet been measured, but the effects of isolation and the deprivation of touch have already been exposed starkly in the 'excess' rate of deaths of dementia sufferers in nursing and care homes. Loss of familiar routines, the stimuli of visits and activities, and above all the absence of physical tenderness are noted as contributory factors to these 'excess' deaths. Hugs it seems are necessary for life.

There is a great weight of sadness at the losses we have sustained which we haven't even begun to allow ourselves to acknowledge and experience.

'Children should be seen and not heard'. The admonition echoed throughout my childhood. I resented it, thought it was stupid (I was right), did everything I could to ignore it. Now here I am, officially old, silent once more. Plus ça change.

Isolation and confinement: two words guaranteed to strike fear in the hearts of most older people. Cut off from the most basic quotidian activities: shopping, going for a walk, greeting our neighbours, getting the bus. There is no law against these activities, but the tone of government 'advice' is severely monitory.[1] You must ... You must not ... You will ... Cowed into acquiescence, many older people believe they may be stopped by the Gardai or fined for leaving their homes. Repeatedly I hear of people terrified to put so much as their nose outside their front door for fear of breaking the law and (therefore) catching 'the Covid'.

This is incarceration, although we are guilty of no crime except to be our age. That's the problem. Being old is high risk, being very old is very high risk. Other people, especially children they said, are dangerous, potentially fatal. The world is your enemy. The only way we can protect you is to lock you up and pocket the key. For your own good.

---

[1] During the Covid-19 pandemic the Irish government was advised by the National Public Health Emergency Team (Nphet), which was established on 27 January 2020 in the Department of Health and chaired by the Chief Medical Officer. For the minutes of the NPHET meetings see https://www.gov.ie/en/collection/691330-national-public-health-emergency-team-covid-19-coronavirus/ (accessed 20 September 2022).

We're not stupid. Older people are aware of the danger: a global fatality rate for the over-80s five times higher than the average; over-65s accounting for 90 per cent of all Covid-19 deaths in Ireland (most, it should be said, with underlying medical conditions). We're not likely to be taking risks. But the thing is, from our perspective, we're not the problem. *You*, out there looking in at us, are the problem. You out there may infect us. So we need you to respect our needs and refrain from engaging in risky behaviours that could endanger our lives. We know very well there's a balance to be achieved here, and everyone has to assume their responsibilities. For the good of all.

But there was to be no balance. In the early panic and chaos, we got locked up. They didn't call it that of course.

Cocooning

In the beginning was the word, and the word was 'cocooning'.[2] Over 70s were to be wrapped in cotton wool, put into hibernation, minimally fed and watered and forgotten about for the duration. There would be no regard for the sharp inequalities and wide variations in the lives and circumstances of older people, just the same (what a surprise) as the deep rifts of inequality that mark all lives in our everyday world. There would be no need for any special financial or social care provision. Sure, weren't we all safe in our own homes, didn't we all have the pension, weren't we all able to look after ourselves, whatever our levels of health, capacity and fitness, and despite being cut off from the vital lifelines of our families, carers and social networks.

After much palaver, the fuel allowance was extended eventually for those in receipt of the old age pension. That was it. We were on our own with our very real fears, our frustration, our loneliness, misery and deprivation. The world had far more important business to be getting on with. It would be very inconvenient to have to be looking after us, and to have us clogging up the hospitals. If that happened, difficult choices might have to be made.

---

[2] The Irish national broadcaster, RTÉ, explained the policy on 'cocooning' on 28 March 2020 as follows: 'The Government has said all those who are over 70 or who are extremely medically vulnerable should "cocoon" … But what does that actually mean? Essentially, people in these two categories should not leave their homes at all. If you are in these categories you should not even go to the shops and you should not leave your home or garden to exercise. This is for your own protection. You should have no interaction or minimal interaction with other people. The Government advises that you should not attend any gathering at all – including religious services and gatherings in family homes. This applies to anyone over 70 even if you're currently fit and well, or anyone at all who is "extremely medically vulnerable".' Available at: https://www.rte.ie/news/2020/0328/1126988-what-is-cocooning/ (accessed 18 September 2022).

They didn't think to consult us. The National Public Health Emergency Team (NPHET) had no members aged over 70, nor from any of the organizations representing older people.[3] Our views didn't count, our agency, dignity and autonomy didn't count. It was quick march, get them out of the way, stack them up where they can come to no harm, hugger mugger. And it will all be grand.

But it wasn't and it isn't.

Because when the chips are down, and this time, they were well and truly down, older people didn't count.

That patronizing word 'cocooning' (perfectly described by our president as 'infantilising')[4] tells a brutal truth about our society's ambivalent attitudes towards older age. We pay lip service to the venerable status, wisdom and experience of older people, but we don't want to be old and we don't want to be reminded that one day we will be. We are obsessed with youth, or more accurately with not ageing.

It is hard to see how such a society can *not* be ageist.

'Cocooning' was heedless of diverse and unequal health, material, social and relational circumstances. Our leaders were disinclined (or unable) to go beyond the dinosauric view of older people as frail, vulnerable and dependent. No one thought to query the rationale of lumping us all together in a 'one-size fits all' box. Why not lower (over 65) or higher (over 80)? Why assume that age is the sole determinant of inclusion in the box – not the existence of underlying medical conditions, not any of the multiple social, economic and other disadvantages which can intersect with age?

Ageing in the twenty-first century is a far more nuanced affair than it was for previous generations and we need to adjust our perception of the stages of ageing accordingly. Medical advances, better health care and education lead to increased longevity for an increasing number of people (although not all, which is sadly true). This means self-evidently that 70 isn't what it used to be, or 80. Or 90 for that matter. We live now in a world where the majority of people aged over 70 are and expect to be active, engaged, often working and healthy, well into their 80s and beyond.

---

[3] For the composition of NPHET see 'Who Sits on the National Public Health Emergency Team?', *The Journal.ie*, 29 April 2020. Available at: https://www.thejournal.ie/here-is-who-sits-on-the-national-public-health-emergency-team-and-what-they-do-5086703-Apr2020/ (accessed 18 September 2022).

[4] See '*The Irish Times* View On Cocooning: One-Size-Fits-All Needs To Be Reviewed', *The Irish Times*, 4 June 2020. In this editorial the paper quoted President Michael D. Higgins who criticized this one-size fits all policy and the infantilizing term. Available at: https://www.irishtimes.com/opinion/editorial/the-irish-times-view-on-cocooning-one-size-fits-all-needs-to-be-reviewed-1.4269592 (accessed 17 September 2022).

And we do, actually, have views about our lives.

Nothing about us without us! I seem to have been shouting that about one issue and another all my adult life. And on it goes, without end. We have to resist!

Caring

There are any number of crises confronting – in fact already erupting in – our post-pandemic world: from late consumer capitalism to racism, migration and of course health, the economy and the future of our planet. One raised surprisingly rarely but of immense importance is the crisis of care.

As the coronavirus cut swathes across the planet mowing down all in its indifferent wake, the response from country after country was to counter it with CARE. Because, for all our braggadocio and rockets into space, we are not masters of the universe. Until we find a vaccine, the only weapon we have to slow it down, if not to actually halt it, is care. Care by, for and of people.

The countries best prepared for the pandemic seem to be those with strong public health systems and universal, free health care. Most countries, to different degrees, were not 'best prepared'. Including Ireland. It is thanks to the Herculean efforts of dedicated health care and other essential workers that we have done better than might have been expected, although less well than we should.

Where Ireland failed catastrophically, although by no means uniquely, was in the protection of people in nursing and care homes and other congregated residential settings (including for example care facilities for people with disabilities; direct provision accommodation centres for asylum seekers and refugees, among others). The majority of people in nursing and care homes are older adults, and the death rate in these settings has been horrific: 62 per cent of Covid-19 deaths in Ireland are associated with care homes (Pierce, Keogh and O'Shea 2020) (reckoned to be the second highest rate in the world, although the rankings game is hazardous, I know).

The scandal is that for months there was effectively little or no protection for people living or working in these settings, despite the example of other countries, and the warnings, requests and pleas of nursing and care home management and care workers from the start. The fact that 80 per cent of these homes are privately owned may have been a contributory factor to the failure to support them. It may partly explain NPHET and government oversight and inaction but it does not pardon it.

Fundamentally, this was a failure to recognize the extreme vulnerability to Covid-19 of the frailest people in our society. In the maelstrom of initial planning in early March, the needs of this significant group of older adults were not so much at the bottom of the pile, as simply not seen at all. How this 'oversight' continued for so long can only be explained in terms of the abysmally low status of frail older people. They are among the most voiceless, and (living behind closed doors) the least visible members of our society. They were unseen, unheard, untouched – and too many died as a consequence.

That is a disgrace. It raises far-reaching questions about our attitudes to people in 'older' old age and indeed to all those who are frail, debilitated or disabled. About how we shunt their care out of our homes, out of our sight, into places apart which one can only think of as 'dying houses'. This holds true for Ireland, the UK and very many other countries. That doesn't make it any more acceptable.

One of the key lessons from the pandemic is surely that it is our collective responsibility to ensure that such a care-less and, bluntly, uncaring catastrophe will never happen again.

Framing

I was once in a photography class where one of our assignments was to make a family portrait, interpreting 'family' however we wished. I photographed myself sitting on a chair with a paper bag over my head, and called it 'Not in the Picture'. That was how I experienced my life as a lesbian at that time, many years ago.

That has changed in Ireland and I can now be out and proud of my sexuality. But the paper bag still applies to people in many contexts, including older adults. That makes me sad and also angry. We need to change that. We need, in the words of Jennifer Eberhardt and Laura Carstensen, a 'new map of life' and we need it fast (Eberhardt and Carstersen 2021: np).

I notice I am often bone weary by the time evening comes. I think it's the effort of will needed to survive this solitary life, hermetically sealed off from the rest of the world; the energy required to resist invisibility, absence, isolation, silence, the sheer unendingness of it all. Sometimes, I shout out loud: I AM HERE, I EXIST, MY NAME IS AILBHE, and hope that someone will hear. I worry that I am on the road to madness. Because it's there, waiting for us, under the pandemic. You have to guard against that. And it's very hard to do without a helping hand.

2. Coda Summer 2020

As I review this in late June 2020, restrictions have been considerably relaxed. There is now very little group-specific advice for those considered to be 'high risk' for Covid-19, including the over-70s, except that we should use our 'judgement' in deciding which activities we can now participate in. Effectively deprived of agency for almost three and a half months, it turns out that we can now re-activate this faculty. If it's still intact of course. Here's hoping.

3. Da Capo Autumn 2022

At the beginning of September 2022, as I sat down to reflect on what I wrote over two years ago, WHO chief, Dr Tedros Adhanom Ghebreyesus announced apropos Covid-19 that 'we are not there yet. But the end is in sight' (14 September 2022). The 1 million pandemic-related deaths recorded this year clearly indicate it's still an emergency, but the advent of a range of vaccines and therapies means we are managing to manage the virus, more or less.

So it's not really 'da capo', back to the beginning, but we're not most surely home free either. No one I know thinks that we're back to some kind of pre-pandemic normal (whatever that may have been), or that we ever will be. Things have changed, although into what is mostly unclear and, in any case, we have new crises to deal with: war, famine and drought, repression, extremism, the immolation of our planet and a fair few other things as well. Our concerns and anxieties – quotidian and existential – have moved on.

One of my own worries (I have many) is that we haven't paused much to take stock of those high pandemic years to work out what it is we needed to learn so that we can do better and differently next time. That's not the conditional mood. It's a racing certainty: there will be a next time, and more after that. Reprise with variations is inscribed as indubitably as anything can be in our precarious planetary future.

Here in Ireland, we do have a stellar exception: the excellent study by The Irish Longitudinal Study on Ageing (TILDA) of the impacts of the restrictions put in place during the first Covid-19 wave on 4,000 people aged 60 and over (Ward, O'Mahoney and Kenny 2021). It is a mine of precious information on the wide range of mental, emotional, physical, social and economic effects of that first draconian lockdown, and its consequences for the well-being and happiness of older people. As Mark Ward put it at the launch of this important report, the research was undertaken in the 'hope that the information in this report can contribute to our recovery from the pandemic and continue our efforts to make Ireland the best place in the world to grow old' (2021).

Of course – a point is emphatically made in the TILDA research – just as there is not one homogeneous group of 'older adults', there was no one defining experience of the pandemic. It was in truth a mixed bag. Older people – *quelle surprise* – are just like everyone else: subject to the inequalities and injustices of birth and circumstance as well as the unavoidable vicissitudes of an individual life. As we age, our lives are marked and shaped by a whole host of intersectionalities as deeply as at any other life stage. On top of that, advantage and especially disadvantage are both cumulative, tending ineluctably to increase with age. Privilege is by and large maintained, while deprivation or marginalization are invariably magnified or aggravated. It's a lot easier to be resilient if you're relatively healthy, securely housed and economically comfortable.

But above and below all the cross-cutting differences and inequalities, there is a striking and deeply affecting thread which runs throughout the accounts gathered by the TILDA researchers. The pandemic was a desperately lonely experience for so many older people, whatever their familial, household or material situation.

> 'It was hard. I am a widow and live alone. I do not have children, so it was all very lonely for me.' (Cynthia, 60)
> 'No end in sight living alone, the dark long winter nights coming.' (Jean, 85)
> 'I found it very hard to stay home and not see my family and especially not seeing my grandchildren.' (Mary, 71) (Ward et al. 2021)

Throughout the report, there are echoes – it seemed to me verbatim – of my own feelings and experiences. I found this both reassuring – I am not crazy – but also depressing. Pain, sadness, loss and loneliness sit alongside remarkable stoicism and resilience. An acute sense of frustration and anger (especially directed at 'cocooning') often counterpointed by a poignant sense of hope and optimism.

> 'I would hope that we might create a better, more just society, one that is seriously tackling climate change.' (Debbie, 65)

I was struck by the reflection of Edith, an 81-year-old participant, who I think summed up succinctly the hopes of so many, by no means only older people, for a better post-pandemic life. Edith said, quite simply and directly:

'What I'm really looking forward to is lessons to be learned by our politicians to see what is really important in life and to implement the policies to end the health and housing crises.' (Edith, 81). (Ward et al. 2021)

This depressed me greatly because to date the large majority of 'our politicians' have given no sign whatsoever that they have learned any meaningful lessons from this extraordinary pandemic. They are back to 'business as usual', which does not include any particular understanding of the urgent need to take specific and strategic action to ensure that older people do not pay the highest price in any future pandemic.

The reality is that Ireland is light years away from being 'the best place in the world to grow old' (and, I might add, is highly unlikely to have caught up by the time I reach later stages of older age). Major strategic thinking and planning, never mind investment, will have to take place before we can become even a 'reasonably good place' to grow old.[5] Incredibly, Ireland's post-Covid-19 'National Recovery and Resilience Plan 2021' makes no mention whatsoever of planning for increasing longevity. This despite the following (minimal) indisputable and widely known facts:

- Older adults paid the highest price for the scourge of Covid-19: Ninety-one per cent of Covid-19 deaths occurred in persons aged 65 and over. Thirty per cent of Covid-19 deaths occurred in nursing homes.[6]
- Approximately 1 million people in Ireland are aged 60 or over – almost one in four of the population (O'Connor and Murphy 2022: 5).
- By 2051 this is projected to have risen to almost 2 million people.
- *The National Positive Ageing Strategy*, published in 2013, has never been activated and there is no new strategy in the pipeline.[7]

Despite the obvious demographic challenges, exposed and magnified by Covid-19, ageing remains an issue which is definitively 'off-agenda' for our politicians, who would do well to bear in mind that they are themselves a 'no longer young' group with an average age of just 50.

---

[5] See for example *20-First.Com Global Longevity Scorecard January 2022*. Available at: https://20-first.com/wp-content/uploads/2022/02/Longevity-Scorecard_2022.pdf (accessed 8 September 2022).
[6] *Deaths from COVID-19 by Location and Age Groups March 2020-February 2022*, Central Statistics Office Ireland. Available at: https://www.cso.ie/en/releasesandpublications/ep/fpdc19lag/deathsfromcovid-19bylocationandagegroupsmarch2020-february2022/ (accessed 26 September 2022).
[7] *The National Positive Ageing Strategy*, An Roinn Sláinte/Department of Health, 30 April 2013, updated 26 October 2021. See: https://www.gov.ie/en/publication/737780-national-positive-ageing-strategy/ (accessed 6 September 2022).

Those who have been paying attention to the impacts of Covid-19 on older adults are well aware of what went wrong during the pandemic with such devastating results for the over 65s,[8] and while not always explicitly named, I believe that NPHET must bear considerable responsibility for this.

The unrelenting 'top-down' approach of NPHET led to 'one-size fits all' decision-making which was immune to the needs and vulnerabilities of older adults. Apart altogether from the blanket 'cocooning' order, there was the brutal ban on all visits to nursing homes which had severely detrimental impacts on the mental health and overall well-being of the people living in these environments. While much can be forgiven for emergency decisions made in the panic of the pandemic moment, this was unpardonable. There was a real failure to think through the implications of incarceration in high-infection situations and, even more markedly, to take any action for change when the results of this decision began to become all too tragically evident.

To be sure, this failure stems from earlier decades-long failures to provide for the care of fragile older people in more effective, humane – and caring – ways, and to develop policies and services emphasizing supported independent living rather than collective enclosure. We might also say that this failure, in turn, is itself rooted in the wider social desire (never articulated, always present) to close our eyes to our own destiny. We do not want to confront – or be confronted with – the inevitable reality of our own ageing. We push it under the carpet and keep it – literally in the case of the pandemic – behind closed doors. Old age is best dealt with by keeping it well out of the way, and off the agenda. Ageism is insidious and invidious, and none of us is entirely immune – including NPHET, politicians and the general public (of any age). This is the real, fundamental challenge we have to face squarely and deal with honestly.

All the same, there are grounds for hope. I think it's fair to say that awareness of the unacceptable indignities, injustices and inhumanities to which older people are subjected, as well as of the complexities of older age, has become more acute as a result of the pandemic. There is a sense of shame about the huge burden older people carried, and of the cost paid, and a determination to do better. I feel greatly encouraged by initiatives such as the one I have had the good fortune to be able to engage with – Reframing Ageing – as I am too by the work of organizations here in Ireland, and elsewhere, which are insisting on the need for a new vision and map of age and ageing, and of strategic thinking and planning

---

[8] Including academics, many medical professionals, front-line health and social care providers and workers, as well as the major organizations advocating and providing services for older people.

designed to combat ageism and to work with older people to ensure our equality, participation and well-being in the world.

Covid-19 has been a frightening, sobering and immensely challenging experience. I have felt diminished by how I was treated by the State as a woman in my mid-70s. It felt as if I was being hurled without warning, permission or consultation into a state of 'older age' I hadn't bargained on reaching for another decade or more – if at all. I didn't know I was 'old' before the pandemic, but now I do. I also know I am one of the lucky ones who has come through (so far), more or less intact, in no small measure because of my social class privileges and all the advantages that brings me. In fact, that stiffens my backbone even more to campaign for the rights, freedoms and dignity of all older people, without distinction, and to hold our governments and decision-makers to full account.

Bibliography

Deaths from COVID-19 by Location and Age Groups March 2020-February 2022, Central Statistics Office Ireland. Available at: https://www.cso.ie/en/releasesandpublications/fp/fp-dc19lag/deathsfromcovid-19bylocationandagegroupsmarch2020-february2022/ (accessed 3 September 2022).

Eberhardt, Jennifer L. and Laura L. Carstensen (2021), 'Charting a New Map of Life', 26 October 2021. Available at: https://www.psychologicalscience.org/observer/new-map-of-life (accessed 30 September 2022).

Ireland's National Recovery and Resilience Plan 2021, (2021), An Roinn Caiteachais Phoibli agus Athchoirithe/ Department of Public Expenditure and Reform, 1 June 2021, updated 12 August 2021. Available at: https://www.gov.ie/en/publication/d4939-national-recovery-and-resilience-plan-2021/ (accessed 2 September 2022).

O'Connor, Nat and Mary A. Murphy (2022), *Reframing Ageing: The State of Ageing in Ireland 2022*. Dublin: Age Action Ireland. Available at: https://www.ageaction.ie/sites/default/files/reframing_ageing_state_of_ageing_in_ireland_2022_published.pdf (accessed 30 September 2022).

O'Donnell, Orla (2020), 'Explainer: What is Cocooning and Who Needs to Do It?', RTE, 28 March 2020. Available at: https://www.rte.ie/news/2020/0328/1126988-what-is-cocooning/ (accessed 18 September 2022).

Pierce M., Keogh F. and O'Shea E. (2020), 'The Impact of COVID-19 on People Who Use and Provide Long-term Care in Ireland and Mitigating Measures', Country report to LTCcovid.org, International Long-Term Care Policy Network, CPEC-LSE, 13 May 2020. Available at: https://ltccovid.org/wp-content/uploads/2020/05/Ireland-COVID-LTC-report-updated-13-May-2020.pdf (accessed 27 January 2023).

'The End of the COVID-19 Pandemic Is In Sight: WHO', 14 September 2022. Available at: https://news.un.org/en/story/2022/09/1126621(accessed 15 September 2022).

'The *Irish Times* View On Cocooning: One-Size-Fits-All Needs to be Reviewed', *The Irish Times*, 4 June 2020.

The National Positive Ageing Strategy (2021), An Roinn Sláinte/Department of Health, 30 April 2013, updated 26 October 2021. Available at: https://www.gov.ie/en/publication/737780-national-positive-ageing-strategy/ (accessed 6 September 2022).

20-First.Com Global Longevity Scorecard January 2022. Available at: https://20-first.com/wp-content/uploads/2022/02/Longevity-Scorecard_2022.pdf (accessed 8 September 2022).

Ward, M., P. O'Mahoney and R. A. Kenny, eds (2021), 'Altered Lives in a Time of Crisis: The Impact of the Covid-19 Pandemic on the Lives of Older Adults in Ireland', *The Irish Longitudinal Study on Ageing. TILDA*, Trinity College Dublin. Available at: https://www.doi.org/10.38018/TildaRe.2021-01

'Who Sits on the National Public Health Emergency Team?' *The Journal.ie*, 29 April 2020. Available at: https://www.thejournal.ie/here-is-who-sits-on-the-national-public-health-emergency-team-and-what-they-do-5086703-Apr2020/ (accessed 18 September 2022).

12

Views from the living room: Older people speak out on television about the Covid-19 pandemic

Helen Doherty

At the start of the Covid-19 pandemic the Irish government's decision to banish people over 70 from society established a negative stereotype that changed their lives for the worse. This startling intervention was based on long-standing assumptions that equated being older with being frail. Before the pandemic in 2020, older people had been encouraged to be active and engaged in society so that singling out older people as an undifferentiated batch for the most severe lockdown conditions prompted many to question their identity.

This chapter explores cultural identity and the role of public service television in matters of national interest. The documentary *Cocooned*, aired by the Irish public broadcaster RTÉ in 2021, is an example of such broadcasting, a film that prioritized older people's views on their Covid-19 pandemic confinement. The director's intention was to gather a small number of portraits that would calibrate our view of older people as wise and witty and worth listening to. In *Cocooned* we are brought into an engaging narrative about an important topic and involved in a nation-wide conversation with ten individuals. I also refer to a larger scale research study on the same topic to demonstrate how a different methodology establishes that the same views were common among older people. This comparison demonstrates that popular television made with passionate concern can be as reliable in its representation of a social issue as qualitative research. While research may be freely available it is usually confined to academia, whereas popular television in its public service role has the power to contribute to the cultural sphere more widely.

Exploring media representations can provide a useful means of understanding how older people are perceived in culture and society.[1] Culture is broadly understood as 'the whole way of life of a people' in the 'pluralist and potentially democratic sense of the concept' (Jenks 2004: 12). From a cultural perspective, everyone's body is meaningful, 'for as it moves through life it is continuously inscribed with cultural meanings' (Featherstone and Wernick 1995: 3). When the Covid-19 virus spread throughout the world in 2020 and became a pandemic, most people's lives changed significantly. International data showed that older people were at more risk of dying from Covid-19; however, there was a big difference in the likelihood of dying among cohorts over 80 than in the rest of the population. Until April 2020 the worldwide morbidity among the 80+ cohort was 14.80 per cent but it was significantly lower among those in their 70s – range at 8 per cent (Sharma 2021: 19).

Despite the different mortality risks, everyone over 70 in Ireland was told not to leave their homes, an imposed state of inertia that the Irish government couched as 'cocooning' (gov.ie 2020). While other cohorts were allowed to go outdoors for shopping and exercise, people over the age of 70 were categorized as elderly, vulnerable and unable to form their own judgements. No convincing rationale was provided for this decision. As older people were deprived of their social pleasures and commitments, many people became very angry. The great Covid-19 immobilization of 2020 had practical implications for how older people's lives shrank and disappeared and, indeed, it was argued that the government's decision was not only unnecessary (Reville 2020) but could be considered unconstitutional (McDowell 2020). From a governance point of view, cocooning was a fast response that was considered an expedient decision but for older people it was seen as an enforced policy of home-detention without their informed consent. As a consequence, many formerly active people over 70 tended to become inert through 'staying at home and reducing face-to-face interaction with other people' (Bailey et al. 2021). Thus, many older people were arbitrarily rendered powerless when deemed by the Irish state as feeble and past it.

The television documentary *Cocooned* was filmed across two phases of social lockdown in 2020 by Venom Films, directed by Ken Wardrop and broadcast on RTÉ, the Irish public broadcaster, in 2021. The filming process enabled

---

[1] I would like to thank the film director Ken Wardrop for a lengthy conversation about the making of *Cocooned* and thank him for his contributions to Irish culture throughout his film-making career. The film was available on the RTÉ iplayer for a limited period. Those interested in viewing the film should contact Venom Films (www.venom.ie): info@venom.ie.

older people to speak on camera about their cocooning experiences while the pandemic unfolded during two periods of restrictive 'lockdown' in Ireland. During the first lockdown, from March to December 2020, the centre for the Irish Longitudinal Study on Ageing supported a survey of older people in Ireland that generated a response rate of 71 per cent with 3,964 returned questionnaires (Costello et al. 2021). Both projects demonstrate that older people were equally assertive and insightful about their life experiences during Covid whether recorded anonymously or filmed for television on the public record. Most older people expressed their anger about the lack of consultation, about being corralled for convenience and being denied the power to choose appropriate actions for themselves and for the public good. Since *Cocooned* was commissioned by RTÉ, it is important here to note the role of the Irish public service broadcaster in contributing to a sense of national community and identity within its territory. Paul Gilbert argues that the formation of a sense of national cultural identity can be formed through an engagement in the arts:

> Now it is widely accepted that cultural identities, and in particular national identities, are constituted, at least in part, by distinctive artistic productions – literature, painting, music and so on – to which the members of a cultural group will have responses of a sort not shared by those outside it. (Gilbert 2010: 152)

Gilbert proceeds to argue that cultural identity can be manipulated for political bias. However, public service television broadcasters are required to address national cultural interests and to serve the public for the benefit of society:

> Public service broadcasting binds together and integrates an increasingly privatized and fragmented society. It ensures that everyone has access to a shared, unifying experience, because it does not discriminate against outlying areas or low-income groups on the grounds of cost or profitability. Its approach is inclusive, seeking to draw together society in its diversity and to frame public discussion in terms of what serves the general good. (Curran and Seaton 2018: 501)

Since RTÉ commissions programmes which represent Irish society, often these are confined to a local or national interest; however, the Covid-19 pandemic has universal appeal since there are shared experiences of the lockdown effects in different countries. In this context, the *Cocooned* documentary is an interesting case study for exploring how public service media can play a vital role in overturning the negative framing of older people in wider social and political discourses, by presenting the 'cocooned' as individuals with their own critical viewpoints and life experiences. In this way, *Cocooned* contributes to widening our cultural understanding of older people in Ireland and elsewhere.

Saunders presents the commonly agreed view that the standard documentary (in contrast to experimental work) should be formed from a coherent and compelling narrative: 'Narrative is what distinguishes a story from a mere list of events, and sets a documentary apart from raw footage' (Saunders 2010: 16). Professional documentary makers are aware that their subjective views are involved in narrativizing a topic. There is a balance to be struck between subjective views and objective facts – there is no single truth. In the words of Stella Bruzzi 'documentaries are predicated upon a negotiation between the polarities of objectivity and subjectivity, offering a dialectical analysis of events and images that accepts that no non-fictional record can contain the whole truth' (Bruzzi 2000: 39). Nevertheless, Bruzzi further explains that there is another form of intersubjective truth which is generated through the activities of filming, being filmed and viewing. It is 'the truth that emerges through the encounter between filmmakers, subjects and spectators' (9). The principles of trustworthiness, narrative engagement and participant's agency are important considerations for documentary making within the public service remit.

Since the increasing number of older people worldwide has implications for how societies will change (Morgan and Kunkel 2011: 15), it is useful to consider cultural identity and older people. In recent decades, terms such as 'the third age' and 'positive ageing' have emerged – particularly in the affluent West – to encapsulate how ageing can be a good experience and how older people can engage in society (286). In their third age many people expect freedoms 'in which they can, within fairly wide limits, live their lives as they please' (Weiss and Bass 2001: 15). While the ideas of the third age and positive ageing can be useful because they work against negative stereotypes, there are indications of encroaching interests that narrow the definitions in ways that are less beneficial. From an economist's point of view, many older people have surplus money, 'the old, at their late stage in the life cycle, don't save, but spend' (Coyle 2020). People reaching the stage of positive ageing can be seen as potential consumers which creates a biased view that favours the wealthy: 'positive ageing is in part a response by marketers anxious to stimulate response … conditional on the possession of sufficient income, cultural capital and mental and physical health' (Blaikie 1999: 22). An additional negative consequence of the positive ageing message occurs when the complexities of the ageing experience are side-lined. This problem is highlighted by Featherstone and Wernick who argue that the obligation to be relentlessly positive while ageing sends out a message 'of denial, keep smiling and carry on consuming' (1995: 10). Thus older people are stereotyped by the limited selection of 'one façade only of a group's activities and potentialities' (Featherstone and Wernick 1995: 5), whereas we all have a 'multiplicity of identities and differences rather than one singular identity' (Hall and du Gay 1996: 90).

In this vein, the media often circulate and fix generic images of older people: after all, simple messages are easier to create and communicate than complex representations. For example, on television older people are regularly portrayed for superficial comic effect to the point where 'we no longer see our elders as sources of wisdom but as feeble yet lovable, doddering but dear' (Nelson 2004: 64). In this way the media are 'a strong contributor to a cultural frame in which aging is portrayed and experienced as decline and as a state of lack' (Harrington et al. 2014: 181). Media research suggests that children and teens who have little contact with older people are more likely to form stereotypical views about them from television viewing. Older viewers show a differentiated response: while some get upset about negative representations of their peer group, others simply shrug them off (10). Given the broad set of cultural experiences in people's lives, television is only one contributor to social stereotyping (Harrington et al. 2014: 182). However, television continues to have an important role in constructing identity, more deeply layered portrayals of older people should encourage a positive self-identity about and among older people (Ylänne 2015: 371). Research by the European Broadcasting Union (EBU) shows that the largest audience for public service television is aged 60+ and that older people watched television for longer durations in 2022: people aged 60+ view five and a half hours daily compared to the three and a half on average (EBU 2022). As people age, television and radio become more important in their domestic space (Harrington et al. 2014: 182).

Considering the range of stereotypes that depict older people with simplistic gestures, a television programme is noteworthy when it enables older people to portray their life circumstances in more complex ways. The television documentary *Cocooned* is a good example of a deeply layered and empathetic portrayal of older individuals who speak out into the public domain from the confines of their own homes. *Cocooned* was commissioned and nurtured by the Factual, Documentary and Series department of RTÉ (2021), produced by the Irish independent production company Venom Films and directed by Ken Wardrop. It was assigned a one-hour prime-time slot on the main broadcaster's schedule and remained on the RTÉ Player for online viewing. When broadcast it generated a strong 25 per cent share of the viewership and

245,000 viewers, another 20,000 and 3 per cent on RTÉ plus one, and it was expected to do well on the RTÉ Player online (Venom films). *Cocooned* was intended to be different from other factual programmes – the central aim was to feature the views of older people and to incorporate lighter tones into a strong narrative-driven programme. The participants who agreed to be filmed and make their views public were courageous, given the backdrop of fractious public debate and misinformation about Covid-19 at that time. Because of lockdown restrictions, the production team had to work out special procedures to meet with older people at a socially safe distance: the director visited each home in various locations across Ireland to talk from outdoors on a mobile phone with eye contact to each contributor who was indoors on their mobile phone. The documentary was styled to create a chatty familiarity with the contributors who appeared like close neighbours, bringing their sense of fun, quirky characteristics and, on occasion, sparring banter to the conversations. This filming technique from the outside into the homes of the contributors enabled the television audience to witness their difficulties and understand the level of personal suffering arising from their confinement. The resulting programme is a series of rounded portraits of people who were comfortable to be themselves while speaking out from their living rooms.

The viewer gets to know the ten contributors by their first names when they appear on-screen. Their age is not specified, they do not know each other and they are represented as ordinary people willing to share their opinions. Discussions of serious pandemic topics may segue into riffs about domestic themes such as appreciation of home cooking or needing a hair-cut. Their responses to cocooning and outside events are interwoven in post-production into an engaging narrative. Their experiences of the pandemic involve various stages of emotions across time, ranging from anger, hope, appreciation of life to resilience, and – at the second more harsh lockdown in October 2020 – deep despondence until a vaccine became available. The chronological plot-points that occur in the exterior world governing their lives and shaping their biographies are revealed in short sequences. From afar, government politicians and public health professionals decide on closing society, they decide when to open up and when to close again; and, they decide who is old and who is not. Those in authority are not seen in *Cocooned*: instead their voices are heard over shots of empty towns and cities. Only An Taoiseach (the Irish Prime Minister) is given a title when making public announcements. This 'facelessness' of the decision-makers emphasizes the social distance between the representatives of power and the people whose lives are affected by their policy decisions.

Figure 6 Four film stills from the documentary *Cocooned,* 2021. Courtesy of Ken Wardrop, Venom Films.

A dominant motif in *Cocooned* is the frame inside a frame which contributes to the mood of enclosure (Figure 6). The filming style creates a series of visual connections: the contributors are framed by their living room windows, the camera films through a frame and the audience views the programme through the frame of a screen. The line of sight leads the audience through the screen frame and onwards through the window that frames the speaker who looks out at us as we look in at them.

The viewer is positioned in the role of a neighbour, rather than an anthropologist, who over time, gets to know these selected strangers, discovering their thoughts, feelings and values. This one-to-one connection, creates the conditions for empathizing with people whose lives may or may not be similar to our own. While talking into their phones, one participant is shown to fiddle with the curtains, another leans an elbow on the window ledge, and a third one sits in their armchair but they are all animated by the conversational intervention into their lives.

Most of the filming took place at night: in contrast to the darkness outside which communicates a sense of menace, the indoor spaces appear bright exuding a sense of cosy warmth. While the audience sees and hears them talking into their phones inside their homes – they are usually alone – the director remains unseen and unheard. The visual effect of looking into their homes through the window frame gives the sense that each person is illuminated on a stage. Everyone's living room becomes a theatrical setting, and we, the audience, can deduce their biographies and lifestyles through glimpses of personal belongings, from curtains and wallpaper to ornamental objects. In this way each participant's habitual space is transformed into a theatrical space where they perform themselves for us. While these filming techniques were motivated by Covid-19 restrictions, they enhance the viewer's intimacy and engagement with personal stories, while the window motif emphasizes the sense of confinement. The result is a multidimensional portrait of older people's experiences of 'cocooning' and an important record of that momentous time of Covid-19 in Ireland in 2020.

Mickey has a heart condition and is happy to cocoon but cannot stop washing his hands; Evelyn's hands are 'like tripe from washing them'. William scorns the new terminology: 'cocooning is not a good metaphor'. With a renewed appreciation of his partner and her cooking, Mickey admits: 'I am learning there are two of us in this relationship after thirty-five years … it helps that the pubs are closed'. By contrast Anne and her partner of 56 years 'permanently fight' but she declares that she wouldn't be without him. Ann worries about her dog which 'means more to me than my family (dreadful to say)', while giggling. People long for social gatherings: Dick and his friends used to sing Irish ballads in the local pub but, as he wryly states, 'that's gone now'. With exercise outdoors forbidden, Gerry is sorry that he cannot do anything energetic now, while Phil has resorted to doing Jane Fonda exercises since she has been 'closed in'.

Radio and television are important for all participants. For Mickey, the radio is on from early morning as he is: 'insatiable for more news'. Dick greatly enjoys watching Westerns or cowboy films he finds online. Gerry yearns for good quality television repeats. All contributors prioritize the news, Ann enjoys entertainment too: 'I do catch up with the news every day but I also want programmes that make me laugh.'

From the midpoint of the documentary, the tone becomes decidedly darker. As government and public health advisers are stepping up their public warnings about this 'once-in-a-century health crisis', the contributors articulate gloomy emotions and ominous thoughts. William reflects that every country is equally suffering during this pandemic, but Ann believes that the poor will suffer most as they always do. Referring to the very high frequency of deaths in care homes for older people in Ireland, Evelyn observes that they are 'facing a firing squad'. On the other hand, they appreciate lower pollution levels worldwide and the quieter environment. Mickey quips that walking in the countryside, the birdsong would 'nearly blow my ears off!'. In a sequence signalling their lowest ebb, the audience watches the participants closing their curtains at the end of the day while hearing a montage of their externalized anxieties:

> 'I just hope we all survive.'
> 'Everybody out there is doing their best.'
> Please God, it will be over soon.

After a brief respite for Christmas, a more strict 'lockdown' order was issued by the Irish government at the end of December 2020. The Taoiseach publicly announced: 'No visitors are permitted in private homes or gardens. We must stay at home and eliminate contact with others now.' The participants in the documentary are now shown to lose hope. William observes: 'Any progress we made is thrown out the window'; Dick is also disheartened: 'I'm cocooning again, the same as last March and there's no definite stop to it'; and Evelyn despairs: 'Where is it going to end?' They are particularly aggrieved by the arbitrary creation of the 70+ age cohort: Ann perceives that people slightly younger than 70 are smirking about their good luck: 'People of sixty-eight are going around saying ha-ha' to those over 70. All participants are now bored with their usual pastimes, and the continuing lack of social interaction with the outside world is threatening their mental well-being. Anne describes this state of hopelessness as follows: 'I don't like to say I've no hope, but at the moment I'm not in a good place about it.' Ethel who lives in a care home is on the phone to her son Ken Wardrop, the director of this documentary, and this is the only time Ken is heard to speak as his mother expresses her deep longing:

> Ethel: I think that's the hardest, not seeing you that often and all the others.
> Ken: And we're missing you mum.
> Ethel: I know, I know.
>   I miss the hugs Ken.
>   I do miss the hugs.
>   I miss the hugs big time.

Cocooned ends with a caption on the screen informing us that the vaccine rollout in Ireland has begun on 4 January 2021 and that older people are prioritized. Over the end credits Evelyn rolls up her sleeve for the nurse and after she has been injected with the vaccination she offers this final comment: 'That was wonderful. I was looking forward to that all day'.

While *Cocooned* was in production in 2020, a university research survey was underway to gather the thoughts of older Irish people about their experiences during the first phase of Covid-19. Working in parallel, but unknown to each other, the research project team systematically gathered data on a large scale about older people's experiences of lockdown. The research findings demonstrate that the views expressed by the small number of contributors in *Cocooned* are indeed representative of their cohort in the larger population. The research publication *In Their Own Words: The Voices of Older Irish People in the COVID-19 Pandemic* (Costello et al. 2021) was published by the Irish Longitudinal Study on Ageing (TILDA) and the findings reported in *The Irish Times* (Keena 2021). The survey enjoyed a very high response of a total of 3,964 questionnaires which is a 71 per cent return rate. The questionnaires were self-completed by people aged over 60 living in Ireland during the first period of lockdown in 2020. The findings provided the evidence that most older people thought that cocooning was unnecessary, the policy in need of a better rationale and that public health advice was confusing. While fictional names were assigned to the respondents to ensure anonymity, actual ages were retained. Nora, aged 73, wrote: 'I resent the singling out of the aged and older for "cocooning". It is not age as such which is relevant, but frailty'; and 80-year-old Willie observed: 'I feel victimised as if a prisoner not allowed out' (Costello et al. 2021: 18). As illustrated by 70-year-old Bernie, there was a sad recognition of abandonment:

> I feel older and my physical fitness levels have declined because of being ordered to sequester at home where I had no means of exercising – home is a first floor, tiny one bedroom flat, without access to a garden. (Costello et al. 2021: 16)

While many were grateful for what they retained in life and any new skills gained, the themes of loneliness, marginalization and powerlessness prevailed.

Comparing the empirical findings from the study with the television documentary highlights a stronger emphasis in the study on themes such as: the exclusion from intergenerational family connections and responsibilities; a heightened awareness of negative and collective representations of older people as incapacitated; the lack of access to religious congregations and services; greater emphasis on being strongly disregarded by policy makers. Empirical research thus provides reliable evidence based on rigorous academic research practices and methodologies.

Trust in the media enables shared goals among a community and confidence in civil society (Debrett 2010: 208). Trust is an important consideration for public service broadcasters who are licensed to act in the public good and consequently are the standard-bearers for trustworthiness in the media domain.[2] While

---

[2] Mary Debrett points to a cluster of research that demonstrates high levels of trust in public media broadcasters around the world (Debrett 2010: 206).

research in Europe indicates that trust is conditional on the public broadcaster being independent from the government (EBU 2021: 58), levels of trust in the traditional media of radio and television in Ireland are among the highest in Europe (EBU 2021: 14).[3]

According to Dee Forbes, the former Director General of RTÉ, the public service broadcaster has to provide fair and comprehensive news coverage and 'entertain, inform and illuminate. Never was that mission more acute, and more demonstrable, than in 2020' (RTÉ 2020). *Cocooned* accrued high status from being commissioned and broadcast by RTÉ in a prime-time slot after the evening news. Entrusted by RTÉ to match its aims as a public service broadcaster, the documentary was extremely well reviewed in the Irish newspapers. *The Business Post* chose the headline 'Knocking a much-needed laugh out of lockdown' and reported that 'Ken Wardrop's documentary tackles a touchy subject with a light touch, full of both charm and pathos' (Kehoe 2021). *The Independent* newspaper headlined 'Wit and wisdom of elderly shielding during the pandemic shine in RTÉ film', praising its emotional range: 'the film's subjects mostly exude cheerful acceptance. There are moving scenes too' (Kelleher 2021). The tabloid paper *The Sun* reported that 'RTÉ viewers say they're "emotional" watching *Cocooned*', with viewers flocking to Twitter 'following the documentary as they praised everyone that was on in this special film' (Conaty 2021). Even though *Cocooned* may have gaps in the content it covered – such as religious life and occupational life – its popular documentary format and sense of intimacy with the participants generated widespread public praise and appreciation. Wardrop's particular filming style enabled viewers to see and hear the older contributors at a time when they were told to be 'unseen and unheard'.[4] In so doing the documentary accentuated the individuality and uniqueness of each and every contributor, who – even though they struggled with the duration and severity of the lockdown – showed remarkable resilience.

Documentaries choreograph a performance from real life for the screen; they 'are a negotiation between filmmaker and reality and, at heart, a performance' (Bruzzi 2000: 154). They can empower contributors, as Anand Patwardan has stated, 'to make their unheard voices heard, by recording things that are actually happening, that are not being represented in the mainstream media' (quoted in de Jong et al. 2007: 22). *Cocooned* has given us a filmed record of older people

---

[3] As RTÉ has two funding sources, the licence fee and commercial advertising, the broadcaster has to be vigilant about delivering a sufficient proportion of public service programming that is not commercially driven (Corcoran 2004: 98).
[4] See Ailbhe Smyth's chapter in this volume.

who let us into their lives at a time of extreme crisis. *Cocooned* is an exemplar of public media television and an important social document that foregrounds the views of older people during the 2020 Covid-19 pandemic.

Bibliography

Bailey, L., M. Ward, A. DiCosimo, S. Baunta, C. Cunningham, R. Romero-Ortuno, R. A. Kenny, R. Purcell, R. Lannon, K. McCarroll, R. Nee, D. Robinson, A. Lavan and R. Briggs (2021), 'Physical and Mental Health of Older People while Cocooning during the COVID-19 Pandemic', *QJM: An International Journal of Medicine*, 114(9): 648–53. Available at: http://www.tara.tcd.ie/handle/2262/94775 (accessed 26 October 2022).

Blaikie, A. (1999), *Ageing and Popular Culture*, Cambridge: Cambridge University Press.

Bruzzi, S. (2000), *New Documentary: A Critical Introduction*, London: Taylor & Francis.

Cocooned (2021), [Television Programme] RTÉ, 28 September, Dir. Ken Wardrop, Ireland: Venom Films. Available at: https://www.rte.ie/player/movie/cocooned-s1-e1/230485031981 (accessed 28 September 2021).

Conaty, A. (2021), 'RTÉ Viewers Say They're "Emotional" Watching *Cocooned* as They Say People on Show are "Great Characters"', *The Irish Sun*, 27 September. Available at: https://www.thesun.ie/tvandshowbiz/7667526/rte-viewers-emotional-cocooned-people-show-great-characters/ (accessed 30 December 2021).

Corcoran, F. (2004), *RTÉ and the Globalisation of Irish Television*, Bristol: Intellect.

Costello, N., M. Ward, P. O'Mahoney and R. A. Kenny (2021), 'In Their Own Words: The Voices of Older Irish People in the COVID-19 Pandemic', Dublin: The Irish Longitudinal Study on Ageing (TILDA). Available at: https://www.doi.org/10.38018/TildaRe.2021-04 (accessed 23 August 2022).

Coyle, D. (2020), 'Why Economics Needs to Wake up to Ageing Populations', *Financial Times*, 2 December. Available at: https://www.ft.com/content/fcbccad8-491e-4f5b-a859-6622bc368e5c (accessed 22 August 2022).

Curran, J. and J. Seaton (2018), *Power without Responsibility: Press, Broadcasting and the Internet in Britain*, London: Taylor & Francis.

de Jong, W. (2011), 'What is Creativity', in W. de Jong, and E. Knudsen and J. Rothwell (eds), *Creative Documentary: Theory and Practice*, 9–17, Abingdon: Taylor & Francis.

Debrett, M. (2010), *Reinventing Public Service Television for the Digital Future*, Bristol: Intellect.

European Broadcasting Union (EBU) (2022), 'Audience Trends'. Available at: https://www.ebu.ch/files/live/sites/ebu/files/Publications/MIS/login_only/audiences/EBU-MIS-TV_Audience_Trends_2022_Public.pdf (accessed 20 September 2022).

European Broadcasting Union (2021), 'Trust in Media 2021'. Available at: https://www.ebu.ch/files/live/sites/ebu/files/Publications/MIS/login_only/market_insights/EBU-MIS-Trust_in_Media_2021.pdf (accessed 20 September 2022).

Featherstone, M. and A. Wernick, eds (1995), *Images of Aging: Cultural Representations of Later Life*, London and New York: Routledge.

Gilbert, P. (2010), *Cultural Identity and Political Ethics*, Edinburgh: Edinburgh University Press.

gov.ie (2020), 'Briefing on the Government's Response to COVID-19 – Saturday 28 March 2020'. Available at: https://www.gov.ie/en/publication/cfc502-daily-briefing-on-the-governments-response-to-covid-19-saturday-28-m/# (accessed 1 September 2022).

Hall, S. and P. du Gay, eds (1996), *Questions of Cultural Identity*, London: Sage.

Harrington, C. L., D. D. Bielby and A. R. Bardo, eds (2014), *Aging, Media, and Culture*, New York and London: Lexington.

Jenks, C. (2004), *Culture*, London: Taylor & Francis.

Keena, C. (2021), '"I Loathe the Word Cocooning": Over-60s Share Experience of Lockdown: Loneliness, Anxiety and Feeling "Diminished" among Issues Cited in Trinity College Report', *The Irish Times*, 17 August. Available at: https://www.irishtimes.com/news/health/i-loathe-the-word-cocooning-over-60s-share-experience-of-lockdown-1.4649487 (accessed 26 August 2022).

Kehoe, E. (2021), 'TV Review: Knocking a Much-Needed Laugh out of Lockdown', *Business Post*, 21 January. Available at: https://www.businesspost.ie/life-arts/tv-review-knocking-a-much-needed-laugh-out-of-lockdown-a85a0486 (accessed 30 December 2021).

Kelleher, L. (2021), 'Wit and Wisdom of Elderly Shielding during the Pandemic Shine in RTÉ Film', *The Independent*, 26 September. Available at: https://www.independent.ie/irish-news/health/wit-and-wisdom-of-elderly-shielding-during-the-pandemic-shine-in-rte-film-40888584.html (accessed 30 December 2021).

McDowell, M. (2020), 'There Needs to be Greater Oversight of the Covid-19 Response', *The Irish Times*, 30 September. Available at: https://www.irishtimes.com/opinion/michael-mcdowell-there-needs-to-be-greater-oversight-of-the-covid-19-response-1.4367717 (accessed 26 August 2022).

Morgan, L. A. and S. R. Kunkel (2011), *Aging, Society and the Life Course*, 4th edn, New York: Springer Publishing.

Nelson, T. D., ed. (2004), *Ageism: Stereotyping and Prejudice against Older Persons*, Cambridge, MA: MIT Press.

Patwardan, A. (2011), 'What is Creativity', in W. de Jong, E. Knudsen and J. Rothwell (eds), *Creative Documentary: Theory and Practice*, 9–17, Abingdon: Taylor & Francis.

Reville, W. (2020), 'Blanket Cocooning for Over-70s Has Done More Harm than Good', *The Irish Times*, 21 May. Available at: https://www.irishtimes.com/news/science/blanket-cocooning-for-over-70s-has-done-more-harm-than-good-1.4254477 (accessed 23 August 2022).

RTÉ (2020), *Annual Report*. Available at: https://www.rte.ie/annual-report-2020/business-review/director-generals-review.html (accessed 29 August 2022).

Saunders, D. (2010), *Documentary*, Abingdon: Taylor & Francis.

Sharma R. (2021), 'History and Epidemiology of COVID-19', in A. Kumar (ed.), *COVID-19: Current Challenges and Future Perspectives*, 11–26, Singapore: Bentham Science Publishers.

Weiss, R. S. and S. A. Bass, eds (2001), *Challenges of The Third Age: Meaning and Purpose in Later Life*, Oxford and New York: Oxford University Press.

Ylänne, V. (2015), 'Representations of Ageing in the Media', in J. Twigg and W. Martin (eds), *Routledge Handbook of Cultural Gerontology*, 369–76, London: Routledge.

13

Born old: Race, judgement and the limits of 'late style'

Julia Langbein

Introduction

This chapter probes a gap in the discourses of old age and visual art, describing a puzzling absence of encounter. In the past five to ten years, many Black American artists who have had long careers have been suddenly 'discovered' by a 'mainstream' art market. This 'discovery' entails a dramatic increase in the price of their work and its more consistent presence in major art institutions. Many of these artists – like Howardena Pindell (1943–), Faith Ringgold (1930–) and Melvin Edwards (1937–) – have come into wider fame and more significant earning power in their 70s and 80s. And yet very little attention has been paid to the fact that they are in late phases of their careers, or to the possibility that, at the end of long careers, they might currently be making work that is conditioned by old age, that represents 'late style' or 'old-age style' in relation to their oeuvre. On the other side of this missing encounter, the literature on 'late style', 'old-age style' and 'old-age creativity' overwhelmingly excludes people of colour from consideration.

A 2019 *New York Times* article captures how Black artists are suddenly seen by the art market, but not placed within their own life courses or considered as ageing subjects: 'Discovered after 70, black artists find success, too, has its price.' 'Once on the margins,' continues the heading, 'older African-American artists are suddenly a hot commodity' (Sheets 2019). The 'price' that these artists have to pay for being 'hot commodities' is that 'precisely when many artists are slowing down' – i.e. in old age – 'they are gearing up.' The article describes the tension between the artists' opportunity for market success and the inconvenient limitation of age. One New York dealer who represents three prominent Black artists in old age admits 'he has been guilty of overestimating the speed of his older artists. "With the enthusiasm of the marketplace," he said, "we forget the age of these human beings …'" (Sheets 2019).

The New York Times article is a piece of cultural reporting and not a work of art history or criticism. Despite appearing in the 'Art & Design' section, and not, say, in the 'Business' section, it made a chilling equation of market value with value *tout court* – a particularly tone-deaf equation in the case of Black artists (their 'names, in some cases, are worth millions on the auction block' (Sheets 2019)). In contrast, a 2019 *Art Newspaper* review of recent work by Jasper Johns – then 89-years-old and celebrated for half a century – raises the possibility of Johns' 'late style' as a kind of obvious or inevitable critical consideration: '[V]isitors to [the gallery's] sampling of his recent work may wonder, as I do, whether it exemplifies the artist's "late style"' (Baker 2019).

In *The New York Times* article about Black American artists, the phrase 'we forget the age of these human beings' hints at a problem that has not been the focus of much academic enquiry, perhaps precisely because the problem is an interdisciplinary one. Taking the case of Black American artists, although similar questions could be raised regarding the Black British context, I want to ask why it is that the work of Black visual artists is seldom, if ever, understood as an example of 'late style', 'old-age style' or indeed 'late-life creativity'. The first two categories were developed with the discipline of art history in the early twentieth century and are problematic yet persistent in humanities scholarship and wider cultural literature. But questions of 'late style' have framed the way scholars across disciplines approach 'late-life creativity' as both a historical subject and a contemporary ideal, an attractive and historically sanctioned aspect of 'successful ageing'. However, studies on late-life creativity smuggle the race and gender prejudices of dated 'late style' discourses into so-called objective, data-driven conclusions about present possibilities for older people.

The missing encounter between Black artists and 'late style' shows us that 'late style' is not equally available to all artists and that 'lateness' is not merely a chronological or sequential marker but a loaded qualitative judgement. Is there, as Gordon McMullan and Sam Smiles have asked, an 'ethical obligation to find a more appropriate … means of validating the productions of old age or of proximity to death …?' (2016: 12). Can we rescue 'late style' from its persistently biased application to whiteness? Can or should 'late style' be recuperated by those who may be eager to highlight the work of older artists, or is lateness fatally overdetermined by ever more powerful market imperatives and age-old cultural bias?

Valuing the work of older artists: The origins of 'late style'

The idea of 'late style' and 'old-age style' – *Spätstil* and *Altersstil* – emerged in the writing of German-language formalists in the early twentieth century who wanted to develop Art History as a modern scientific discipline. In contrast to an earlier practice of anecdotal accounts of artists' lives or professions of taste, the new scientific Art History or *Kunstwissenschaft* established a methodology based on style as a means to access collective ideas of historical and philosophical change. The founding texts of this new discipline, like Alois Riegl's *Spätromanische Kunstindustrie* (1901, reprinted 1927; translated as *Late Roman Art Industry*, 1985) and Heinrich Wölfflin's *Kunstgeschichtliche Grundbegriffe: Das Problem der Stilentwicklung in der neueren Kunst* (1915; translated as *Principles of Art History*, 1932), set up a framework for valuing art produced in epochs long understood as ones of 'decline' (Smiles 2016: 16–30; Hutchinson 2016: 11–12; Sohm 2007: 8–9).

This reassessment of epochal decline opened the way for reassessment of individual accomplishment late in life. Whereas from the Renaissance through the nineteenth century, old age was seen as an unequivocal negative – nothing but a physical and mental limitation even for such revered artists as Titian and Turner – these German-language writers in the early twentieth century found particular value in the later output of such artists. For example in Georg Simmel's book *Rembrandt: ein kunstphilosophischer Versuch* (1916, *Rembrandt: An Essay in the Philosophy of Art*, 2005), Albert Brinkmann's seminal *Spätwerke grosser Meister (Late Works of the Great Masters*, 1925) and other 'late works' studies, writers tended to see in late stylists a heightened expressivity, the falling away of mere technique and the revelation of spiritual essence (Simmel: '[Late] Rembrandt's artistry has been transformed into the subjectivity of his life.' Cited in Smiles 2016: 22). Importantly, there was something transcendent or shared among the late stylists – even across disciplines – so that by the 1920s Beethoven, Shakespeare and Titian began to be spoken of in relation to each other as artists who had surged into new and superlative modes as death approached.

'Old-age style' has come to be used interchangeably with 'late style' to mean 'exceptional or significant style in late life' (e.g. in Munsterberg 1983; Lindauer 2003), a telling elision which extends the exceptionalism of 'late style' to those who reach the general condition of 'old age'. Strictly speaking, according to the original art-historical conception, 'old age style' merely manifests the conditions of old age, but not all old artists will possess a 'late style'. The latter is reserved for the greatest of them, who accelerate towards new aesthetic achievement in their last years. Beethoven and Shakespeare are two repeatedly cited examples of artists who possessed 'late style' although they were not particularly long-lived (McMullan and Smiles 2016: 1, 3).

In the foundational early twentieth-century texts of 'late style', candidates for such critical consideration were drawn from a pre-existing canon of Old Masters. This is unsurprising given the limited purview of the field in general at the time and the overarching romanticism of the theorists' interest in the extraordinary and deeply felt. And it is perhaps, then, logical that 'late style' as a critical term fell out of fashion with subsequent generations of academics, particularly after art history was revolutionized in the 1970s and 1980s by poststructuralism, feminism, critical race and queer theory and as postmodern art itself – often conceptual or performance-based – resisted designations of 'style' (Painter 2006: 5).

And yet, in humanities scholarship 'late style' has been hard to do away with completely: it is a critical trope that 'has survived seemingly unscathed' compared to terms that have long been discredited like 'genius' and 'masterpiece' (McMullan and Smiles 2016: 1) Outside the humanities, the longevity of this somewhat arcane critical framework deserves scrutiny. In the interdisciplinary volume *Creativity in Later Life: Beyond Late Style* (McMullan 2019), editors Amigoni and McMullan note that 'the most obvious limitation' of the term is its traditional attachment to 'white middle-class men' (3). And yet they persist in probing the possibilities of a connection between the 'force of creativity ... traditionally associated with the received canon of late stylists' and 'the possibilities of creativity as it applies to later life' today, for gerontologists, creative-ageing practitioners, art therapists and public health and age-related policy experts (5). The model of an ageing and suffering Rembrandt or Turner, overcoming the effects of age to produce sublime masterpieces, has been powerful enough that even scholars who admit to its obvious gender and race, not to say historical and theoretical limitations, still desire to use the term to designate a contemporary, broadly available ideal of late-life cognitive flourishing.

In the past twenty years, 'late style' has found its way into two opposing discourses. Edward Said's *On Late Style* (2006) sparked a renewal of interest in the idea, mostly among literary scholars and musicologists, not scholars of visual art; nevertheless Said's thinking has led some scholars to apply 'late style' to artists of colour. Second, studies on age and creativity, purporting to a new objectivity and relying heavily on analysis of visual artists, covertly promote the most simplistic and exclusionary aspects of the 'late style' discourse.

The critical position of old age: Said, Adorno and the contemporary

Edward Said's *On Late Style: Music and Literature Against the Grain*, written in 2003 as the author was dying and published in 2006, revived interest across the humanities in the relation between art and late life. *On Late Style* opens with a key essay on Theodor W. Adorno's writing on late Beethoven and applies the critical terms of that essay to further meditations on composers and writers from Mozart to Jean Genet. If there is a persistent racial blind spot to the discourse of late style, Said's book is no exception: he looks only at white European artists and theorists. As Said acknowledges, this reflects Adorno's cloistered, elite European tastes (Said 2006: 21).

Said finds in Adorno a means of understanding late-life as a particularly *critical* position, a being out of time, out of sync with history. Said describes how certain artists in late life reject ideals of wisdom and momentarily go 'against the grain' of contemporary culture. The dying subject can act as a powerful critical counterpoint to the naturalized ideologies of the present, to what Adorno called the 'general culture of the age' (cited in Said 2006: 15). For Said, 'lateness' – outliving one's timeliness – can permit a 'self-imposed exile' from this suffocating generalness, from the ideological conventions of a given historical moment that limit even the most solitary thought (2006: 15–16).

Said's development of 'late style' charges the contemporary experience of old age with significant, if rarely actualized, potential. 'Lateness' is not synonymous with old age; but lateness exists in relation to society as old age relates to the life course ('retains in it the late phase of a human life', 2006: 13). Old age, in its difficulty and isolation, *nourishes*, is a *propitious condition for* what Said describes as a wilful exile or alienation from the established social order (2006: 8). The experience of illness and isolation permitted Beethoven a site outside 'the general culture of the age', a site from which bourgeois ideology could be seen, critiqued, rejected (2006: 13, 18). If we can extrapolate from the historically contingent model of Beethoven, then late life can generate work that is singularly alienated, out of time and therefore a reminder of modernity as a 'fallen, unredeemed reality' (18).

Robert Spencer (2019), in an essay on Derek Walcott's late-life poetry collection *White Egrets* (2010), defends Said's model of 'late style' as particularly apt for a poet of colour living and working in a contemporary neo-colonial context.¹ Just as Adorno saw Beethoven as a figure whose own lateness permitted him to lay bare the catastrophic and conflictual nature of his own modernity, so Spencer sees Walcott exposing the decrepitude and decline of imperial capitalism from its periphery in St. Lucia. It is precisely Walcott's 'inescapable experience of old age, with its attendant frailties and its … acute consciousness of mortality' that the poet shapes into a vision of the 'senescence and mortality' of 'capitalist modernity's neo-colonial mode' (Spencer 2019: 78). For Spencer, Walcott's *White Egrets* 'vindicates Adorno's approach to the study of late work' (77), reminding us that for Adorno (*contra* the early German-language theorists of 'late style'), what mattered was not merely a surprising crescendo of aesthetic expressivity. Rather the power of late works lies in their ability to 'direct us away from the merely aesthetic sphere to a critical engagement with the unsatisfactory and antagonistic order in which those works originate' (2019: 96).

For Spencer, Said's vision of 'late style' – strongly linked to the bodily, lived experience of old age – *still*, in our historical moment, might be available as a critical position that derives its power and clarity from being out of sync, out of time, with the present.

Although 'late style' has not been common as a framework for analysing Black American visual artists, the marginalization and repression that they have experienced has often been invoked with the language of untimeliness, of being forcibly out of sync with 'the contemporary'. The artist Alma Thomas (1891–1978), for example, who worked as a junior high school art teacher for thirty-five years, was the subject of the first solo exhibition by an African American woman at the Whitney Museum of American Art in New York at the age of 81 in 1972. While Alma Thomas is now understood as a major figure of twentieth-century painting, Thomas J. Lax (2019) writes that her 'anomalous position extends far beyond her biography to broader considerations of how one can be in or of one's time or place while, at the same time, making images of and for someplace else' (38). Lax's comment here does not come from an essay about lateness – merely grappling with Alma Thomas in an introductory catalogue essay, Lax has to frame her as out of time, not seen by or producing for a contemporary 'art world'.

---

¹ For another application of Said's 'late style' to the analysis of a poet of colour, see Sandy Alexandre's (2014) analysis of Richard Wright's late-life turn to haiku, arguing that this late form allowed Wright to 'divest himself of the weight of his socio-historical and racial circumstance', to transcend the suffocating, oppressive label of 'African-American literature' (247).

Courtney J. Martin (2019), in describing the watershed *Freestyle* exhibition at the Studio Museum in Harlem (2001) which had a major impact on the visibility of Black artists in America, makes an important connection between market success and the idea of being out of time. Are those unseen by the 'contemporary art market', marginalized and made difficult, denied vitality and viability, somehow put in a metaphorical position of old age? Martin writes that after *Freestyle*, the 'artists knew themselves to be contemporary artists, and that knowledge was affirmed by the exhibition and by audiences ... who then had to acknowledge that black artists were making art, *in their own time*, that was both museum-ready and viable for the market' (Martin 2019: 197, italics mine). Black artists, Martin argues, with this new visibility, were suddenly in sync, no longer forced into perpetual lateness. Using Said–Adorno's terms, they had left a position *outside* and had joined the general, visible 'culture of the age'. (The sense of loss associated with such a move is part of what makes Martin's a controversial assessment.)[2]

I want to suggest that the missed encounter between Black American visual artists and considerations of 'late style' may have to do with the kind of relationship to the 'contemporary' that Martin describes. For Said and Adorno, the artist's arrival at the end of a long public career is the condition for the production of 'late style'. But in the case of many Black American artists, particularly across a twentieth-century American landscape of segregation and inequality – e.g. the biographies of the artists listed in the *Times* article cited above – they were born 'old', born into the conditions of lateness, denied mainstream visibility for so long that they are only entering 'contemporary' time now (defined purely as an unjust contemporary media visibility), experiencing a 'newness' more associated with youth. This may explain something of the gallerist's refusal to see 'these human beings' as old – they are, culturally now, in the position of youth or midcareer, not alienated but celebrated, not struggling against but 'gearing up'.

Negativity and criticality at disciplinary borders

For Said and Adorno, old age can nurture a critical clarity that is *negative* – not as in pessimistic but in its refusals of palliative resolution, commercial ease and wisdom: 'Thus the power of Beethoven's late style is negative, or rather it is

---

[2] See Eddie Chambers (2021), *World is Africa*, London: Bloomsbury, 4–7.

negativity: here one would expect to find serenity and maturity, one instead finds a bristling, difficult – perhaps even inhuman – challenge'[3] (Said 2006: 12). Said and Adorno's model of lateness is, like Adorno himself, thorny and theoretical, sheltered from superficial consumer culture by its own volition. This 'negativity' has contributed to the difficulty of importing 'late style' with any integrity into positivist and therapeutic disciplines.[4] For example, there is a nearly comical attempt by Gordon McMullan in *Creativity in Later Life* to reconcile Adorno on 'late style' to a 'positive', successful-ageing narrative – McMullan regrets that Adorno is 'willfully downbeat' (2019: 64). This is a telling moment: the criticality of the humanities cannot pass the positivity barrier of an interdisciplinary successful-ageing imperative. McMullan's interpretation of Adorno as 'negative' rather than 'critical' suggests that to position old age as alienated, difficult, existing in contrapuntal or critical relation to society at large, is to conform to a decline narrative. Of course, it is not – rather, it is to consider contemporary late-life's culturally imposed marginality and biologically imposed difficulty as perhaps productive or important.

In some recent, prominent work on creativity and age, we find a full-on effort to purge 'late style' of criticality and to make it broadly applicable to an optimistic vision of old-age creativity as a key to 'successful' ageing or as an economic driver, and we find a troubling concomitant naturalization of late-life creativity as a white possibility.

Creative ageing

One might assume that, while attention to creative achievement in late life was *originally* limited by early theorists to white European Old Masters, surely a modern psychological, sociological or economic lens would do away with this outmoded disciplinary boundary. As it turns out, such studies have reinforced

---

[3] My chapter tracks the particular emphasis in Adorno and Said on the negation manifest in Beethoven's late works and what it demonstrates about 'late style'; however, negation has an overarching role in the aesthetic purpose of the work of art in modernity. As Espen Hammer writes, glossing Adorno's aesthetic theory, 'Significant works are works of negation: they come into being through determinate negation of past works (2015: 187); and 'the central preoccupation of modern art is the negation of aesthetic synthesis' (200).

[4] For example, see 'Why do so many artists do their most interesting work in their final years' (2017), *The Economist*, 18 February, in which Said is wrongly credited with 'coining' the term 'late style'. In fact, the terms goes back to the eighteenth-century art historian J. H. Winckelmannn. See: Ben Hutchinson: 'Spätstil'. *Zeitschrift für Ideengeschichte* 11/2 (2017): 5–14.

a racially biased possibility of late-life creativity but, more dangerously, present that bias as completely objective or scientifically validated.

Studies on life cycle creativity, notably foundational texts by physician W. A. Dorland (1908) and sociologist Harvey Lehman (1953) analysed the age of achievement of white, male 'geniuses', coming to fairly dismal conclusions about old age against which scholars have pushed in more recent years. Psychologist Martin S. Lindauer's 2003 *Aging, Creativity and Art: A Positive Perspective on Late-life Development*, as the title suggests, tries to come to more positive conclusions, and part of that aim is proving the objective existence of 'old-age style'.

Lindauer begins his study with a data set comprising in total 225 long-lived artists drawn from art history textbooks expanded with the input of a handful of art historians on the assumption that textbooks would objectively identify 'the "giants" of the art world' (2003: 174). (We will return to the problem of textbooks). He calls this list a 'fairly complete set of most of the Western world's recognized artists' (174). Unsurprisingly, he ends up with a sample exclusively of white male Old Masters (Rembrandt, Titian) and Modernists (Braque, Mondrian).

Lindauer's 'scientific' method consists of submitting these lists to thirty art historians, all specialists in 'historical and modern European and American Art'; twelve in total responded, identifying from the lists those whose 'style significantly changed in old age' (174). This method – 'consensual criterion' – indicated statistical significance, permitting him to conclude with a list of the definitive possessors of 'old-age style', a picture of aged, white, Western mastery that is supposed to stand for the 'positive' possibilities of older people in general.

Beyond the problem of Lindauer's biased data set, it is not clear what the purpose of this study is. Lindauer claims that objectively confirming the existence of 'old-age style' should be 'of considerable interest to gerontologists, developmental psychologists, and other professionals interested in extreme forms of successful ageing' (2003: 152). Again we find an attempt to link the cultural romanticism that saw Titian or Turner as examples of late-life genius and the neoliberal boosterism of 'successful ageing' discourses. Yet what would it mean to 'objectively' confirm the ahistorical existence of old-age style? Would it affirm a technique of 'successful ageing' because it would *prove* that this positive possibility existed for all ageing people? The narrowness of the original sample, racial, historical and as a canon of 'greats', seems to render that conclusion laughable – 'If Rembrandt and Braque can do it, so can I'? – while implying whiteness as a prerequisite for old-age creativity.

One finds similar problems in the work of economist David Galenson, whose initial study *Painting Outside the Lines* (2001) predates Lindauer's by two years. Galenson has returned to and repackaged the main idea of this book repeatedly since 2001, including in *Old Masters and Young Geniuses* ([2006] 2011), which positions itself for a broader readership on the model of Malcolm Gladwell's nifty statistics-based bestsellers (Gladwell's endorsement is on the 2001 cover.)

Galenson poses the question that motivates his study in *Painting Outside the Lines* thus: '[I]s it merely by chance that some [artists] have made their greatest contributions early in their careers and others late in theirs, or is there some general explanation that accounts for the variation?' (2001: 4). Galenson's analysis – foreshadowed already in the binary structure of his question – can be summed up simply: there are two models of 'creative life cycle', 'Old Masters', i.e. people who achieve more and more as they age (possessors of 'late style'), and 'Young Geniuses', who have early breakthroughs and flame out.

This is not the place for a wholesale critique of Galenson's work on artistic quality and the life cycle, which has been ignored in the humanities (his misuse of citations is particularly striking), while his fellow economists have shown that his conclusions cannot be replicated with different data sets (Ekelund et al. 2015). I want to focus on just a few of the ways that Galenson's supposedly scientific study systematically excludes artists of colour from consideration as ageing creative subjects.

Like Lindauer, Galenson imports biased data sets and attributes a scientific neutrality to them. For example, he uses the complete auction sales records for 1970 to 1997 compiled by *Le Guide Mayer* as the basis for 'age-price' profiles of the artists contained there. While this presents a host of problems – including the basic methodological one of isolating age versus other factors – the only potential weakness of this data that Galenson acknowledges is that of collector or gallerist manipulation. But with his 100 per cent white data set before him (2001: 6-10), which is about half twentieth-century Americans, he never addresses the possibility that auction sales might be a racially biased sample. He never considers that the careers of many of his subjects unfolded under segregation and racist exclusion, or that, for example, art school admission, acceptance by dealers, or the publicity given to exhibitions might affect the way that this sample represents 'all the artists whom art historians consider to have been the most important figures' (Galenson 2001: 5) in the periods he selects. You don't have to look far to find accounts like those of Norman Lewis (1909–1979), an influential Black Abstract-Expressionist absent from Galenson's book, who described in 1968 how the 'race question hindered many things [my gallerist] wanted to do for me' (Oral History Interview 1968). Whereas Lewis' gallerist also represented Lyonel Feininger (1871–1953), whom Galenson incorporates in his data as 'creative', contemporary racism trammelled Lewis' gallerist from promoting him in the same way. And if you don't get in the gallery in the 1940s, you don't get in the museum collection, you are not the subject of a retrospective, and you don't figure in the art-history textbook – invisibility compounds.

Like Lindauer, Galenson uses textbooks as a major data source and a metric of 'influence'. Yet as Celeste Bernier has noted, 'mainstream' US art history textbooks have a 'disheartening' record of under-representation (2019: 7). Galenson uses the presence of photographic reproductions in textbooks as quantitative evidence of an artist's importance, reasoning that reproductions are costly and therefore a mark of value. Yet as Mary Ann Calo has described:

> A paucity of basic information and lack of ready access to images make it difficult to bring the work of African American artists into the discursive field … The result is that their work often resides in a separate space, marginalized or poorly understood, especially in relation to mainstream historical analysis. (2003: 12)

Galenson's flattened economic view of the life course – of the possibilities of old-age creativity – naturalizes outmoded art-historical models as universal, particularly the exclusionary modernist-formalist model of artistic achievement as a chain of breakthroughs. As Linda and Michael Hutcheon point out, quantitative ageing research into 'late style' has tended to make 'productivity' a marker of 'creativity' although the two are not necessarily related (2016: 61–3) – an artist can drastically reduce her output while heightening imagination or originality. In a similar way, Galenson wants to make 'innovation' (measured as 'influence' – high prices and textbook visibility) a marker for 'creativity' yet he does so by uncritically adopting modernism's historically contingent valorizing of large-format paintings by heroic white males as natural, continuous or given. This is one of several ways in which Galenson presents time, history and cultural visibility as unitary and stable backgrounds for achievement.

A defence of Galenson's work might be, 'Now these Black artists *are* in collections, have entered the auction records and will soon be in textbooks. A historical wrong has been righted – let's update the data and move on.' But that is too optimistic – first, in that it supposes that this 'wave' of recognition will not recede, and second, in that we have to ask, 'Who else is invisible?' Such a defence misunderstands the crucial idea, articulated above by Mary Ann Calo, of shifting, separate, uneven discursive fields. The 'contemporary' is not a given – not everyone is invited to live out a life course in its light. Consider how Howardena Pindell – one of the artists profiled in *The New York Times* article I cited at the top of this chapter – describes the *experience* of being an artist in the 'separate space' of Black visibility:

> When I see our people working, dedicated, and avoided by the so-called mainstream, I am infuriated. We are now going through a ten-year crest in the wave. Every ten years, the Euro-Americans come out and it's 'please tell us where you've been all this time?' Suddenly we are of great interest and then the interest dips and we hear nothing. Then suddenly they get interested and it's 'Oh my God!! Where were they?' Every time the crest of the wave comes, there we are. We were there all along. We've been doing our work, we've been plodding along. (Jones 2011: 231)

Against the quantitative certainties of Galenson's 'age-price' profiles, which either rise early and fall (Young Geniuses) or climb steadily up to old-age achievement (those capable of 'late style'), Pindell describes a wave cycle of mainstream visibility, a turbulence and inconsistency that has nothing to do with Black artists' 'creativity' and everything to do with the vicissitudes of a prejudiced market, and which Galenson cannot account for. For him, Pindell is not important, literally not quality, not 'innovative', because for most of her career she did not generate 'influence' *according to his metrics*. To chart her age-price profile, one would presumably see a flatline and a sudden leap in old age (now that she's been 'discovered'), a graph that would tell you that while she was 'plodding along' – studying at Boston University and Yale University, working at the Museum of Modern Art, teaching, generating wildly innovative pictorial surfaces using textiles, stencils and various techniques of deconstruction and assemblage – she was inactive, unimportant. Life courses do not play out in a void, and the truth is that Galenson's method does not measure quality, innovation or influence, but 'market visibility', which, historically, has often meant 'white attention'. The most dangerous simplification of Galenson's study is not the ridiculous idea that there are *two* kinds of 'innovators' – that *some people* can achieve old-age creativity and others not – but that 'creativity' at any point in the life cycle plays out against a flat, ahistorical and textureless plane of opportunity, one in which white artists happen to dominate.

Galenson covertly imports the structures of 'late style' into his Old Master designation, and his simplistic plotting of late-life creativity reflects an aspect of 'late style' that goes back to its very origins. With its transcendental linking of exceptional individuals (Beethoven, Shakespeare, Titian), it was a kind of early, unscientific data set – a cohort-formation that already, in its romantic isolation of greatness, de-historicized its subjects and repressed social, cultural and material difference. 'Late style' may owe its longevity to the way that it precisely invites and seems to legitimize this kind of ahistorical, spurious linking. This ahistorical cohort-formation reinforces a vision, comforting to some, of creative achievement modeled by a canon of white Euro-American masters.

Importantly, the criticism of 'late style' as de-historicized does not apply to Adorno's or Said's understanding of 'late style,' which embedded it concretely in the historical progress of modernist aesthetics (Hammer 2015: 181–92). Adorno would have seen Galenson as merely an example of the culture industry, the commodification of culture that the negative aesthetics epitomized by Beethoven and other late stylists can resist. In other words, Galenson's watered-down image of the individual as late-life cultural producer is completely antithetical to the critical tradition in which Said stands, and yet they have a common ancestor in a 'late style' which identifies and links exceptional individuals.

The artist's perspective and the practical invalidation of 'late style'

In the same volume cited above, Lindauer conducted a different and to my mind, more interesting study. In order to discover how older artists considered their *own* late-life creativity, he gave questionnaires to a random sample of over 150 artists (predictably, race was not indicated, but the sample contained equal numbers of men and women). The questionnaires asked the artists to rate the quantity and quality of their output across their lives, into their 60s, 70s and 80s. They overwhelmingly reported that despite some decline after 60, they remained productive and were doing higher quality work than in their youth or midcareer – whether because they kept learning, were freed from work or family obligations or freed from producing art for the market (2003: 125–33). These results remind us that 'late style' is a theoretical construct that comes completely from the outside artistic experience. In fact, artists – and, we may speculate, creative amateurs – are much more likely to feel their relation to art-making in old age to be continuous with that of an integrated and long-lived self. However, as a theoretical tool, 'late style' and more generally a critical interest in lateness, will surely remain vital to humanities scholars, especially as the climate crisis and the increasing dysfunction of capitalism generate metaphors of a civilization near death.[5]

But as soon as 'late style' morphs into a vague vision of 'old-age creativity', it sneaks exclusionary and outmoded notions of 'quality' into the realm of what is possible, or interesting, or remarkable, in the work of older artists. It also tends to rob the artist of any agency over his or her own ageing. Philip Sohm's *The Artist Grows Old* (2007) is a particularly circumspect analysis of old-age artistic production, in which Sohm considers how Titian, for example, did not merely reflect the conditions of old age in his late paintings, but he *worked*, manipulated, even exaggerated the image of himself as ageing, keenly aware of the negative expectations for older artists in sixteenth-century Italy. Sohm's analysis points to the way that 'late style' or 'old age style' in a work like Lindauer's is the sudden onset of an identity – old age – in a life considered void of identity. Perhaps Sohm's method can, in its exceptional inclusion of so much rich social and cultural context for the 'late style' of a visual artist, further explain the missing encounter between 'late style' and Black artists: questions of identity, representation and social expectations have consistently overdetermined the reception of Black American artists (English 2010). Perhaps such consistent overdetermination makes it difficult for critics to pluck Black American artists out of their social, political, historical context in the simplistic way that, this chapter reminds us, Galenson's or Lindauer's models of old-age creativity require.

In probing this 'missing encounter', I do not suggest that Black artists are being denied a valuable designation, that anyone should want or deserve 'late style' consideration. Rather, the absence of encounter throws light on the rigidity and conservatism of 'late style' itself, particularly when it moves out of the humanities into the social sciences (economics, psychology) or when it is held up as a model for gerontologists, therapists, and policymakers (e.g. in Amigoni and McMullan). So, is there a way to valorize the productions of old age, without the baggage of 'late style' or 'old-age style'? Absolutely. Pay attention to old-age artists: write about them, show them, give them opportunities, make them a vital part of 'the contemporary'. In 1988, Roni Feinstein curated a show of work by older artists (*Enduring Creativity*) in which she dismissed 'old-age style' off the bat: 'There does not in fact seem to be a stylistic or thematic syntax basic to artists in advanced age, any more than there is one basic to, say, young artists or women artists' (3). She nevertheless

---

[5] Ben Hutchinson's *Lateness and Modern European Literature* (2016) is a multidimensional account of European modernism as a function of its lateness *without* leaning heavily on problems of 'late style'.

argued that in a world 'oriented toward the young', to expose older artists was itself to work against a damaging prejudice. Without seeking in old age a unified, transcendent achievement, we will be conceptually freer to appreciate late-life art-making not in comparison with Rembrandt, Picasso or Pollock but as a continuation of lives shaped by difference, irreducible to the curve of a graph, and deserving of more nuanced attention than hollow and prejudicial designations of greatness.

Bibliography

Alexandre, S. (2014), 'Culmination in Miniature: Late Style and the Essence of Richard Wright's Haiku', in A. Craven, W. Dow and Y. Nakamura (eds), *Richard Wright in a Post-Racial Imaginary*, 245–62, London: Bloomsbury.

Baker, K. (2019), 'Jasper Johns' Latest Work Is Unmistakably His Own, Transmitting Traces of the Past', *The Art Newspaper*, 23 February.

Bernier, C. (2019), *Stick to the Skin: African American and Black British Art, 1965–2015*, Berkeley: University of California Press.

Brinkmann, Albert (1925), *Spätwerke grosser Meister*, Frankfurt: Frankfurter Verlag.

Calo, M. A. (2003), 'Recovery and Reclamation: A Continuing Project', *American Art*, 17(1): 10–13.

Chambers, E. (2021), *World is Africa*, London: Bloomsbury.

Dorland, W. A. N. (1908), *The Age of Mental Virility*, New York: Century Co.

Ekelund, R. B., Jr., J. D. Jackson and R. D. Tollison (2015), 'Age and Productivity: An Empirical Study of Early American Artists', *Southern Economic Journal*, 81: 1096–116.

English, D. (2010), *How to See a Work of Art in Total Darkness*, Cambridge, MA: MIT Press.

Feinstein, R. (1988), *Enduring Creativity*, Stamford, CT: Whitney Museum of American Art.

Galenson, D. (2001), *Painting Outside the Lines: Patterns of Creativity in Modern Art*, Cambridge, MA: Harvard University Press.

Galenson, D. (2006), *Old Masters and Young Geniuses: The Two Life Cycles of Artistic Creativity*, Princeton: Princeton University Press.

Hammer, E. (2015), *Adorno's Modernism: Art, Experience, and Catastrophe*, Cambridge: Cambridge University Press.

Hutcheon, L. and M. Hutcheon (2016), 'Historicizing Late Style as a Discourse of Reception', in S. Smiles and G. McMullan (eds), *Late Style and its Discontents*, 51–68, Oxford: Oxford University Press.

Hutchinson, B. (2016), *Lateness and Modern European Literature*, Oxford: Oxford University Press.

Hutchinson, B. (2017), 'Spätstil', *Zeitschrift für Ideengeschichte*, 11(2): 5–14.

Jones, K. (2011), 'Interview with Howardena Pindell (1989)', in Kellie Jones and Amiri Baraka (eds), *Eyeminded: Living and Writing Contemporary Art*, 231–2, Durham, NC: Duke University Press.

Lax, T. J. (2019), 'Thomas J. Lax on Alma Thomas', in Courtney J. Martin (ed.), *Four Generations: The Joyner/Giuffrida Collection of Abstract Art (revised and expanded)*, 38–43, New York: Gregory R. Miller & Co.

Lehman, H. C. (1953), *Age and Achievement*, Princeton, NJ: Princeton University Press.

Lindauer, M. S. (2003), *Aging, Creativity and Art: A Positive Perspective on Later Life Development*, New York: Kluwer Academic/Plenum.

Martin, C. J. (2019), 'Style, Influence, and the *Freestyle* Generation,' in Courtney J. Martin (ed.), *Four Generations: The Joyner/Giuffrida Collection of Abstract Art (revised and expanded)*, 193–201, New York: Gregory R. Miller & Co.

McMullan, G. (2019), 'Constructing a Late Style for David Bowie: Old Age, Late-Life Creativity, Popular Culture', in G. McMullan and D. Amigoni (eds), *Creativity in Later Life: Beyond Late Style*, 61–76, London: Routledge.

McMullan, G. and S. Smiles (2016), *Late Style and its Discontents: Essays in Art, Literature and Music*, Oxford: Oxford University Press.

Munsterberg, H. (1983), *The Crown of Life: Artistic Creativity in Old Age*, San Diego, CA: Harcourt Brace Janovitch.

Oral History Interview with Norman Lewis, July 14, 1968, Archives of American Art, Smithsonian Institution, Washington, DC. Available at: https://www.aaa.si.edu/collections/interviews/oral-history-interview-norman-lewis-1146 (accessed 14 November 2022).

Painter, K. and T. Crow (2006), *Late Thoughts: Reflections on Artists and Composers at Work*, Los Angeles, CA: Getty Research Institute.

Riegl, A. (1901), *Die spätrömische Kunstindustrie nach den Funden in Österreich-Ungarn, I. Teil*, Vienna: K. K. Hof- und Staatsdruckerei; reprinted in 1927 as *Spätrömische Kunstindustrie*, Vienna: Österreichische Staatsdruckerei.

Riegl, A. (1985), *Late Roman Art Industry*, trans. Rolf Winkes, Rome: Bretschneider.

Said, E. (2006), *On Late Style: Music and Literature against the Grain*. London: Bloomsbury.

Sheets, H. M. (2019), 'Discovered after 70, Black Artists Find Success, too, has its Price', *New York Times*, 23 March.

Simmel, G. (1916), *Rembrandt: ein kunstphilosophischer Versuch*, Leipzig: K. Wolff Verlag.

Smiles, S. (2016), 'From Titian to Impressionism: The Genealogy of Late Style', in S. Smiles and G. McMullan (eds), *Late Style and its Discontents*, 16–30, Oxford: Oxford University Press.

Sohm, P. L. (2007), *The Artist Grows Old: The Aging of Art and Artists in Italy 1500–1800*, New Haven, CT: Yale University Press.

Spencer, R. (2019), 'An "Old Man in the Dimming World": Theodor Adorno, Derek Walcott and a Defense of the Idea of Late Style', in G. McMullan and D. Amigoni (eds), *Creativity in Later Life: Beyond Late Style*, 77–98, London: Routledge.

Wölfflin, H. (1915), *Kunstgeschichtliche Grundbegriffe: das Problem der Stilentwicklung in der neueren Kunst*, Munich: Bruckmann.

Wölfflin, H. (1932), *Principles of Art History: The Problem of the Development of Style in Later Art*, trans. M. D. Hottinger, London: G. Bell and Sons.

14

Race, ethnicity, culture and later life: Problematic categorizations and unsatisfactory definitions

Moïse Roche, Claudia Cooper and Paul Higgs

In 2020, the differential impact of Covid-19 mortality and morbidity accentuated the need to interrogate the role of race and ethnicity in the field of health and ageing (Bhala et al. 2020), and to understand the interconnections between race and ethnicity, and history and inequality (Taylor 2020). The growth of older populations in the UK, as in other high income countries, has also added renewed urgency to academic and professional interest in 'ethnogerontology' (Crewe 2005). Making sense of the language that is used to describe populations and to frame how racial and ethnic disparities are experienced whilst considering how race and ethnicity as identification grounds contribute to inequalities is an important discussion to be had, if we are to advance the gerontological imagination on race, ethnicity and ageing well.

This chapter provides a critical commentary on the nature of the plurality of terminology and meanings of racial and ethnic categories used in gerontological research. It argues that the collective categorization and labelling of minoritized[1] ethnicities (ME), as the groups bearing the brunt of this homogenization, offers little clarity and perpetuates a culture of racial binary of 'Whiteness versus Otherness'. Attention is drawn to the problematic history and unscientific basis

---

[1] The use of 'minoritized' underlines that people are actively minoritized by others, as a consequence of socio-political construction processes shaped by power dynamics, rather than existing naturally as a minority, as conferred in widely used terms, such as Minority Ethnic or Ethnic Minority (ME). Minoritization is a socially created process that places individuals into minority status based on circumstances rather than their own characteristics. This approach allows description of any 'specific' group of people who, by virtue of numerical size and place of residence, in relation to current understanding of ethnicity, is in a minority, and, while heterogeneous, may have, to some extent, overlapping experiences of inequalities and marginalization.

of the key concepts – of race and ethnicity – on which the formulation of these categories and collective terminologies are predicated. The chapter also queries their value and appropriateness to modern research and practice. It concludes that their use should be limited to rare and specific circumstances instead of becoming ubiquitously routine. Advice and recommendations are made on information that should be included in ethnicity-focused research that might better meet the needs of a diverse and racialized society.

Introduction

Historically, there has been a proliferation of terminologies to categorize minoritized ethnicities because of ongoing debates that resemble an absolute 'battle of the name' (Banton 1987). Terms and labels such as Black and Minority Ethnic (BME), Black, Asians and Minority Ethnic (BAME), People of Colour (POC), Black and Indigenous People of Colour (BIPOC), non-White, and many more, have been used in the UK and other countries. These continue to evolve and alter, giving rise to a range of nebulous, problematic and unwieldy terms, creating an *ersatz* 'homogeneous' group as the obverse of an equally flawed notion of a 'White group'. These terms create a general sense of confusion and lack of clarity, even among policymakers and political officials who are responsible for the population's health and managing disparities within it. On 7 June 2020, the then-UK Secretary of State for Health and Social Care, Matthew Hancock, was asked in a televised interview: 'How many Black people are in the current Cabinet?', to which he replied with hesitation: 'Well, there's a whole series of people from a Black and Ethnic Minority background'. But he then proceeded to name the Chancellor of the Exchequer (Rishi Sunak) and the Secretary of State for the Home Office (Priti Patel), neither of whom identifies with a Black ethnicity. This occurred even after Priti Patel had already warned Conservative colleagues not to 'label [her] as BME', calling it 'insulting' and 'patronising' (BBC 2018). Whether this homogenization was intended to express the shared experiences of those who do not identify with the White population, or to demarcate population groups, the fashioning of categorical descriptors for minoritized ethnicities remains a powerful preoccupation of British society.

The scholarly controversy concerning the political and social debates that continue to plague the formulation of collective terminologies for minoritized ethnicities has largely bypassed the terms 'White' and 'Caucasian', which in public discourse are unjustifiably accepted as normative and treated as self-explanatory

(Bhopal and Donaldson 1998). They have also tended to be exempted from indices or definition in censuses, statistical records and research. Despite the apparent normalization of 'White' as the standard category of reference, all these terms are open to equal levels of obscurity and imprecision. They all aggregate groups of disparate people based on socially constructed and poorly understood concepts such as race and ethnicity, and a flawed and imagined 'cultural essence' that connect *all* members. Ironically, these concepts that in their very nature imply and share an idea of commonality in ancestry, heritage and characteristics have essentially created a dichotomy between White skin people and people of all other skin colours (Allen 2014). For example, the acronym and initialism BAME and BME were arguably introduced in the UK to address the complexities of a multicultural society under the guise of political good intentions; however, they have in effect created a superordinate divide between the White majority British population and all others by conflating racial and ethnic characteristics. Although BME and BAME officially include certain White minorized groups such as Irish and Gypsy, the assessment of racial and ethnic affiliation of these terms, which draws on commonplace assumption, general narrative, popular usage and the social zeitgeist, has gravitated towards minoritized people with black, brown and other skin colour – except those whose skins are white. The exclusion of 'national minoritized ethnicities', such as Cornish, Welsh and Scottish, reinforces the preponderance of skin tone, a racial attribute, in the formation of these terminologies.

Despite undergoing surface evolution through socio-political advances, these terms are unhelpful, misleading and conflict with the rigour of modern research. They continue to perpetuate a culture of racial dichotomy of 'Whiteness vs Otherness' that was invented under the flawed and biased 'science' of race (Malik 1996). Why do researchers still use racial and ethnic administrative categories that are acknowledged as having no scientific or anthropological validity? Why has the quest for the appropriate classification and terminology for race and ethnicity solely focused on minoritized ethnicities when they are recognized to be conceptually, sociologically and politically problematic across the board? There is an argument to be made against their use and in favour of a more reliable and objective approach that would uphold the unbiased and systematic values of science.

This conversation about the conceptual and moral implications of the language that is used to talk about race, ethnicity and the disparities that relate to these concepts has particular importance in ageing research, as older people are, by the shared experience of the consequences of older age and ageing, often disempowered from participation in research and society, in the same way that ageism excludes older people from the formulation of policies. Researchers in health, social gerontology and any fields that involve human subjects should reflect on how the use of catch-all terminologies might escape the realm of academic research and negatively impact popular views of older peoples' experiences, needs and sense of identity and agency. There is a risk these terminologies might compound the sense of disempowerment among minoritized older people to whom researchers set out to give voice. Moreover, given racial and ethnic divide is pervasive and entrenched in society, this conversation about the categorization of race and ethnicity extends beyond any specific field and discipline.

The use of collective terms

The racial and ethnic classifications and naming conventions in countries such as the UK are largely grounded in civil and political rights and were devised initially as part of a broader strategy to foster equity and reduce inequalities, driven by political responses to social movements, public opinion and pressure from race equality organizations, advocates and equality debates. The emergence of the initialism BME in the late 1980s followed the Scarman Report, commissioned by the British Government after the 1981 Brixton riots (Scarman 1986; Saeed et al. 2020). At the time, the rationale was to retain the word *Black* in the descriptor, not for its racial, ethnic or cultural significance but for its political overtone, which had begun to drift from a historically derogatory connotation to a sense of shared experience of racial discrimination faced by all people who did not fit the 'White group' descriptor. This initiative, which clearly had no scientific objective, forged an *ersatz* group with a flawed politically racialized meta-identity that inappropriately dichotomized the growing multicultural UK population into White vs everyone-else-who-is-not-White, often labelled as 'non-white', a term now also considered derogatory.

New debates ensued among sociologists, activists and politicians within their respective fields mostly around superficial concerns regarding political correctness and issues of the ambiguity, usefulness and practicality of these terms. This led to the proliferation and continual iteration of terms both in their full form and as acronyms and initialisms such as, Black, Asians, BAME, ABME, WOC, BIPOC, ME, etc., elongating an already lengthy and confusing list of terminologies (Bhopal 2004). For example, some argued for reframing these descriptors to reflect the importance of South Asians who had become the largest minoritized ethnicity, and to make clear that Black groups were also a minoritized population, by adding 'other' to the terms (e.g. Black, Asians and *Other* Minority Ethnic) (Cole 1993). Sociologists have pointed out multiple problems with these collective terminologies, starting from their failure to distinguish race from ethnicity (Torres 2020). The two concepts, which are discussed in more detail later, are often confused, combined or treated as synonymous.

This disposition to conflate and confuse race and ethnicity is apparent not only in the use of ordinary language and official nomenclature of collective terms that utilize racialized ethnic categories to group people, but also in census questions (ONS 2011). The US census, where the concept of race appears to be more accepted and acceptable, does make this distinction (U.S. Census Bureau 2020). Sociologist Peter Aspinall (2002) has highlighted what he regarded as 'persistent problems' with existing terms. He underlined their ambiguity and acceptability with respect to the populations they purport to describe, questioning whether the collectivities they embody have any substantive meaning and representativeness (Aspinall 2020), concealing as they do some minoritized groups, notably White minoritized groups. The incoherence in the pattern of inclusion of certain White minoritized groups and the exclusion of others, the masking of the *true* reality of the experience of some groups whose marginalization and exclusion are exacerbated, diminished or elided, and the exposure of others to false realities through a process of assimilation, render these collective terms impractical and inappropriate for research and practice. Unless categories are clearly defined and the individuals included in studies described accurately, it becomes impossible to understand to whom study findings refer and apply. In most studies, it would be feasible to use descriptors with greater specificity in the place of BME/BAME and avoid perpetuating a culture of racial dichotomy of 'Whiteness vs Otherness'.

This is not to say that there is no rationale or circumstance when these collective terms can be used. In accordance with their monitoring purpose, they have value in revealing broad disparities based on skin colour or phenotype. Lin and Kelsey (2000: 187) list a number of epidemiological purposes in categorizing populations by race and ethnicity, ranging from 'elucidating disease aetiology, to applications in clinical settings, to [identifying and] targeting specific groups for prevention and intervention on a public health scale'. However, as they noted, 'race and ethnicity are less objective and more difficult to conceptualize and measure than other factors such as age and sex' (187). They also lack scientific basis and are more prejudicial as they are too often and too promptly transformed into risk factors for ill health (but not good health), poor socioeconomic conditions and other areas of attainment. Despite lacking objectivity, validity and reliability, they have been operationalized and are used routinely as default analytic tools to make evaluations and judgements in research and practice, and to inform policies.

Unlike in the UK and US, in France, in line with 'laïcité' that seeks to foster greater integration of all citizens and give equal treatment to everyone, the French government prohibits collection of data based on race, ethnicity or religion (Romain 2008; Lenoir 1983). Despite laudable aims, this model has not eliminated discrimination and may have created new systemic forms of it, by rendering minoritized populations and the difficulties they face almost invisible (Ndiaye 2020). Absence of questions about race or ethnicity from the French national census precludes any form of targeted measures for specific groups that might experience unequal treatment (Chevalier 2020).

Beyond the labels: Conceptual difficulties

Regardless of how these terms are formulated and presented, their nexus in demarcating population groups is race. Even when ethnicity or culture or national identity is introduced in the process, racial considerations remain the commanding factors that lead population grouping and classification, feeding into an underlying context to serve political, economic or social purposes. Both race and ethnicity are concepts laden with problematic historical, political and social contents.

Although related, race and ethnicity are distinct concepts that are often mistakenly used interchangeably. The appropriate assessment of race and ethnicity is crucial to research and practice, as researchers and government officials employ them routinely in their analysis and to make judgements. For example, studies have associated South Asians with stigma of mental illness and dementia, attributing their apparent reluctance to engage with services for these conditions to ethnocultural characteristics (Seabrooke and Milne 2004; Giebel et al. 2015; Mukadam et al. 2015; Werner et al. 2012). Following a similar line of reasoning, the Social Care Institute for Excellence (SCIE) advice for professionals working with minoritized ethnic people affected by dementia, utilizes racial and ethnic characteristics as a frame of reference for their guidelines (SCIE 2020). Race and ethnicity are complex, multidimensional, overlapping and highly controversial constructs. They denote belonging to a constructed social group in which members allegedly share presumed and/or apparent similarities that distinguish them from other groups.

Race

The idea and classification of race originate from eighteenth-century naturalists and philosophers (Smedley, Takezawa and Wade 2017), who used observation of geographical location and phenotypic traits such as skin colour to categorize people into racial groups. This flawed, Eurocentric and pseudoscientific idea of racial types gained wider currency throughout the eighteenth and nineteenth centuries, particularly as it served the needs of colonialist and imperialist expansion and domination. Writings from people with vested interests in maintaining racial distinction such as Edward Long, a former British plantation owner and jurist in Jamaica, and Charles White, an English physician, were given great weight as 'scientific' vehicles to confirm the delineation of races and deepen the rift between groups of people on the basis of skin colour (Smedley et al. 2017). Not long after, Arthur de Gobineau's essay on *The Inequality of the Human Races* further helped to legitimize racism using scientific racist theory and racial demography (de Gobineau 1855). He argued that intellectual differences existed between races and the mixing of races between those he considered superior with others led to the decline of civilization.

The biological positioning of race as an indicator of distinct, genetically different population groups has not stood the test of time and is now widely considered to be 'non-existent' in scientific terms (Beutler et al. 1996; Bradby 1995; Chaturvedi and McKeigue 1994; McKenney and Bennett 1994; Senior and Bhopal 1994; Williams, Lavizzo-Mourey and Warren 1994). There are no genetic variants that occur in members of one socially constructed racial group that cannot be found in another. Research has shown that genetic differences between humans are 'inconsistent and typically insignificant' (Cornell and Hartmann 2006; Cashmore 2004). In fact, there are greater intraracial genetic variations than interracial ones (Senior and Bhopal 1994; Williams et al. 1994).

Ethnicity and culture

Whilst race tends to be ascribed to individuals, ethnicity is more likely to be a matter of choice, with individuals able to subscribe to more than one ethnic group. This makes ethnicity an even more elusive construct from an observer perspective, and it can remain difficult for the individual to self-assign ethnic identity. It is a multifaceted construct that conflates multiple characteristics, some of which are assumed to be inherited, and others taught, learned and/or passed on across multiple generations. Ethnicity has also a sense of peoplehood as it refers to closeness in physical characteristics and commonality in historical, ancestral, cultural, culinary, linguistic, national, social, behavioural and religious heritage. Although less controversial than race, ethnicity too evolves in the context of social and political phenomena and movements and brings into the mix a cultural dimension that relates to shared and learned values, behaviours, beliefs and attitudes that make people behave in a certain way. According to Corin (1995), culture is 'a system of meanings and symbols that shape every area of life', which binds individuals together into communities. Like ethnicity, culture is not static, varies largely within groups, and certainly cannot apply to every individual within a specific subculture.

Identity

Although race and ethnicity have no genetic or scientific basis, the concepts of race and ethnicity are important and consequential to identity, as much in the ways people see themselves as in how they are perceived by others. Jenkins's (2008, 2014) work on social identity points to the notion of ethnicity as being intimately connected to identity. In a similar vein, it refers to identity in terms of a process rather than a 'thing' that people have. Jenkins's social-constructionist perspective rejects the essentialist notion that race and ethnicity somehow condition – or shape – people to be who they are. For Jenkins, ethnicity is 'rooted in, and the outcome of, social interaction' (Jenkins 1997), and is about cultural differentiation, just like identity is invariably concerned with difference and similarity. In this regard, ethnic identity is both internally imposed in personal self-identification and externally constructed in social interaction; hence, both collective and individual. As identification grounds, race and ethnicity cannot be separated from the social context within which they occur because without social interaction there is no ethnicity.

The importance of social context and social interaction in the determination of ethnicity is evident in how society uses concepts of race and ethnicity. They are designed to divide and categorize people into groups ranked by assumed similarities and differences, which are applied to people to establish whether they belong or do not belong to a social group. Still, for reasons that are clearly not rooted in science, when racial and ethnic disparities become apparent in any context, no attempt is made to peek behind the surface of race and ethnicity, to gaze into the social antecedents and the social determinants of these inequalities. Instead, enquiries about racial and ethnic disparities remain focused on highlighting differences between groups. By not peeking beyond the surface of racial and ethnic disparities into what lurks behind, research that draws attention to race and ethnicity risks buttressing beliefs and ideologies that perpetuate the social divisions and social injustices they seek to address.

It is noteworthy that despite ethnicity's close connection to identity, the ethnic group responsible for constructing the *concept* is less likely to associate with it. Even though everyone is in some sense 'ethnic', the term tends to be erroneously applied only when dealing with minoritized groups. Surveys conducted in the US over a number of years reported that Black adults are more likely than other groups to say that race or ethnicity is central to their identity and to feel connected to a broader Black community (Barroso 2020). Nearly three-quarters of Black adults surveyed said that being Black is extremely (52 per cent) or very important (22 per cent) to how they think about themselves, whereas only 15 per cent of White adults say that race is central to their identity (Barroso 2020). The surveys did not mention how important members of racial groups felt race or ethnicity was for them in the identification of groups that are different to theirs. However, it is very telling that the group historically culpable of racial segregation is less likely to say that race or ethnicity is central to their identity.

Racial and ethnic categorization in dementia research

The problem of categorization in gerontology generally reflects and amplifies the taxonomic problems described above. Minoritized ethnic populations have become the focus of increased attention in dementia research as the issue rises up the global health agenda. In the UK, using conventional terminology, researchers continue to demonstrate racial and ethnic inequalities in dementia outcomes, with minoritized ethnic populations documented to be at pronounced disadvantage on most facets of dementia treatment and care (Knapp et al. 2007; Prince et al. 2014; Mehta and Yeo 2017). Quantitative empirical research repeatedly flags the higher risk of dementia for Black and other minoritized populations in comparison to 'the White population'. It also reports higher prevalence and incidence of the condition, earlier onset, lower diagnosis rates, poor engagement with services, lower participation in research and reduced treatment uptake for these groups (Adelman et al. 2011; Mayeda et al. 2015, 2016; Pham et al. 2018; Tuerk and Sauer 2015).

While monitoring disparities in dementia is well intentioned, there is a risk that minoritized ethnic populations can be presented in these reports as problematized collectivities based upon their racial, ethnic and cultural affiliation. This message is amplified in qualitative research that describes minoritized ethnic groups as holding misconceptions, poor knowledge and inappropriate beliefs about dementia (Adamson 2001; Ayalon and Arean 2004; Werner et al. 2014; Mukadam et al. 2011). Generally, inequalities in dementia are correlated with 'preformed' ethnic categories, which are often combined with cultural components that determine both outcomes and risk factors proposed as mediators. Researchers tend to use existing administrative categories created by national and local government out of convenience, uncertainty or lack of better options, often omitting to include clear definitions or important characteristics of the individuals under investigation. There is an irony that studies with the explicit purpose of highlighting unfairness for individuals in receipt of care, treatment and services, may themselves perpetuate inequalities.

In a review of qualitative research looking at experiences of dementia among people from Black, African and Caribbean backgrounds, only four out of the twenty-eight papers provided a definition for the ethnicity of the participants involved, and only two papers reported participants' background information, such as sociodemographic characteristics, migration history, and more. What was also apparent was that there was little attention given to the specific differences between those of African American descent and those from Black backgrounds in countries such as the UK or the Netherlands (Roche et al. 2020). In the UK, the origins and cultures of Black African and Black Caribbean as well as other minoritized ethnic populations vary greatly. Added to this is the linking together of different populations such as those from South Asia as part of a composite BAME category in dementia research (Johl, Patterson and Pearson 2016; Lawrence et al. 2008). Acknowledging the greater variety of cultural backgrounds warrants greater attention if researchers are to make meaningful contributions to our knowledge of diverse populations and development of culturally informed, effective, inclusive care and policy.

Categorization of human characteristics and experiences is an essential component of research, certainly of quantitative analyses; but categories need to be meaningful, experienced as legitimate and not disempowering to those who are being researched. This principle that research should be in partnership with, rather than 'done to' communities is widely accepted (Burton, Ogden and

Cooper 2019), and yet ethnic categories are rarely challenged or opened to this scrutiny. The framing of dementia research, and indeed other conditions or phenomena experienced by ageing populations, must acknowledge the layered plurality of subgroups that exist within these predefined ethnic categories. It would be amiss to presume that all the individuals confined under the umbrella term Black ethnicity/Black British/Black Caribbean constitute a uniform entity with a unified cultural element that can be measured. This will be even less likely possible for terms that include multiple groups such as BME or BAME, yet much research and government information are reported using these terms.

Conclusion

There is much controversy around using race, ethnicity and ill-defined collective terminologies such as 'BME' and 'BAME' as classification and/or identification devices. This continues to be done in much thinking about health and ageing, as we have shown in the case of dementia research. Continuing to use these forms of classification risks overemphasizing a flawed unscientific sense of *'nature'* over nurture or vice versa, or falling into damaging stereotypical generalization. In many countries such as the UK, the development of collective terms to describe minoritized populations has exacerbated historical divides and caused confusion, ambiguity and discord. By attempting to combine large heterogeneous groups of people with little objectively in common, these labels often cloud interpretation of research relating to the very cultural and ethnic considerations that studies seek to elucidate (Aspinall 2002; Bhopal and Donaldson 1998; Cole 1993; Polenberg 1980). These terms, ones that are generally devised by members of the majority population with little or indirect contribution from minoritized ethnicity representatives, can underestimate the impact they can have on groups' and individuals' sense of identity.

The use of race, ethnicity and culture as identifiers and indeed their lexicon of terms should be limited to rare and specific circumstances, such as monitoring broad disparity based on skin colour and numerical size, and cautious elucidation of health (good and bad) aetiology. Even in these circumstances, additional information such as background, demographics and socioeconomic details should be provided and inform our analysis, instead of allowing racial and ethnic characteristics to be the determining factors when they may distract from the real causes of an effect. Using the most appropriate and specific ethnicity label is also essential, not only at the stage of selecting the study population but also at the design and reporting stages of any study. Where granularity is not possible, the use of terms such as 'minoritized ethnicity', as used in this chapter, is advisable (Khunti et al. 2020), provided researchers reflect on the use of ethnicity in the context of their research and report on the extent they think it has played a role in their findings. Additionally, researchers should justify *why* they identify race or ethnicity in studies: often it is unclear why ethnicity or race features in many health and medical studies other than to provide a source of contrast between groups. This can ultimately detract from finding important information about minoritized groups, or more egregiously lead groups to be understood in terms of 'artefactual' problems linked to perceived cultural differences.

Given the ambiguity and difficulty around the categories and terms of classification systems and their underlying concepts, as well as their problematic historical development and political resonances in racism, it is troubling that they continue to be used in research, practice and policy about and for groups of people who have little to no direct involvement or say in their development or validation. It is something that current researchers reframing ageing need to be both cognizant of, and critical about.

Bibliography

Adamson, J. (2001), 'Awareness and Understanding of Dementia in African/Caribbean and South Asian Families', *Health & Social Care in the Community*, 9: 391–6.

Adelman, S., M. Blanchard, G. Rait, G. Leavey and G. Livingston (2011), 'Prevalence of Dementia in African-Caribbean Compared with UK-born White Older People: Two-stage Cross-sectional Study', *The British Journal of Psychiatry*, 199(2): 119–25.

Allen, T. W. (2014), *The Invention of the White Race, Volume 2: The Origin of Racial Oppression in Anglo-America*, London: Verso.

Aspinall, P. J. (2002), 'Collective Terminology to Describe the Minority Ethnic Population: The Persistence of Confusion and Ambiguity in Usage', *Sociology*, 36(4): 803–16.

Aspinall, P. J. (2020), 'Ethnic/Racial Terminology as a Form of Representation: A Critical Review of the Lexicon of Collective and Specific Terms in Use in Britain', *Genealogy*, 4(3): 1–15. Available at: https://doi.org/10.3390/genealogy4030087 (accessed 26 January 2023).

Ayalon, L. and P. A. Arean (2004), 'Knowledge of Alzheimer's Disease in Four Ethnic Groups of Older Adults', *International Journal of Geriatric Psychiatry*, 19(1): 51–7.

Banton, M. (1987), 'What We Now Know about Race', *New Community*, 13: 349–58.

Barroso, A. (2020), 'Most Black Adults Say Race is Central to Their Identity and Feel Connected to a Broader Black Community'. Available at: https://www.pewresearch.org/fact-tank/2020/02/05/most-black-adults-say-race-is-central-to-their-identity-and-feel-connected-to-a-broader-black-community/ (accessed 24 November 2022).

BBC (2018), 'BME Label Insulting, Says Ex-Minister Priti Patel'. Available at: https://www.bbc.co.uk/news/uk-politics-43350527 (accessed 24 November 2020).

Beutler, L. E., M. T. Brown, L. Crothers, K. Booker and M. K. Seabrook (1996), 'The Dilemma of Factitious Demographic Distinctions in Psychological Research', *Journal of Consulting and Clinical Psychology*, 64: 892–902.

Bhala, N., G. Curry, A. R. Martineau, C. Agyemang and R. Bhopal (2020), 'Sharpening the Global Focus on Ethnicity and Race in the Time of COVID-19', *The Lancet*, 395: 1673–676.

Bhopal, R. (2004), 'Glossary of Terms Relating to Ethnicity and Race: For Reflection and Debate', *Journal of Epidemiology & Community Health*, 58: 441–45.

Bhopal, R. and L. Donaldson (1998), 'White, European, Western, Caucasian, or What? Inappropriate Labeling in Research on Race, Ethnicity, and Health', *American Journal of Public Health*, 88: 1303–307.

Bradby, H. (1995), 'Ethnicity: Not a Black and White Issue. A Research Note', *Sociology of Health & Illness*, 17: 405–17.

Burton, A., M. Ogden and C. Cooper (2019), 'Planning and Enabling Meaningful Patient and Public Involvement in Dementia Research', *Current Opinion in Psychiatry*, 32(6): 557–62.

Cashmore, E. (2004), *Encyclopedia of Race and Ethnic Studies*, London: Routledge.

Chaturvedi, N. and P. M. McKeigue (1994), 'Methods for Epidemiological Surveys of Ethnic Minority Groups', *Journal of Epidemiology & Community Health*, 48: 107–11.

Chevalier, J. (2020), 'TOUT COMPRENDRE - Pourquoi les Statistiques Ethniques font Débat en France'. Available at: https://www.bfmtv.com/societe/tout-comprendre-pourquoi-les-statistiques-ethniques-font-debat-en-france_AN-202006150240.html (accessed 24 November 2020).

Cole, M. (1993), '"Black and Ethnic Minority" or "Asian, Black and Other Minority Ethnic": A Further Note on Nomenclature', *Sociology*, 27: 671–73.

Corin, E. (1995), 'The Cultural Frame: Context and Meaning in the Construction of Health', in B. C. Amick, S. Levine, A. R. Tarlov and D. Chapman Walsh (eds), *Society and Health*, 272–304, New York: Oxford University Press.

Cornell, S. and D. Hartmann (2006), *Ethnicity and Race: Making Identities in a Changing World*, London: Sage.

Crewe, S. E. (2005), 'Ethnogerontology: Preparing Culturally Competent Social Workers for the Diverse Facing of Aging', *Journal of Gerontological Social Work*, 43: 45–58.

Giebel, C. M., M. Zubair, D. Jolley, K. S. Bhui, N. Purandare, A. Worden and D. Challis (2015), 'South Asian Older Adults with Memory Impairment: Improving

Assessment and Access to Dementia Care', *International Journal of Geriatric Psychiatry*, 30(4): 345–56.

de Gobineau, A. (1855), *Essai sur L'inegalité des Races Humaines*, vol. 1 Paris: Librairie de Firmin Didot Freres.

Jenkins, R. (1997), *Rethinking Ethnicity: Arguments and Explorations*, London: Sage.

Jenkins, R. (2008), *Rethinking Ethnicity: Arguments and Explorations*, 2nd edn, London: Sage.

Jenkins, R. (2014), *Social Identity*, London: Routledge.

Johl, N., T. Patterson and L. Pearson (2016), 'What Do We Know about the Attitudes, Experiences and Needs of Black and Minority Ethnic Carers of People with Dementia in the United Kingdom? A Systematic Review of Empirical Research Findings', *Dementia*, 15(4): 721–42.

Khunti, K., A. Routen, M. Pareek, S. Treweek and L. Platt (2020), 'The Language of Ethnicity', *British Medical Journal*, 371. Available at: https://doi.org/10.1136/bmj.m4493 (accessed 26 January 2023).

Knapp, M., M. Prince, E. Albanese, S. Banerjee, S. Dhanasiri and J. L. Fernandez (2007), *Dementia UK: The Full Report*, London: Alzheimer's Society. Available at: https://www.alzheimers.org.uk/sites/default/files/2018-10/Dementia_UK_Full_Report_2007.pdf?fileID=2 (accessed 26 January 2023).

Lawrence, V., J. Murray, K. Samsi and S. Banerjee (2008), 'Attitudes and Support Needs of Black Caribbean, South Asian and White British Carers of People with Dementia in the UK', *The British Journal of Psychiatry*, 193(3): 240–6.

Lenoir, N. (1983), 'La Loi 78-17 du 6 Janvier 1978 et la Commission Nationale de L'informatique et des Libertés: Elements Pour un Premier Bilan de Cinq Années D'activités', *La Revue Administrative*, 36(215): 451–66.

Lin, S. S. and J. L. Kelsey (2000), 'Use of Race and Ethnicity in Epidemiologic Research: Concepts, Methodological Issues, and Suggestions for Research', *Epidemiologic Reviews*, 22(2): 187–202.

Malik, K. (1996), *The Meaning of Race: Race, History and Culture in Western Society*, London: Bloomsbury.

Mayeda, E. R., M. M. Glymour, C. P. Quesenberry Jr, J. Y. Liu, J. Johnson and R. A. Whitmer (2015), 'Racial/Ethnic Differences in Dementia Survival in a Cohort of 59,494 Dementia Patients from a Healthcare Delivery System', *Alzheimer's & Dementia*, 11(7S_Part_6): 294–5.

Mayeda, E. R., M. M. Glymour, C. P. Quesenberry and R. A. Whitmer (2016), 'Inequalities in Dementia Incidence Between Six Racial and Ethnic Groups over 14 Years', *Alzheimer's & Dementia*, 12(3): 216–24.

McKenney, N. R. and C. E. Bennett (1994), 'Issues Regarding Data on Race and Ethnicity: The Census Bureau Experience', *Public Health Reports*, 109(1): 16–25.

Mehta, K. M. and G. W. Yeo (2017), 'Systematic Review of Dementia Prevalence and Incidence in United States Race/Ethnic Populations', *Alzheimer's & Dementia*, 13(1): 72–83.

Mukadam, N., C. Cooper, B. Basit and G. Livingston (2011), 'Why Do Ethnic Elders Present Later to UK Dementia Services? A Qualitative Study', *International Psychogeriatrics*, 23(7): 1070–7.

Mukadam, N., A. Waugh, C. Cooper and G. Livingston (2015), 'What Would Encourage Help-Seeking for Memory Problems among UK-Based South Asians? A Qualitative Study', *BMJ Open*, 5(9): e007990. Available at: doi: 10.1136/bmjopen-2015-007990.

Ndiaye, S. (2020), 'Sibeth Ndiaye: "Nous Payons Aujourd'hui L'effacement de L'universalisme Républicain"'. Available at: https://www.lemonde.fr/idees/article/2020/06/13/sibeth-ndiaye-nous-payons-aujourd-hui-l-effacement-de-l-universalisme-republicain_6042708_3232.html (accessed 24 November 2021).

ONS (2011), 'Household Questionnaire'. Available at: https://census.ukdataservice.ac.uk/media/50966/2011_england_household.pdf (accessed 26 January 2023).

Pham, T. M., I. Petersen, K. Walters, R. Raine, J. Manthorpe, N. Mukadam and C. Cooper (2018), 'Trends in Dementia Diagnosis Rates in UK Ethnic Groups: Analysis of UK Primary Care Data', *Clinical Epidemiology*, 10: 949–60.

Polenberg, R. (1980), *One Nation Divisible: Class, Race, and Ethnicity in the United States since 1938*, New York and London: Penguin.

Prince, M., M. Knapp, M. Guerchet, P. McCrone, M. Prina, A. Comas-Herrera, R. Wittenberg, B. Adelaja, B. Hu and D. King (2014), *Dementia UK: Update*, London: Alzheimer's Society. Available at: https://www.alzheimers.org.uk/sites/default/files/migrate/downloads/dementia_uk_update.pdf (accessed 26 January 2023).

Roche, M., P. Higgs, J. Aworinde and C. Cooper (2020), 'A Review of Qualitative Research of Perception and Experiences of Dementia among Adults from Black, African, and Caribbean Background: What and Whom are We Researching?', *The Gerontologist*, 61(5): e195–e208.

Romain, G. (2008), 'La Décision n 557 DC du 15 Novembre 2007 du Conseil Constitutionnel sur la Loi Relative à La Maîtrise de L'immigration, à L'intégration et à L'asile', *Publications Doc Du Juriste*. Available at: https://www.conseil-constitutionnel.fr/decision/2007/2007557DC.htm (accessed 26 January 2023).

Saeed, A., E. Rae, R. Neil, V. Connell-Hall and F. Munro (2020), 'To BAME or Not To BAME: The Problem with Racial Terminology in the Civil Service', *Civil Service World*, 4 October. Available at: https://www.civilserviceworld.com/news/article/to-bame-or-not-to-bame-the-problem-with-racial-terminology-in-the-civil-service

Scarman, L. G. (1986), *The Scarman Report: The Brixton Disorders 10–12 April 1981: Report of an Inquiry*, London: Puffin.

SCIE (2020), 'Black and Minority Ethnic (BME) Communities and Dementia', *Social Care Institute for Excellence*. Available at: https://www.scie.org.uk/dementia/living-with-dementia/bme/ (accessed 13 April 2021).

Seabrooke, V. and A. Milne (2004), *Culture and Care in Dementia: A Study of the Asian Community in North West Kent*, Northfleet: Alzheimer's and Dementia Support Services.

Senior, P. A. and R. Bhopal (1994), 'Ethnicity as a Variable in Epidemiological Research', *British Medical Journal*, 309(6950): 327–30.

Smedley, A., Y. I. Takezawa and P. Wade (2017), 'Race: Human', *Encyclopædia Britannica*. Available at: https://www.britannica.com/topic/race-human/Hereditarian-ideology-and-European-constructions-of-race (accessed 26 January 2023).

Taylor, K. Y. (2020), 'Of Course There Are Protests: The State is Failing Black People', *The New York Times*, 29 May.

Torres, S. (2020), 'Racialization without Racism in Scholarship on Old Age', *Swiss Journal of Sociology*, 46(2): 331–49.

Tuerk, R. and J. Sauer (2015), 'Dementia in a Black and Minority Ethnic Populations: Characteristics of Presentation to an Inner London Memory Service', *The British Journal of Psychiatry Bulletin*, 39(4): 162–66.

U.S. Bureau Census (2020), 'Questions Asked on the Form'. Available at: https://2020census.gov/en/about-questions.html.

Werner, P., D. Goldstein, D. S. Karpas, L. Chan and C. Lai (2014), 'Help-Seeking for Dementia: A Systematic Review of the Literature', *Alzheimer Disease & Associated Disorders*, 28(4): 299–310.

Werner, P., M. S. Mittelman, D. Goldstein and J. Heinik (2012), 'Family Stigma and Caregiver Burden in Alzheimer's Disease', *The Gerontologist*, 52(1): 89–97.

Williams, D. R., R. Lavizzo-Mourey and R. C. Warren (1994), 'The Concept of Race and Health Status in America', *Public Health Reports*, 109(1): 26–41.

15

JR's *Wrinkles of the City* project: Representing global old age, 2008–2015

David G. Troyansky

Confronting the overlooked

This chapter, like the book in which it appears, grows out of a series of interdisciplinary dialogues, and it involves one historian's attempt to engage with photography and the media in their treatment of old age. For me this is a relatively new departure. More typical is my monographic study of French magistrates seeking to retire in the first half of the nineteenth century (Troyansky 2023). Their retirement dossiers combine proof of service with first-person accounts of career, family life and politics as well as plans for retirement. The authors provide verbal portraits of their late life. While the monograph includes some illustrations (portraits, letters, bureaucratic forms), it is based essentially on textual sources that permit a social history of the life course, old age and retirement, a cultural history of representations of the ageing self against the backdrop of an evolving national historical narrative, and a political history of changing regimes and anticipations of welfare-state formulas for determining pension rights. In short, the book is concerned with how a population's experience of ageing is put into words. The cultural history of old age has often privileged literary representations (Skagen 2021). Largely absent is the 'look' of the aged.

Historians who have studied old age have sometimes used images for purely illustrative purposes, as artistic representations often clarify themes of moral philosophy, literary characterization, and religious belief and practice. A prime

---

The author wishes to thank the volume editors and Professor Shirley Jordan for their valuable comments on an earlier draft of this chapter.

example is the richly illustrated *Long History of Old Age*, edited by Pat Thane, where the image of the aged body serves some moral purpose, and the aged character illustrates cultural stereotypes (Thane 2005). Historians have to some extent begun to shed their discomfort with figural representations, and cultural history has seen a resurgence in the context of ageing, moving from simple illustration to a focus on deeper meanings and constructions of the ageing self, including the gendered ageing self. Indeed, some historians are using age as a category on par with race, gender and class, as is made evident in a roundtable in the pages of the *American Historical Review* (2020). And images of ageing individuals feature prominently in a recent issue of the *Radical History Review* devoted to the history of old age (*RHR* 2021). I once authored a chapter on artistic representations of old people in a book on eighteenth-century France, but there as well the imagery was subservient to other kinds of sources and themes (Troyansky 1989). My experience of viewing a recent exhibition of the work of JR and the encouragement of the editors of this volume led me to attempt to cross disciplines and consider JR's images of ageing faces displayed outdoors in urban space in the early twenty-first century. Moreover, in contrast to an analysis which gives primary importance to texts and sees visual data as mere illustration, this essay starts with images and moves out into the social, economic and historical discourses where image and text intersect.

JR's *Wrinkles of the City* project occupied its own space in his recent retrospective exhibition at the Brooklyn Museum (*JR: Chronicles*, Brooklyn Museum, Brooklyn, New York, 4 October 2019–3 May 2020, extended to 18 October 2020). Those who are familiar with JR generally know him from the 2017 film on which he collaborated with the late Agnès Varda, whose own *oeuvre* has paid much attention to the experience of ageing (Jordan Forthcoming). In *Visages Villages* (*Faces Places*) they travelled around France photographing ordinary people and pasting larger-than-life portraits on the walls of their towns or workplaces. The public in the Paris region may recall him as the photographer from the working-class/immigrant *banlieue* who pasted portraits of people from his neighbourhood on the walls of central Paris. He has undertaken a portrait project on Israelis and Palestinians, a project on the US–Mexican border, a series of portraits of impoverished women around the world, a series of portraits of New Yorkers, and a number of projects in which he has asked ordinary people to become photographers themselves. In all these efforts he has produced work that forces the viewer to confront people who are often overlooked. Along with the large pasted portraits, he has created books, documentary films and audio files in which his subjects speak for themselves.

I originally wrote this piece in the time of Covid-19 and was very aware of the indoors and the outdoors, and consequently of the importance of the outdoors for JR's aged subjects. We do glimpse some interiors, but the emphasis is on the aged out of doors, their portraits pasted on exterior walls. We often expect to see old people indoors, in spaces they themselves have created or in institutions that may or may not allow individual adaptation of their surroundings. In other words, they have grown less visible to anyone who hasn't made a special trip to see them. But JR's world is different. His pasted images will not last, for the walls behind them and even entire neighbourhoods are in the process of disappearing. And we may think of the subjects themselves, with their long historical memories, reaching their own ends. But for a time, in the streetscape, they remain visible and out of doors.

Photographing ageing

JR is not the only artist to document ageing individuals, but JR's project is unique in the way he uses photography as large-scale, site specific and importantly *public*, reinforcing or supplementing those photographic installations with narratives that appear in books, websites, films, etc.

Other artists have tried to trace ageing individuals over time. Consider projects of photographing the same family members annually over the course of decades, such as Zed Nelson's 'Family Project' and Nicholas Nixon's 'Brown Sisters'. Nelson began photographing friends with their newborn son in 1991 and returned to them in essentially the same pose every year 'from then on, forever' (Nelson 2015). Thus, it was possible to see a maturing child and a couple growing into middle age, although old age is presumably to come. Nixon photographed his wife and her three sisters annually since 1975. A book of photos was published in 1999, and the images appear on the websites of the Fraenkel Gallery and the Munich Pinakothek, which mounted an exhibition of the photographs taken from 1975 to 2020 (Nixon 2018, 2021).

Nixon's photographic portrait of ageing involved a long-term artistic and emotional investment and a focus on family life and privacy, rather different from JR's emphasis on a moment of life captured and displayed in public. Or consider Rick Schatzberg's *The Boys*, which depicts a circle of childhood friends in late middle age, juxtaposing youthful snapshots with recently staged portraits (Schatzberg 2020). Those efforts to depict ageing in a longitudinal fashion may have another purpose in mind. They may allow for reflections on self and, most evidently, ideas of decline.

(I am thinking about how one of Schatzberg's photographs combines wrinkles with surgical scars, as if to emphasize the medical interventions associated with age.)

The comparison with Schatzberg and Nixon highlights also the importance of the non-photographic data that JR makes available. JR's project, after the initial photographic encounter in the street, requires us to listen to recorded voices or to read text in order to fully appreciate the passage of time in individuals' lives. Those features permit a certain visibility to extend across the life course, but the literal visibility of what appears on the wall exists in the moment and makes the viewer ponder what old age now represents, a kind of evanescence that can only be made lasting in further reproductions.

Wrinkles of the City: Past and present, private and public

JR's work forces an examination of aged faces and the identities they represent in multiple cities around the world. We are invited to gaze at wrinkles themselves and appreciate individual older persons – we are told that JR himself was very close to his grandmothers – but we are also encouraged to view those faces as representing a time, a place and a history. As in some of his other projects, most notably work produced in a public-housing project undergoing demolition, he uses his characters to mark a moment of dramatic change in the urban landscape. His aged subjects have a sense of past and present at a critical moment. So in the portraits, the films and the books, we confront individuals who are witnessing the world being transformed around them. He speaks of the walls themselves as also having wrinkles. In a catalogue essay about a Paris-based installation, he writes of his grandmothers, born in 1915 and 1923:

> They were telling me about their childhood spent on two different continents, their husband who had been chosen for them by their parents. One spoke to me of decolonization which had transformed her country, the other of the war which had obliged her to run away, alone with her son. One mentioned her choice to work when women were supposed to stay at home, the other of her difficulty to learn French ... (JR 2015: 36)

But even those grandmothers, representing the private or personal side of the question of ageing, permit him to connect private histories to public ones: 'With them, I crossed the twentieth century, I shared their secrets, I was in touch with sexism, racism, fear, stupidity, war, difference, submission, revolt, success, exile, failure, sadness and joy and I wanted to continue travelling in the past' (JR 2015).

So too in depicting older people he had just encountered and whose portraits he was pasting on city walls, he writes: 'I wanted to confront the facades with the people, the collective history with the individual's narrative' (2015).

The exhibition catalogue describes *The Wrinkles of the City* as having grown out of an earlier project, *Women Are Heroes*, which consisted of portraits of working-class women around the world. The transition from *Women* to *Wrinkles* began in 2008 in Cartagena, Spain. Curators of the 2019–2020 Brooklyn retrospective Drew Sawyer and Sharon Matt Atkins juxtapose individual cities' experiences and the biggest of themes in contemporary world history, placing extraordinary interpretive weight on individual portraits.

> This time he photographed the oldest inhabitants of this port, which was the site of a major rebellion during the Spanish Civil War and the last city to surrender to General Francisco Franco. Portraits of elderly townspeople were pasted on the walls of buildings, with the faces and facades both bearing the traces of the city's history. Subsequently, JR traveled to cities in China, Cuba, Germany, Turkey and the United States in order to explore the lives of inhabitants who had witnessed some of the most significant cultural, social, and economic changes of the twentieth century. The resulting series not only reflects on change and memory, modernization and globalization, but also challenges cultural perceptions of the elderly by celebrating their aging appearance as beautiful, at a monumental scale. (Sawyer and Atkins 2019: 33)

While *Wrinkles of the City* began in 2008 with large-format photographs pasted on walls, over the next few years it encompassed gallery exhibits, illustrations in books, and moving images in videos posted to the internet.

Audiences who encountered *Wrinkles of the City* across these various platforms were encouraged to connect past and present. For example, the Cartagena project, as mentioned above, evokes the town's significance in the 1930s. The oldest subjects could have remembered the events themselves, and they certainly would have grown up with stories of that resistance. Similarly, a project based in Istanbul anchored itself in memories of the founding of the Turkish Republic in the 1920s and in nostalgic thoughts of cooperation among different ethnic and religious communities. Yet, few would remember the early days of the Republic, and the elders themselves spoke less of big public events than of their everyday lives. The Berlin project certainly builds on recent memories of the end of the Cold War, but JR's introduction insists on the longer-term history of the city, with special mention of the Nazi period. Even the Los Angeles project, focusing on the careers of people in the film industry, includes individuals who evoke memories of the Holocaust, but it tries to root itself in a longer-term background of American natural, cultural and political history, with several portrait subjects revealing themselves as activists for civil rights.

Perhaps the Havana project best links the sitters' own memories to a historical, in this case revolutionary, background. That past weighs heavily on the lives represented in *Wrinkles of the City: Havana* (2012), an installation project and book produced in collaboration with Cuban-American artist José Parlá (JR and Parlá 2012). Accounts by individual subjects often evoke the Cuban Revolution – their portraits take on the importance of revolutionary images of Fidel, Che, and others (or of the large-scale advertising that routinely appears in the capitalist world) – but they also recount family histories, working lives, music and food.

A double portrait in Havana simultaneously evokes an intimate personal connection between husband and wife and the physical support created by old and distressed walls joined together in a corner that draws the viewer's eye into the scene (Figure 7). An image of affection pasted onto long-standing mutually supporting architectural surfaces makes for a human-architectural embrace. The image exhibits its own strength, whether encountered by a passer-by in the street or a viewer of the photograph online or in a book. The wall-sized photograph

Figure 7 JR, *Wrinkles of the City*, Havana, 2012. *The Wrinkles of the City* is a project presented in various cities around the world where 'wrinkles', human as well as architectural, can be found. Copyright JR.

in the street is obviously startling, but even in the book the reproduction of the pasted image, peeling from the wall, occupies an entire double-page spread.

One learns more about this particular couple from the subsequently published *Wrinkles of the City* book (JR and Parlá 2012): Felo (Rafel Lorenzo), at age 90, recounts a career as a musician who had opportunities to travel even as Cuba experienced Cold War isolation. He describes how his wife Otulia (Obdulia Manzano), age 82, did not travel and devoted herself to their children.

In general, photographs frame individuals – couples are rare – in isolated portraits, but the stories they tell, collected and later published in JR's catalogues and other materials, embed those individuals in family histories. In the text that accompanies the photographs for *Wrinkles of the City: Havana*, Leda Antonia Machado speaks of her Cuban mother and Chinese father, of travel, clothing and the arts, but she mentions never having left Cuba. Alfonso Ramón Fontaine Batista, 83, smiles pensively, looking down, and describes the manual labour that filled his life, the employment that came from membership in the Communist Party, and his love of music. Alicia Adela Hernandez Fernández cocks her head up and speaks of her dentist daughter and chemistry-student granddaughter as well as her Catholicism and love of dancing. Twice-widowed Luisa Maria Miranda Oliva closes her eyes in a way that communicates calm and perhaps satisfaction. Head and top half of torso are pasted to the wall, but the head alone accompanies her text. She has no surviving children, remembers her family's hardships under the Batista dictatorship, spends each day, like other elders portrayed in the project, at a convent and thanks God for the beauty of creation.

Political history is woven into individuals' life stories, as those individuals narrate their stories and as JR frames them. In the context of the overall volume, the reach of the revolution and the impacts of Soviet support and collapse as well as of the American embargo are not far from the surface. As a way of offering an even longer historical context, the book includes a chronology that begins in 1492. The chronology for the Shanghai volume begins in the 1840s, that for the Los Angeles volume in 1602.

Despite that long-term context, the project often focuses attention on a medium-scale temporality. Old subjects remember the events, both public and private, of a half-century before, as living memory goes back to moments in youth that define generations. Here I see a connection with my own project on post-revolutionary France, a cultural world living in the shadow of world-historical events. Individual memories that may be central to people's sense of self take on added importance for subjects and viewers by being linked to larger political and economic narratives.

JR and the commercial image

The large-format visibility of wrinkles on the human face in JR's portrait installations are in and of themselves a disruption of the codes of commercial visual culture; they transcend what might otherwise look like billboard advertising. Indeed, his work stood out already as a counter-example in Margaret Morganroth Gullette's essay on how not to photograph older people. His are the rare images that meet with her approval (Morganroth Gullette 2017).

Because of its play with the large-format commercial imagery associated with the billboard and other forms of modern advertising, Los Angeles, the cradle of so much commercial culture, is a particularly fascinating site for JR's interventions. While JR selects individuals associated with the film industry, their wrinkled images and their narratives of work and migration upend the slick codes of commercial visibility. Carl Virden, at 63, is far younger than most of his fellow Los Angeles subjects. But he recognizes the process of ageing and its connection to his labour as a union carpenter (Figure 8). 'My wrinkles represent

Figure 8 JR, *Wrinkles of the City*, Los Angeles, 2012. Copyright JR.

time spent working, but more so time spent working for my family. They also represent aging: I remember looking down at my own wrinkled hands one day and thinking, "Those are my Dad's hands! I'm becoming my Dad!" That's when I realized I was getting older' (JR, *Wrinkles ... Los Angeles*, 2012: 54). Nonetheless, the image itself puts greater emphasis on the vitality or forcefulness of a man still in middle age.

Others in the Los Angeles project include an electronics store owner, a documentarian, a dancer, a printer, a cafeteria worker and various laborers. Several were political activists, and quite a few were immigrants, having come from Mexico, Guatemala, Thailand and Israel. Rita Guizulfo, a 65-year-old immigrant from Mexico who has lived in Los Angeles for fifty years, claims she has little to say because she didn't have any children, but she goes on to discuss the liberty that came from her divorce, her still-living parents, her love of the climate and geography of the area, and a philosophy that seems to combine a form of stoicism with an American sense of optimism: 'If I had one message for the world, it would be: be happy. If you have a problem, deal with it. And everybody does have problems but be happy as much as you can while you're living in this world' (30).

Many of JR's Los Angeles subjects take particular pleasure in participating in the disruption of the youth-centredness of commercial imagery, commenting on the superficiality or fakery at the heart of Hollywood. Jim Budman proudly displays his wrinkles, as he has experienced much and is critical of the cult of youth that surrounds him (34–7). It's not clear that the exact placement of the image offers a direct comparison with youth-obsessed advertising, but one wouldn't have had to travel far to see it. Karen (Ariana) Manov sees her wrinkles as representing her life story and as a symbol of resistance to ageism and injustice (60–3). Even one of the youngest subjects, at 56, actor Jim Hayes says, 'I want to see my ugly wrinkles on the side of a building because I want to be bigger than life' (64–7).

Changing landscapes and ageing lives

The representation of older people has often historically possessed a symbolic weight, as older people are stand-ins for moral qualities, sometimes representing the decrepit body as distinct from the more youthful soul, sometimes being tied to a desire to hold onto life, a representation of greed and vanity, and sometimes embodying wisdom (Troyansky 2016: 52). JR works against abstract symbolism.

While we may still recognize the 'wisdom' of old age and the beauty of the wrinkled face, the very sites of JR's installations ground the qualities of his portrait subjects in the midst of large social and economic forces that threaten their world, in some cases imminently. As happened in some of JR's *banlieue* images, the faces were pasted on walls that were soon to be demolished.

The precarious placement of JR's photographs is evident in the installation views of JR's *Wrinkles of the City: Shanghai* (2012). In a portrait of Wu Zheng Zhu, we have what appears to be a troubled reaction to the transformation of the city, even perhaps the noise generated by the construction of new towers (Figure 9). The old city is being torn down, and one imagines the subject thinking back to an earlier time.

A photograph that is ephemeral in a rapidly changing landscape nonetheless gives the viewer the impression of the older person's long-time presence. More than the old walls will soon be lost. Yet, the photo of the photo in the landscape will preserve the face of Wu Zheng Zhu. Other aged subjects, such as great-great-grandmother Shi Li, retired school cook Zhou Zhozi, retired nurse Cao Minjia and technician Ji Jinsui, also appear on old walls overwhelmed by new towers rising in the near background. JR has developed a pattern for juxtaposing the expressive aged face and the threat of urban renewal. When one refers to the *Wrinkles of the City: Shanghai* catalogue, one can situate Wu Zheng Zhu's visual

Figure 9 JR, *Wrinkles of the City*, Shanghai, 2012. Copyright JR.

manifestation of consternation or pain within a longer historical trajectory that she narrates herself. Born in 1939 in Shanghai, she recalls the Japanese bombing of the city. She and her family fled when she was three and returned when she was seven. She speaks of school, family, and factory work. She mentions problems associated with the Cultural Revolution and reflects on change in the city (JR, *Wrinkles ... Shanghai* 2012: 91). Virtually everyone speaks of dramatic changes over time, and many refer to particular national events, praising the Liberation and the Great Leap Forward (1958–1962), criticizing the Cultural Revolution (1966–1976), and sometimes singling out individual leaders. Few depart from 'official' memory, but some offer examples of cultural syncretism. Thus, while Yang Yinzhen, born in 1923, recounts the familiar difficulties of the Japanese occupation, she links improvements she has witnessed to a combination of forces: 'I lead a very happy life thanks to both the Communist Party and Buddhism' (95).

If JR's portrait subjects are often threatened by urban renewal, their very materiality sharing a fate with the buildings that will soon give way, they also assume the complex role of witnesses over those changes. In some cases an aged eye is positioned to 'oversee' some neighbourhood activity, as when an eye of Nidia Mulet Rojas oversees children playing soccer in a Havana street. If the camera itself has often been theorized as a kind of disembodied or proxy eye, JR emphasizes his subjects' own eyes not as objective devices or machinic surveillance but as living, vulnerable and integrated witnesses to urban, environmental and historical change. Because the installations have a dual existence – first experienced in situ and later reproduced via installation shots in his books, albums, exhibitions and websites – the image of the older resident watching the neighbourhood in transition reaches a global public, attaining a radical kind of visibility in and even authority over public space, where older people are often erased.

JR's placement of and emphasis on his subjects' eyes encourages an outside/inside consideration of the eye not merely as portal for visual information but as symbolic of a dense and layered interiority. For example, in JR's Los Angeles installation (published 2012) he stages an image of George Cockfield, a 58-year-old African American who led a difficult life. In the subsequent narrative, Cockfield recalls losing an eye when his house was burgled and he was assaulted by the robber. 'Once, I was meditating and I heard a voice say: "Do you know why you lost an eye? Because now you have one eye to see outside and the other to see inside"' (76). Cockfield's particular circumstance literally embodies this inside/outside tension which runs implicitly through the entire project.

Ageing as universal and particular

JR's *Wrinkles of the City* projects represent ageing as individuated, localized and historically contingent. But they also suggest that ageing is something that ties people together. For example, a book aimed at younger readers (JR, *Wrinkles* 2019) is a way of crossing multi-generational divides. Living longer, even today, is a global phenomenon, and old age might break down social and cultural differences (Troyansky 2016). JR's collaborator on the Havana volume, artist José Parlá, describes ageing in universalizing terms:

> The wrinkles of experiences of our beloved Cuban elders are a representation of the grandparents I didn't get to meet. They are the wrinkled palimpsests of human language, the very essence of mankind. Their faces are the universal symbolic carrier of history that all humans share as we reach the third stage of life. Their language, smiles, doubts, mannerisms, memories, celebrations, downfalls, apathy, and triumphs are the drama made of ordinary heroes. (JR and Parlá 2012)

As a historian of public health makes clear in a medical, social-scientific and policy context, there is a danger in thinking in terms of a uniform way of ageing, especially when it derives from a particularly Western model (Sivaramakrishnan 2018). So perhaps we should view *Wrinkles of the City* as pointing out both similarities and differences while recognizing the danger of accepting stereotypical or homogenizing views. We can go from one city to another, focus on wrinkles, and overlook differences, or we can view them as speaking from very different and precise historical, geographic and personal contexts. Those who appear in the photographs, however displayed or viewed (on a city wall, a museum wall, or in a book, looking aside or straight ahead, displaying an earring or hearing aid), constitute a global cast of characters. The viewer is free to generalize about ageing and urban transformations in a collective moment or search for particular stories rooted in individual or national experience.

Importantly, we ought to recognize that JR's subjects are overwhelmingly working-class. Each story of the twentieth (and early twenty-first) century is different, each neighbourhood seems to be experiencing its own form of social life, neglect or gentrification, but all permit an appreciation of non-elite ageing, often an active and assertive old age, sometimes a nostalgic or resigned one. And every different geographic installation of JR's project places great emphasis on the role of memory, its simultaneously private and public nature.

Wrinkles on the walls of Cartagena or Havana or Berlin or Los Angeles allowed a juxtaposition of individual memories and historical transitions, from the Spanish Civil War or the Cuban Revolution to the Cold War or periods of urban renewal. And those images, whether stills on the wall, illustrations in books, or moving images in videos presented in museums or online, try to relate the look of the aged face and the legibility of the urban landscape. Books and videos supplement and amplify the experience of the original photographic installations, always emphasizing the thoughts of the old people themselves rather than objectifying them as mere portrait subjects. The narrative information clearly provides audiences more depth and specificity than a passer-by looking up at a larger-than-life portrait can access, and yet those subsequent documentary efforts can only exist because of the original, monumental, disruptive and site-specific installation that they seek, in turn, to preserve and historicize.

Bibliography

American Historical Review Roundtable (2020), 'Chronological Age: A Useful Category of Historical Analysis', *American Historical Review*, 125(2): 371–459.

Jordan, Shirley (forthcoming), 'Ageing and Care in Agnès Varda,' in Shirley Jordan (ed.), 'Ageism, Ageing and Old Age in Contemporary French Culture,' *French Studies*, 77(4). Available at: https://academic.oup.com/fs/advance-article-abstract/doi/10.1093/fs/knad144/7240037?utm_source=advanceaccess&utm_campaign=fs&utm_medium=email

JR (2012), *The Wrinkles of the City: Los Angeles*, Rome: Drago.

JR (2012), *The Wrinkles of the City: Shanghai*, Rome: Drago.

JR (2015), *Wrinkles of the City, Des rides et des villes*, Paris: Alternatives.

JR (2019), *Chronicles*, Paris: Maison CF; New York: Brooklyn Museum.

JR (2019), *Wrinkles*, London and New York: Phaidon Press.

JR website. Available at: https://www.jr-art.net/project-list/the-wrinkles-of-the-city (accessed 25 July 2022).

JR and José Parlá (2012), *The Wrinkles of the City: Havana*, Bologna: Damiani.

Morganroth Gullette, Margaret (2017), *Ending Ageism of How Not to Shoot Old People*, New Brunswick, NJ: Rutgers University Press.

Nelson, Zed (2015), 'Family Project'. Available at: www.zednelson.com/?TheFamily (accessed 25 July 2022).

Nixon, Nicholas (2018), 'Brown Sisters'. Available at: www.fraenkelgallery.com/portfolios/nicholas-nixon-brown-sisters (accessed 20 July 2022).

Nixon, Nicholas (2021), 'Brown Sisters'. Available at: www.Pinakothek.de/en/exhibitions/Nicholas-nixon-brown-sisters-1975-2020 (accessed 15 July 2022).

Old/Age (2021), special issue, ed. Amanda Ciafone and Devan McGeehan Muchmore, *Radical History Review*, 139: 1–223.
Sawyer, Drew and Sharon Matt Atkins (2019), 'The Public Image: JR's Community Collaborations,' in *JR Chronicles*, introduction by Anne Pasternak, text by Drew Sawyer and Sharon Matt Atkins, 11–47, Paris: Maison CF; New York: Brooklyn Museum.
Schatzberg, Rick (2020), *The Boys*, Brooklyn: PowerHouse Books, 2020.
Sivaramakrishnan, Kavita (2018), *As the World Ages: Rethinking a Demographic Crisis*, Cambridge, MA and London: Harvard University Press.
Skagen, Margery Vibe, ed. (2021), *Cultural Histories of Ageing: Myths, Plots and Metaphors of the Senescent Self*, New York and London: Routledge.
Thane, Pat, ed. (2005), *The Long History of Old Age*, London: Thames & Hudson.
Troyansky, David G. (1989), *Old Age in the Old Regime: Image and Experience in Eighteenth-Century France*, Ithaca, NY and London: Cornell University Press.
Troyansky, David G. (2016), *Aging in World History*, New York and London: Routledge.
Troyansky, David G. (2023), *Entitlement and Complaint: Ending Careers and Reviewing Lives in Post-Revolutionary France*, New York: Oxford University Press.

16

Reframing LGBT+ ageing: Self, others and queer generations

Andrew King and Matthew Hall

Introduction

The literature about ageing amongst lesbian, gay, bisexual and trans (LGBT+) people has grown exponentially over the past few decades both in our own country (UK) and globally (Almack and King 2019; Almack, King and Jones 2022). Key issues that mark LGBT+ ageing as distinct from ageing as a cisgender heterosexual person have been identified in areas as diverse as health, housing, social care, social connections and loneliness amongst others. The purpose of this chapter, however, is not to repeat the findings of existing research. This would risk (re)producing either a celebratory or constraint view of LGBT+ ageing that emphasizes ways in which older LGBT+ people respond to later life in different ways to cisgender heterosexual people (for a critique see King 2016). Instead, the chapter will consider four inter-related questions: what does it mean to re(frame) LGBT+ ageing? Why is this important? How is reframing achieved? Why are generations important?

The chapter is divided into three sections. The first section explores the concept of reframing. It draws on Erving Goffman's sociological writings concerning social interactions and the importance of context, as well as Judith Butler's more poststructuralist philosophical writings about ontology and the power of norms. The section outlines an approach to reframing that helps us to further understand LGBT+ ageing and the lives of older LGBT+ people, as well as how they are shaped by themselves and others. The second section then applies this notion of reframing to data we have collected across several projects over the past decade involving LGBT+ people. We will not give a detailed methodological description of these projects – but, by and large, they all address questions of in/equality experienced by LGBT+ people, including older people, from a largely qualitative perspective. In this section we also explore how reframing is undertaken in relation to the self and others. It therefore illustrates the complicated ways that this happens and why it happens. The third section then brings the notion of queer generations to bear on the notion of reframing. We explain why a generational lens is important to understand LGBT+ ageing and its dynamism. The chapter concludes that reframing LGBT+ ageing means attending to change, both social and individual, that is ongoing, disruptive, productive and that we need to be mindful of imposing simplistic understandings on complex lives.

The concept of reframing

In his book, *Frame Analysis*, Erving Goffman (1974) defined framing as the schemes of interpretation that people use in everyday life, which are organizationally produced and structured yet shape activities and understandings. To explore framing means examining aspects of everyday life and asking: what is going on here? What norms and rules are shaping the tacit understandings that are guiding this interaction? How is the interaction both repetitive but changeable? In short, what frame or frames guide interactions? Goffman (1974) describes several frames in his book, not with the intention of producing a comprehensive taxonomy, but to illustrate the point he is making through detailed examples and interpretations. We contend that the same is possible, indeed important, in respect to LGBT+ ageing and older people.

From a more post-structural and Queer theoretical perspective, Butler (2010) also suggests that a frame 'implicitly guides the interpretation', but never wholly. That is, interpretive frames seek to fix meanings but their ability to do so can always be subverted; something is always 'beyond the frame'. Moreover, in her discussion of the circulation of cultural texts, she notes how such texts shape meaning but can always be reframed, resisted and reconsidered.

It is, therefore, possible to see framing as the way that aspects of everyday social life are guided, but not exclusively determined, by wider social forces – whether they be social or intuitional norms or legal tenets. There is a degree of agency – people are not automata who endlessly repeat themselves or uncritically follow (even tacit) rules and regulations. Yet conversely, the way individuals traverse their lives is not entirely a case of free will.

To extend this, the notion of reframing entails attending to how interactions, and indeed all aspects of social life, are a choreography of both agency and constraint which vary according to the people involved, the historical and spatial contexts, and the social and institutional norms being deployed, resisted and/or reconfigured. For example, how an older person experiences a health care appointment is framed by expectations about the significance of the appointment, which medical staff will be there, and how the individuals, including the older person themselves, ask and respond to questions. It depends upon the medical understandings that the doctor and other medical staff bring to the consultation and the personal and social characteristics of all those involved, including individual and institutional assumptions about those characteristics. In effect, it means exploring how identities, institutions and norms intersect, interact and are (re)produced as a result. However, frames shift, over time and place, they do not stay the same but transform in and through different contexts in relation to the people involved in any specific social interaction and social situation. To return to the older person's health care appointment example, how that interaction takes place in England in 2022 will have resonance with other geographical and national settings, but also differ. It may also vary from how such an interaction took place thirty, forty, or 100 years ago because of changes in medical knowledge and education, in social norms and attitudes, and in institutional rules and regulations. A focus on reframing means exploring framing, how it changes in specific settings, across settings and over time. Reframing is both an interactional encounter – between self and others, and a sociological method of exploring this and thinking 'what is going on here?'

In the introduction to this chapter, we noted areas of LGBT+ ageing that have been studied and regarded as notably different to those of cisgender heterosexual people, e.g. health, housing and care, amongst others. What does connect these diverse areas of LGBT+ ageing is how all are framed by cisnormativity and heteronormativity – the normative assumption that a person's gender identity, expression and presentation align directly with the sex classification they were assigned at birth and that they are, and have always been, heterosexual. This cisheteronormativity (a term combining both gender identity and sexual orientation norms) frames how individuals, institutions and policies relate and respond to all older people and subsequently how older LGBT+ people can be disadvantaged, marginalized and disempowered in comparison to their cisgender heterosexual peers. In attempting to understand our previous example of an older person's health care appointment, it is essential to consider how cisheteronormativity is framing: 1) the doctor's understanding (both their medical and lay knowledge); 2) the older person's prior experiences of medical encounters and their understanding of how medicine and health care have historically treated LGBT+ people; 3) their response to the doctor; and 4) how the medical institution itself does, or does not recognize, stigmatize or engage with LGBT+ people and their lives. However, this chapter is not about LGBT+ ageing in relation to health care, but rather how understandings of LGBT+ ageing and older LGBT+ people are both framed and reframed through social interactions, whether those be in ones reported during research (e.g. in what might be said to the interviewer) or by looking at the actual interview interaction itself. Indeed, it is the constant, reflexive, back and forth that makes reframing LGBT+ ageing a dynamic process between self and others.

Reframing LGBT+ ageing by self and others

As a number of authors have noted, LGBT+ ageing is not a singular, uniform experience but one that is refracted through multiple forms of difference and diversity; in short, it is intersectional (King 2016; Westwood et al. 2020). It is, therefore, imperative that any attempt to reframe LGBT+ ageing explores and encompasses this intersectionality. Whilst this section of the chapter will draw on several intersections, its primary purpose is to give examples of how older LGBT+ people seek to reframe themselves and are reframed by others.

Reframing the self

Reframing is important conceptually to help us consider how older LGBT+ people position themselves in relation to certain social identities and their associated structured constraints and intersections. Questions of age and ageing are often subject to re-contextualization in terms of how temporality and chronology affect LGBT+ people. For instance, who might be classified as an older LGBT+ person, in what circumstances and in relation to what other intersecting forms of social identity, in/equality and social division?

In the following short section of an interview conducted with Ernest, a gay man in his early 70s, we can see a process of framing and reframing in how he identifies himself. The specific research project was exploring how older LGBT+ people experience services and issues of equality. Despite taking part in a study that asked for LGBT+ participants over the age of 50, Ernest had explained why he did not think the sexual identity label 'gay' applied to him in an unproblematic way – he had not lived in a gay community, nor had a civil partnership or same-sex marriage. A little later in the interview, he was asked what he thought about service provision for older people and stated:

> There again I have very rarely got myself involved and not classifying myself as gay I don't classify myself as er old. I just don't think in terms of age ... so that's [his voluntary work] brought me much more in to focus the needs of older people and what older people talk about er which is mainly sitting around chatting about the old days [laughs] it's not really my scene but you know you listen and you try and be as helpful as you can.

In this way, two important intersectional aspects of Ernest's identity and why he was being interviewed, his sexuality and his age, are being called into question by Ernest himself. He is distancing himself from frames of sexuality and ageing as he understands them and in the context of the interview he is reframing them himself. This of course does not mean that these identity categories and ontologies cannot be applied to Ernest, but that he himself wants to reframe them.

As it stands, there is nothing inherently radical about Ernest's reframing. Indeed, there is a sense in which his rejectionist approach towards 'older people' and 'being gay' could be regarded as highly cisheteronormative and ageist. What is analytically interesting, though, is his agency to do this reframing in the interview context. Ernest, despite taking part in a study about older LGBT+ people, is quite prepared to do so on his own terms. In many ways this aligns with Goffman's (1974) work about identity management and framing but it also shows how individuals can attempt to reframe their identities. However, it does not tell us very much about the constraints within which older LGBT+ lives are lived and the deleterious ways that societal structures themselves force LGBT+ people to reframe ageing.

Many participants in our studies spoke of how they had challenged inequalities related to ageing as an LGBT+ person. This sometimes involved calling out discrimination, such as questioning a person's perception of LGBT+ people in an organizational setting. However, such self-reframing is limited – many times structures persist that limit older LGBT+ people's lives more systematically, as the following example illustrates.

Maz was a cisgender, lesbian woman who was in her mid-fifties when interviewed in the mid 2010s. She came out as a lesbian in midlife, having previously identified as heterosexual and been married to a cisgender man, which resulted in several children. Although Maz spoke about the reframing of her identity in her midlife, during the interview she was asked about her possibilities for retirement and later life. She said:

> Oh I don't think about it, but I certainly dream about it. I'd love to have the time to spend in the garden and get the garden, you know, under control and enjoy being in it. I would like to be able to travel because I've not been in a position to do that. I've never had any money, and it's only really since I've been working full time the last few years that I've had any money at all and what I have now is, you know, sort of split ... for the mortgage and about a third for my pension ... which I didn't have at all because it was with my husband and so that's all gone, so I have nothing, and about a third which is ... living and ... a big chunk towards saving things and pension and trying to save some so that I've got something to live on, because otherwise I'm going to have nothing, and a big chunk goes towards supporting the kids.

In this case Maz's capacity to reframe ageing beyond cisheteronormative expectations are circumscribed because of intersecting structural dimensions related to her age, gender, sexuality and arguably social class. Whilst Ernest sought to reframe his identity, both to himself and to the interviewer, Maz is indicating that she cannot reframe how she experiences her retirement, or in this case, opportunities for early retirement. Maz's identity work – coming out as a lesbian later in life – has had material consequences above and beyond already existing gendered inequalities. She has less capacity to reframe what ageing means to her, as an older lesbian, which she recounts in the interview.

Being reframed by others

In many ways, Maz's case is illustrative of how an older LGBT+ person is reframed by cisheteronormative ideologies and inequalities which shape and constrain their lives. One way in which this appears to happen, consistently and structurally, is in relation to institutions and the institutionalized sectors of life that people, including LGBT+ people, age within.

It is well documented that older LGBT+ people have concerns about retirement housing, care homes and care at home in later life (King and Cronin 2016; Westwood 2016a, 2016b; King and Stoneman 2017; Lottmann and King 2020; Savage and Barringer 2021). This includes experiences of discrimination (both actual and anticipated), concerns about precarity of tenure or finance and the loss of or detachment from LGBT+ social networks leading to social isolation, loneliness and loss of support.

In the following quotation from research conducted in 2019, an older cisgender gay man, Michael, recounts an example of where he and his partner felt belittled by nurses who were supposed to be supporting them; the inference being that this was because they became identifiable as a gay couple.

> And I went to pick him up and the nurses that were behind the station were sniggering because I went to pick him up and I was holding him up. And [my partner] got really angry, 'yes he is holding me up and yes he is my partner'.

It is possible to see in Michael's story that he and his partner are reframed as older gay men by the nursing staff, which his partner attributes, at least, to their behaviour towards them. It illustrates one way that those with institutional identities and status reframe older LGBT+ people in negative terms.

Many participants in our studies were acutely aware that despite perceived and actual progress in terms of LGBT+ equality in more recent years, which in effect should enable them to challenge such reframings, getting older could mean they were more vulnerable and less able to 'fight their corner'. As such, they undertook actions themselves to avoid being placed in these positions, as the following quotation from a housing study we conducted in 2018 illustrates.

> We have a sheltered housing manager, but I don't feel safe to express my sexual orientation. Probably she does know but unfortunately there's an awful lot of people in the caring profession who tend to be religious.

In this quote, Liz, a cisgender lesbian in her 60s, is responding to a question posed by the interviewer about whether she has told anyone in a position of authority at her sheltered housing complex about her sexuality. Liz indicates that she has not, because she does not feel safe to do so on the grounds of the manager's religiosity. She anticipates that this religious frame will be used to judge her, and she may experience discrimination. In this sense, Liz is seeking to avoid being reframed as an older lesbian by her housing manager, although she does note that this woman 'probably does know'.

A similar example of avoiding being reframed by others can be seen in the following quote from Kent, a cisgender gay man in his early 50s. Kent reflects the concerns of many of the gay men in our studies about potential discrimination from other (cisgender heterosexual) men if they were to become aware of their sexuality. This leads Kent to modify certain aspects of his home – in this instance, hiding photographs of himself and his partner:

> [Housing providers] have got various different engineers for whatever it is … and I'm very, very wary of who they're going to be sending here. Are they going

to pick up the fact that I'm gay? When it's a male coming here, is there enough time for me to get rid of those pictures or whatever, they all come off the shelf.

Whilst Liz and Kent provide examples of older LGBT+ people who seek to avoid being reframed as not cisgender or heterosexual, Trish, an older trans woman, discussed the harassment she experienced in and around her home due to others knowing she was trans. Whilst this harassment could sometimes be very overt – in terms of abusive comments and threats of violence – more often it was insidious and symbolic. When asked by the interviewer how this affected her life and what could be done about it, she said with incredulity: 'But how do you deal with, you know, the guy next door who won't even get in a lift with me?'

Positive reframing

The examples discussed so far in this section have primarily detailed ways in which older LGBT+ people are reframed by others, which can have negative impacts on their experiences of ageing – they reproduce stigmatization and discrimination, emanating largely from cisheteronormativity. However, many other participants in our projects cited related examples whereby they felt people in institutional positions of support, care or responsibility had reframed ageing as an LGBT+ person in positive ways. In short, we must not always assume that reframing is problematic for LGBT+ people.

When interviewed about her care home, one older cisgender lesbian, Lacy, explained that she felt safe and supported. She attributed this to the care home manager who had been on equality, diversity and inclusion (EDI) training and responded very positively. This had led to Pride events at the home and clear policies related to LGBT+ inclusivity. Lacy made particular reference to the visibility of the LGBT rainbow flag and information displayed on a notice board and the inclusive environment communicated by the care home staff. Hence, we can see a reframing of the context in which Lacy lives and how important symbolism and communication can be in this process.

Many other participants across our projects had discussed wider social, political and legal changes that had affected their lives in more positive terms. Examples included the Stonewall Inn uprisings of 1969, the partial decriminalization of male homosexuality in the Sexual Offences Act (1967), the introduction and later repeal of Section 28 of the Local Government Act (1988), the Civil Partnership Act (2004), the Gender Recognition Act (2004) the Marriage (Same-Sex Couples) Act (2014), alongside the introduction of equalities legislation more broadly. Whilst discrimination, harassment and violence against gender and sexually diverse people continues to exist and have deleterious impacts (Bayrakdar and King 2023), such legislative changes had, it was felt by many participants, contributed to a meaningful society-wide legal and institutional reframing of LGBT+ lives and ageing. However, many of the older LGBT+ people in our studies were also wary of complacency – that rights once fought for and won, could be subject to backlash and rescindment. It was, furthermore, when thinking about these changes and their impact across the life course that we began to think about applying a generational lens to LGBT+ lives, including LGBT+ ageing and older people. For our purposes in this chapter, it is important to consider reframing LGBT+ ageing in relation to queer generations.

Queer generations

The concept of generations is an important one within Sociology and the wider social sciences, with frequent use also found in popular culture and media commentary (Bristow 2016). Emanating from the pioneering writings of Karl Mannheim (1952), a generation can be considered to form when an age-based cohort comes of age and experiences formative life course experiences during their youth in such a way as to create a *zeitgeist*, or world view, that they carry with them through their lives. This generational location is like an imprint on the self and social group and has led to contemporary popular categorizations of generations such as Baby Boomers, Generation X, Millennials, etc. All are marked by significant social, cultural and historic events.

It has long been considered that different age-based cohort groups will experience LGBT+ ageing in diverse ways. For instance, several writers have separated LGBT+ people into the 'young-old' and the 'old-old' when writing about those aged over 50 years of age (Rosenfeld 2002; Cronin 2006). In part this reflects differences related to employment activity and retirement, but also to when people became aware of their sexuality. Indeed distinct age-based generational groups have been discussed by Knauer (2011) and others (Rosenfeld, Bartlam and Smith 2012), wherein differences are noted between those who came of age prior to the emergence of the modern LGBT+ rights movement in the late 1960s. This is a distinction between what Knauer refers to as the Silent Generation and the Stonewall Generation, with the latter understanding their sexuality based on a celebratory and affirmative discourse, rather than one that is hidden and shameful.

Other writers, such as Dunlap (2014), have begun to discuss the idea of queer generations. This involves exploring differences in coming-out narratives amongst lesbian, gay and bisexual peoples in order to interrogate the applicability of generations, as a concept, to non-heterosexual lives across the life course. Dunlap argued that a staged model of coming out was more redolent with older groups, rather than the more complex and less sequential experiences of those who were younger. Dunlap identified five identity cohorts which he argued 'queered' the popular notion of generations. Rather than those often cited in generational research and popular culture within many Western countries (noted earlier), Dunlap identified the following five: Pre-Stonewall, Stonewall, AIDS crisis, post-AIDS/Millennial and the Youngest generation. These partly reflected birth date, but also key aspects of LGBT+ history. Thus, the Youngest generation have had more access to celebratory, rights-based notions of being LGBT+ and have not experienced engrained or, at points, legalized homophobia, biphobia and transphobia in the ways that older LGBT+ have. However, others have argued that the generational concept can be overly simplistic and universalistic (Marshall et al. 2019) as it does not take into account difference and diversity. Nor does it, as we have also argued elsewhere (King and Hall, forthcoming), account for the non-linearity of many LGBT+ lives and LGBT+ history.

In our most recent project, titled *Comparing Intersectional Life Course Inequalities amongst LGBTQI+ Citizens in Four European Countries (CILIA-LGBTQI+)*, we specifically asked participants who ranged from 18 to 83 years of age about their lives now, in the past and their thoughts about the future. This provided us with a range of stories about how LGBT+ people can challenge (or queer) cisheteronormative notions of generation, which are often embedded in familial and institutional histories.

An example of this can be seen in the following quote from Rahul, a cisgender gay man in his late thirties, who defined his ethnic identity as Asian/British Indian. He noted the importance of familial generativity in his own background, but also how it had been challenged by his sexuality:

> Because at that time, I'm sure the experiences of younger gay Asians are different now, because the generation of parents is, they'll be my age will be parents now. And so, if I had a gay son, I'd be like, 'Yeah, whatever'", kind of thing, 'Just be safe.' But at the time, we were, I suppose, pioneers, because there was nobody else like it. And so, we defined the way things kind of went, I suppose, in some way ... our parents were of a generation where they weren't exposed to things like LGBT and stuff.

Reframing himself as a 'pioneer', Rahul here imagines generational differences in the coming-of-age experiences of younger Gay British Asians, compared to his own experiences. Although not explicitly discussing ageing, there is a sense in which this will make his experiences of later life different from previous generations in the ways that he attributes to his own parents.

It is important to note that such generational reframing is not confined to experiences or events from earlier in an individual's life. Indeed, one of the main findings of our project was that older LGBT+ people often reframed themselves in relation to more contemporary discourses and events that were not accessible to them earlier in life. A good example of this was recounted by one older bisexual woman with intersex variations, Liv, who spoke about the recent practice of identifying one's pronouns, something that she would have found important and useful when younger. Now she felt it was influencing interactions as she got older:

> But I've only become aware of people using pronouns in the last six months, they've generally started putting it on their correspondence and I thought, 'Oh yes maybe I ought to do that.'
> [Interviewer: Is it a useful thing? Is it a useful thing to do?]
> In certain circumstances I think, yes. Next time I go to hospital I will say, 'My pronouns are ... ' In the care home, I've been going to the care home for a year now and somebody asked me a couple of weeks ago, 'What do we call you? Do we call you him, her?' I had to tell them but it's nice that they asked. Why did it take them a year though?

In this quotation, not only does Liv indicate how she has reframed herself, but that a generational reframing has wider implications and consequences for others ('why did it take them a year though') beyond younger people with whom it is more often associated.

Conclusion

In this chapter we have outlined the concept of reframing and how this can be applied to LGBT+ ageing and older people. It enables us to understand LGBT+ ageing as a dynamic process, which involves elements of identity (re)positioning by both self and others. We have also argued that reframing is itself positional and changing – which is why understanding it through a generational lens remains important. Above all, the concept of reframing allows us to view LGBT+ ageing as changeable, both in terms of individual lives and across time. Ageing as an

LGBT+ person comes with challenges and complications, but also wisdom and agency. Tracing these reframings across time, contexts and lives is, we contend, an important component to our conceptual understanding of ageing.

Bibliography

Almack, K. and A. King (2019), 'Lesbian, Gay, Bisexual, and Trans Aging in a U.K. Context: Critical Observations of Recent Research Literature', *The International Journal of Aging and Human Development*, 89(1): 93–107.

Almack, K., A. King and R. L. Jones (2022), 'Care in Late Life, End of Life and in Bereavement for the Oldest LGBT Generations around the Globe', *Sexualities*, 25(1–2): 3–8.

Bayrakdar, S., and A. King (2023), 'LGBT Discrimination, Harassment and Violence in Germany, Portugal and the UK: A Quantitative Comparative Approach', *Current Sociology*, 71(1), 152–72.

Bristow, J. (2016), *The Sociology of Generations: New Directions and Challenges*, London: Palgrave Macmillan.

Butler, J. (2010), *Frames of War: When Is Life Grievable?* London: Verso.

Cronin, A. (2006), 'Sexuality in Gerontology: A Heteronormative Presence, a Queer Absence', in S. O. Daatland and S. Biggs (eds), *Ageing and Diversity: Multiple Pathways and Cultural Migrations*, 107–22, Bristol: Policy Press.

Dunlap, A. (2014), 'Coming-Out Narratives across Generations', *Journal of Gay & Lesbian Social Services*, 26(3): 318–35.

Goffman, E. (1974), *Frame Analysis: An Essay on the Organization of Experience*, New York: Harper & Row.

King, A. (2016), *Older Lesbian, Gay and Bisexual Adults: Identities, Intersections and Institutions*, London: Routledge.

King, A. and A. Cronin (2016), 'Bonds, Bridges and Ties: Applying Social Capital Theory to LGBT People's Housing Concerns Later in Life', *Quality in Ageing and Older Adults*, 17(1): 16–25.

King, A., and M. A. Hall (forthcoming), 'Re-Thinking Generations from a Queer Perspective: Insights and Critical Observations from the CILIA-LGBTQI+ Lives in England Project', in H. Kingstone and J. Bristow (eds), *Studying Generations: Multidisciplinary Perspectives*, Bristol: Bristol University Press.

King, A. and P. Stoneman (2017), 'Understanding SAFE Housing – Putting Older LGBT* People's Concerns, Preferences and Experiences of Housing in England in a Sociological Context', *Housing, Care and Support*, 20(3): 89–99.

Knauer, N. J. (2011), *Gay and Lesbian Elders: History, Law and Identity Politics in the United States*, Farnham: Ashgate.

Lottmann, R. and A. King (2020), 'Who Can I Turn To? Social Networks and the Housing, Care and Support Preferences of Older Lesbian and Gay People in the UK', *Sexualities*. Available at: https://journals.sagepub.com/doi/full/10.1177/1363460720944588?casa_token=ND13rTrhB_UAAAAA%3AdfzOUg9FK1JLZa6i4-gnu48kRh3K-Jz9h_bIh2yO9qzCV8ASYeT8Uvti-R0yBVi2TcVPBB_nPus- (accessed 27 January 2023).

Mannheim, K. (1952), *Essays on the Sociology of Knowledge*, London: Routledge and Kegan Paul.

Marshall, D., P. Aggleton, R. Cover, M. L. Rasmussen and B. Hegarty (2019), 'Queer Generations: Theorizing a Concept', *International Journal of Cultural Studies*, 22(4): 558–76.

Rosenfeld, D. (2002), 'Identity Careers of Older Gay Men and Lesbians', in F. Gubrium and J. Holstein (eds), *Ways of Aging*, 160–81, Oxford: Blackwell.

Rosenfeld, D., B. Bartlam and R. D. Smith (2012), 'Out of the Closet and into the Trenches: Gay Male Baby Boomers, Aging, and HIV/AIDS', *The Gerontologist*, 52(2): 255–64.

Savage, B. and M. N. Barringer (2021), 'The (Minority) Stress of Hiding: The Effects of LGBT Identities and Social Support on Aging Adults' Concern about Housing', *Sociological Spectrum*, 41(6): 478–98.

Westwood, S. (2016a), 'LGBT* Ageing in the UK: Spatial Inequalities in Older Age Housing/Care Provision', *Journal of Poverty and Social Justice*, 24(1): 63–76.

Westwood, S. (2016b), 'We See it as Being Heterosexualised, Being Put into a Care Home: Gender, Sexuality and Housing/Care Preferences among Older LGB Individuals in the UK', *Health & Social Care in the Community*, 24(6): 155–63.

Westwood, S., P. Willis, J. Fish, T. Hafford-Letchfield, J. Semlyen, A. King, B. Beach, K. Almack, D. Kneale, M. Toze and L. Becares (2020), 'Older LGBT+ Health Inequalities in the UK: Setting a Research Agenda', *Journal of Epidemiology and Community Health*, 74(5): 408–11.

Index

Note: *Italic* page numbers indicate figures.

Adorno, Theodor W. 185–8, 193
ageism, internalized 44
agency, exploration of alternative forms of 121–2
Ahmed, Sara 100–1
Alexandre, Sandy 186n1
Allenby, Braden 28–9
Amigoni, D. 184
archaeology of literary communication group 55
'Archaïscher Torso Apollos' ('Torso of an Archaic Apollo') (Rilke) 31–2
Aristotle 98–9, 99n2
art
    biomedicine/technology as problem of and in 30–1
    care for works of art 33–5
    embodied attitude 31–3
    empty-handedness evoked by 35–6
    finitude, living with and 45–6
    presence created for beholder 31–3
    responsibility for meaning of 35
    risk in making and viewing 23, 25, 33
    tremors 30
    see also late style
The Artist Grows Old (Sohm) 194
'art of ageing', successful ageing vs 41–3
arts
    benefits of focus on ageing 16–17
    in gerontology organizations 15
    perspectives from 13–14
Aspinall, Peter 203
assemblages 150
As You Like It (Shakespeare) 57–8
Atkins, Sharon Matt 219

Baars, Jan 42–3
Bakhtin, Mikhail 117
Baltes, Margaret 62
Baltes, Paul 62, 63–5
Banville, John 36
Beauvoir, Simone de 126–7, 135, 136

Benjamin, Jessica 127
Berlin Wisdom Paradigm 64–5
Bernier, Celeste 191
Berridge, C.W. 113n2
biomedicine/technology
    commercialization of old age 27–8
    complexities and ambiguities of humanity as ignored by 29
    dementia and 79
    healthy ageing and 25–9
    humanities and 28
    longevity as focus of 26–7
    as problem of and in art 30–1
    tremors, art and 30
    unexpected consequences of developments in 28–9
Black artists
    contemporary, relationship with the 187
    critical position of old age 186–7
    discovery of by mainstream 181
    late style and 181–2, 194
    out-of-time, being 186–7
    racial bias towards late style 189–93
    wave cycle of mainstream visibility 192
Bluck, S. 141
Boddice, Rob 99n2, 100
bodily functions, failing of 118–20
The Boys (Schatzberg) 217
Bracken, Louise 2
Brecht, Bertolt 56
'Brown Sisters' (Nixon) 217
Bruzzi, Stella 170, 177
Butler, Judith 230

Calo, Mary Ann 191, 192
care
    ethics 33n6
    for works of art 33–5, 33n5
care and nursing homes
    Covid-19 159–60, 164
    LGBT+ ageing 234–6

care industry 93
Carstersen, Laura 160
The Caucasian Chalk Circle (Brecht) 56
Chamisso, Adalbert von 104, 106
Children of Violence series (Lessing) 131, 134
chronotope 117
cisheteronormativity, LGBT+ ageing and 231–2
Cocooned (TV documentary)
   aim of 167, 172
   discussions from participants 172
   filming process 169–70, 172
   framing as motif in 173–4
   gloomy emotions and thoughts 174–5
   national cultural identity and 169
   one-to-one connection 173
   personal stories from 173
   radio/television, importance of 173
   reviews and reception of 177
   stills from *173*
   In Their Own Words: The Voices of Older Irish People in the COVID-19 Pandemic (Costello) 176
cocooning 157–9, 168
cognitive learning capacity in old age 62
comics
   dementia and 72–95
   Life Costs a Lot of Time (Das Leben kostet viel Zeit) (Sparschuh) 103–8
coming-out narratives 238
commercialization of old age 27–8
concrete 34–5
conferences
   humanities access to 16
   as overcoming interdisciplinary barriers 17
Conway, Kathlyn 43
Corin, E. 206
Couser, Thomas 42
Covid-19 pandemic
   care and nursing homes 159–60, 164
   cocooning 157–9, 168
   consultation, lack of 157–8
   context of 2
   framing 160
   invisibility of old-age 3
   Irish Longitudinal Study on Ageing (TILDA) 161–3
   lessons from 161–3
   mortality risks for older people 168
   National Public Health Emergency Team (NPHET) 158
   older people 156–7
   relaxation of restrictions 161
   resistance 160
   touch, absence of human 155–6
   see also *Cocooned* (TV documentary)
cultural gerontology
   funding partnerships 19
   future developments 19
   in gerontology organizations 15
   increasing interest in 14
   journals 15
   networks developed 15
   perspectives from 13–14
cultural identity
   Cocooned (TV documentary) 169
   older people and 170–1
   television and 171
culture
   arts, national cultural identity and 169
   commercial visible *222*, 222–3
   identity, cultural 169, 170–1
   terminologies of racial/ethnic categories 206
   wisdom and 54–9, 61

Darius-Kopp trilogy (Mora)
   age-focused perspective on 140
   ageist gaze 144
   alternative work and social relations in *On the Rope* 149–52
   ambiguity of 149
   decline in *The Monster* 146–9
   decline in *The Only Man on the Continent* 143–6
   de-institutionalization of the life course 146
   instability, social security and 150
   marriage failure 147–8
   midlife as narrative 140–3
   midlife progress narratives 146–52
   possibility or decline after disruption 146–52
   precarization of employment 146
   resilience 146, 148–9, 152
   as story of a midlife crisis 139–40
   time as disorder 145–6
   trauma and grieving 148–9

death
  biomedicine/technology and 83
  peaceful 87, 92
decline narratives 142, 142n2
Dee, John 56
de-institutionalization of the life course 146
Deleuze, Gilles 29, 30
dementia
  detoxifying 72–95
  racial/ethnic categorization in research 207–9
desynchronization 145–6
documentaries
  subjectivity and objectivity in 170
  see also *Cocooned* (TV documentary)
Dorland, W.A. 189
doubled consciousness of women 126–7
double standard of ageing 125–6, 127–8
  subverting 134–5
Dulle Griet (Breughel the Elder) 45–6
Dunlap, A. 238

Eberhardt, Jennifer 160
embodied attitude, art and 31–3
empathetic realism 112, 116–20
employment, precarization of 146
ethnicity
  dementia research 208
  identity and 206–7
  and race, confusion between 203, 204–5
  specific situations, use of term in as recommended 209–10
  terminologies of racial/ethnic categories 205–6
  see also terminologies of racial/ethnic categories
eudaemonic happiness 99
European Geriatric Medicine (journal) 15
everydayness
  exclusion and 47
  Olive Kitteridge and *Olive, Again* (Strout) 117
  practical wisdom of 56–7
exclusion, everyday 47

'Family Project' (Nelson) 217
Featherstone, M. 170
Feigel, Lara 136

Feininger, Lyonel 191
Feinstein, Roni 194–5
female agency, absence of older women from 111–12
femininity, old age and loss of 127–8
feminist literature, use of as resource 129
finitude, art and living with 45–6
Fischer, Hannah 102–3
flexibilization of employment 146
fools and sceptics, wisdom of 57–8
Fourth Age
  dread of 119–20
  friendship in 122
  Olive Kitteridge and *Olive, Again* (Strout) 119–22
Fourth Age/Third Age 41–2
frailty 120–1
Frame Analysis (Goffman) 230
framing
  cisheteronormativity, LGBT+ ageing and 231–2
  defined 230
  post-structuralism/Queer theory and 230
  see also reframing
France 204
Frank, Arthur 43
friendship in the Fourth Age 122
funding partnerships 19

Galenson, David 190–193
gay people
  lesbians, male gaze and 127n1
  see also LGBT+ ageing
gender
  doubled consciousness of women 126–7
  politics of, absence of older women from 111–12
  sexuality and ageing 125–6, 127–8
generations, queer 237–9
Germany,
  happiness and ageing 102–3
  Life Costs a Lot of Time (Das Leben kostet viel Zeit) (Sparschuh) 103–8
Gerontological Society of America (GSA)
  cultural gerontology and 14
  Humanities, Arts and Cultural Gerontology Advisory Pane 15
The Gerontologist (journal) 15

gerontology
    disease and disability as focus 13
    pillars within 13
Gilbert, Paul 169
Gilleard, Chris 41–2, 118, 119, 120
Goffman, Erving 230
The Golden Notebook (Lessing) 136
graphic storytelling, dementia and 72–95
Greenaway, Peter 56
grotesque (the), ageing and 46–9
Gullette, Margaret Morganroth *see* Morganroth Gullette, Margaret

Hamlet (Shakespeare) 56–7
Hammer, Espen 188n3
Handbook of Humanities and Aging (Cole, Van Tassel and Kastenbaum) 14
happiness
    and ageing, issue of 97–8
    co-constructed 107–8
    desire for, inequality and exclusion and 101
    as disciplinary tool 100–1
    as dominant contemporary theme 97
    eudaemonic 99, 107
    Germany, ageing and 102–3
    hedonic 99
    Life Costs a Lot of Time (Das Leben kostet viel Zeit) (Sparschuh) 103–8
    narrative methodologies 99–100
    performative approach 105
    performing 100–1
Haraway, Donna 33n5
Harms Selfies (Kinder) 46n6, 48n7
health humanities 17n2
    see also medical humanities
healthy ageing
    biomedicine/technology approach to 25–9
    defined 25–6
    humanities and 26
    see also The Way of All Flesh (Kinder)
hedonic happiness 99
Heim, Wallace 33
Higgs, P. 41–2, 118, 119, 120
homosexuality *see* LGBT+ ageing
humanities
    benefits of focus on ageing 16–17
    biomedicine/technology and 28

    in gerontology organizations 15
    healthy ageing and 26
    in journals 15
    perspectives from 13–14
    see also art; arts; medical humanities
human touch, absence of 155–6
Hutcheon, Linda and Michael 191

identity
    cultural 169, 170–1
    ethnicity and 206–7
    race, importance of to 207
illness narratives 42–3
    triumphant/untriumphant 43
    see also The Way of All Flesh (Kinder)
images of ageing
    historians' use of 215–16
    non-photographic data and 218
    outdoor settings 217
    over time 217–18
    photographing ageing 217–18
    textual representation as norm 215
    see also Wrinkles of the City (JR)
incontinence 118–20
instability, social security and 150
interdisciplinary scholarship
    challenges of 16
    challenges of trend towards 2
    collaboration issues 18
    funding partnerships 19
    old age and 2
    publications, low level of 17–18
    rewards of 16
    transparency in authorship 18–19
internalized ageism 44
intersectionality, LGBT+ ageing and 232, 233, 234
In Their Own Words: The Voices of Older Irish People in the COVID-19 Pandemic (Costello) 176
invisibility in old-age 2–3, 111–12
Ireland
    ageing in 163
    potential improvements for older people 164–5
    Reframing Ageing 164
    see also Covid-19 pandemic
Irish Longitudinal Study on Ageing (TILDA) 161–3, 169

isolation during Covid-19 lockdowns, impact of
  care and nursing homes 159–60, 164
  cocooning 157–9
  consultation, lack of 157–8
  framing 160
  Irish Longitudinal Study on Ageing (TILDA) 161–3
  lessons from 161–3
  National Public Health Emergency Team (NPHET) 158
  older people 156–7
  relaxation of restrictions 161
  resistance 160
  touch, absence of human 155–6

Jenkins, R. 206
Journal of the American Geriatrics Society 153
journals, humanities in 15
JR 216
  grandmothers 218
  see also *Wrinkles of the City* (JR)
judges/rulers, wisdom of 56

Kahn, R.L. 3, 113n2
Kant, Immanuel 60
Kelsey, J.L. 203
Kim, Eunjung 121
Kinder, Hermann
  death and illness as focus of work 39n1
  Harms Selfies 46n6, 48n7
  life and death 39
  see also *The Way of All Flesh* (Kinder)
Kircher, Athanasius 56
Knauer, N.J. 237
Knopp, Julian 102–3
knowledge, wisdom as type of 58–61
Kohlberg, Lawrence 61–2

late style
  The Artist Grows Old (Sohm) 194
  Black artists and 181–2, 194
  critical position of old age 185–7
  longevity of 184, 193
  negativity and criticality 187–8
  opposing discourses on 184
  origins of idea 183–4
  out-of-time, being 186–7
  racial bias towards 189–93
  survey of artists 193
  as theoretical construct 193–4
Lax, Thomas J. 186
learning to live a finite life 42–3
Lehman, Harvey 189
lesbians
  male gaze and 127n1
  see also LGBT+ ageing
Lessing, Doris 126
  The Golden Notebook 136
  Love, Again 129–30, 133
  A Proper Marriage 131, 134–5
  The Summer Before the Dark 130–2, 133
Lewis, Norman 190–1
LGBT+ ageing
  cisheteronormativity, framing by 231–2
  coming-out narratives 238
  institutions, concerns about 234–6
  intersectionality 232, 233, 234
  key issues 229
  legislative changes, impact of 236–7
  positive reframing 236–7
  pronouns, identifying 239
  queer generations 237–9
  reframing 232–7
  reframing by others 234–6
  self-reframing 232–4
Life Costs a Lot of Time (Das Leben kostet viel Zeit) (Sparschuh) 103–8
life narratives, happiness and 99–100
  Life Costs a Lot of Time (Das Leben kostet viel Zeit) (Sparschuh) 103–8
lifespan psychology 62, 63
life's work of an author 128–9
Lin, S.S. 203
Lindauer, Martin S. 189, 193
literature
  feminism and 129
  illness narratives 42–3
  life's work of an author 128–9
  midlife progress narratives 142–3
  triumphant/untriumphant tales 43
  see also Lessing, Doris; *The Way of All Flesh* (Kinder)
longevity
  as focus of biomedicine/technology 26–7
  of late style 184, 193
  as problem of the arts 31

looking, politics of 111
Love, Again (Lessing) 129–30, 133

magicians and sages, wisdom of 56
male experience of social
    disempowerment 114–15
male gaze 111
    doubled consciousness of women
        126–7
    emasculation by 14–16
    lesbians and 127n1
Mannheim, Karl 237
Mantel, Hillary 23
Martin, Courtney J. 187
Martin, Wendy 14, 16
Martinson, M. 113n2
McMullan, G. 184, 188
McWeeny, Jennifer 127
media
    representations of older people 171
    trust in 176–7
    see also *Cocooned* (TV documentary);
        images of ageing
medical humanities
    development of 14
    emergence of 17
medicine, systemic inequalities of 75–6
midlife
    crisis, origin of term 141
    defining 141
    duration 141
    events and transitions 141
    as gendered and hetero-normative
        141
    progress narratives 142–3, 146–52
    society/individuals' framing of age
        141–2
    see also Darius-Kopp trilogy (Mora)
minoritization 199n1
    see also terminologies of racial/ethnic
        categories
The Monster (Mora) *see* Darius-Kopp
    trilogy (Mora)
Mora, Terézia *see* Darius-Kopp trilogy
    (Mora)
Morganroth Gullette, Margaret 99, 100,
    107, 141–2, 222
Mulvey, Laura 111
'A Mutating Story' (Van der Beugel) 23,
    24, 25, 33–6

Nachtwey, Oliver 143
narratives
    decline narratives 142, 142n2
    of illness 42–3
    *Life Costs a Lot of Time (Das Leben
        kostet viel Zeit)* (Sparschuh) 103–8
    methodologies of, happiness and
        99–100
    triumphant/untriumphant 43
    see also *The Way of All Flesh* (Kinder)
National Collaboration on Ageing
    Research (NCAR) 19
national cultural identity, *Cocooned* (TV
    documentary) and 169
Nelson, Zed 217
New Dynamics of Ageing (NDA)
    Programme 19
Niedecken, Wolfgang 53
Nixon, Nicolas 217
nursing and care homes
    Covid-19 159–60, 164
    LGBT+ ageing 234–6
Nussbaum, Martha 44

old-age style
    The Artist Grows Old (Sohm) 194
    Black artists and 181–2, 194
    critical position of old age 185–7
    longevity of 184, 193
    negativity and criticality 187–8
    opposing discourses on 184
    origins of idea 183–4
    out-of-time, being 186–7
    racial bias towards 189–93
    survey of artists 193
    as theoretical construct 193–4
Olive Kitteridge and *Olive, Again* (Strout)
    ageing depicted in 113
    agency, exploration of alternative
        forms of 121–2
    bodily functions, failing of 118–20
    empathetic realism 112, 116–20
    ethnographic perspective 113, 117, 123
    everyday life, significance of 117
    Fourth Age, dread of 119–20
    frailty 120–1
    friendship in the Fourth Age 122
    male gaze, emasculation by 14–16
    multiple perspectives in 113
    narrating the Fourth Age 120–2

ordinariness and uniqueness of ageing 117–18
self-perceptions, changes in 113–14, 117
social disempowerment, male experience of 114–15
On Late Style (Said) 185
The Only Man on the Continent (Mora) *see* Darius-Kopp trilogy (Mora)
On the Rope (Mora) *see* Darius-Kopp trilogy (Mora)
Oughten, Elizabeth 2

Parlá, José 226
Patwardan, Anand 177
Pellegrino, Ed 17
performative approach to happiness 100–1, 105
Peter Schlemihl's Miraculous Story (Peter Schlemihls Wundersame Geschichte) (Chamisso) 104
Phillipson, Chris 42
photographing ageing 217–18
  see also *Wrinkles of the City* (JR)
Piccinini, Patricia 32–3
Pindell, Howardena 192
Port, Cynthia 107
positive ageing 170
practical wisdom of everyday experience 56–7
precarization of employment 146, 151
pronouns, identifying 239
A Proper Marriage (Lessing) 131, 134–5
Prospero's Books (Greenaway) 56
psychology of ageing, wisdom and 61–2
publications,
  collaboration issues 18
  interdisciplinary, low level of 17–18
  transparency in authorship 18–19

queer generations 237–9
  see also LGBT+ ageing
queer temporality 107

race
  classification of 205
  importance of to identity 207
  specific situations, use of term in as recommended 209–10
  see also Black artists; terminologies of racial/ethnic categories

reality of ageing, lack of willingness to confront 164
reframing
  LGBT+ ageing 232–7
  notion of 231
  by others 234–6
  positive 236–7
  self-reframing 232–4
The Rest is a Matter of Luck: On Satisfaction in Old Age (Der Rest ist Glückssache: Über Zufriedenheit im Alter) (documentary) 102–3
Reuchlin, Johannes 56
Ricoeur, Paul 117
Rilke, Rainer Maria 31–2
risk in making and viewing art 23, 33
Rosa, Hartmut 145
Routledge Handbook of Cultural Gerontology (Twigg and Martin) 14
Rowe, J.W. 3, 113n2
rulers/judges, wisdom of 56

Said, Edward 185–8, 193
Sarewitz, Daniel 28–9
Saunders, D. 170
Sawyer, Drew 219
sceptics and fools, wisdom of 57–8
Schatzberg, Rick 217
Segal, Lynn 128
self-healing concrete 34–5
sexuality
  and ageing, gender and 125–6, 127–8
  doubled consciousness of women 126–7
  double standard of ageing 125–6, 127–8
  subverting the double standard of ageing 134–5
Shakespeare, Tom 48
Sivaramakrishnan, Kavita 10
Small, Helen 99n2
social disempowerment, male experience of 114–15
Sohm, Philip 194
Solomon, wisdom of 56
Sontag, Susan 125
Sparschuh, Jens 103–8
Spencer, Robert 185–6
Staudinger, Ursula 63, 64–5, 141
Strout, Elizabeth see *Olive Kitteridge* and *Olive, Again* (Strout)

structural bodily exclusion 47
successful ageing 3–4, 113n2
  vs 'art of ageing' 41–3
  individual responsibility for 41
  midlife progress narratives compared 143
  new paradigm in gerontology 62
The Summer Before the Dark (Lessing) 130–2, 133
systemic inequalities of medicine 75–6

The Techno-Human Condition (Allenby and Sarewitz) 28–9
television
  cultural identity and 171
  representation of social issues 167
  representations of older people 171
  see also *Cocooned* (TV documentary)
The Tempest (Shakespeare) 56
terminologies of racial/ethnic categories
  ageing research and 201–2
  confusion and lack of clarity regarding 200–1
  culture 206
  dementia research 207–9
  emergence and development of 202–3
  epidemiological purposes for 203
  ethnicity 205–6
  France 204
  in gerontology 207
  identity, ethnicity and 206–7
  minoritized groups 199
  problems with 203–4, 209
  proliferation of 200
  race 205
  race/ethnicity confusion 203, 204–5
  skin tone and 201
  specific situations, use in as recommended 209–10
Third Age/Fourth Age 41–2
time as disorder 145–6
'Torso of an Archaic Apollo' ('Archaïscher Torso Apollos') (Rilke) 31–2
touch, absence of human 155–6
tremors, art and biomedicine/technology 30
triumphant/untriumphant narratives 43
Tsing, Anna Lowenhaupt 150
Twigg, Julia 14, 16, 114n3

untriumphant/triumphant narratives 43

Van der Beugel, Jacob 33–6
  'A Mutating Story' 23, *24*, 25, *25*
Varda, Agnès 216
visibility in old-age 2–3, 111–12

Walcott, Derek 185–6
Ward, Mark 162
The Way of All Flesh (Kinder)
  art of ageing 49
  attentive living 45
  darker sides of ageing 39
  finitude, art and living with 45–6
  grotesque, ageing and 46–9
  holding on to life, importance of 49
  illness trajectory 39
  illustrations 39, *40*, 46–9
  internalized ageism 44
  life as worth living 44–5
  reconsideration of healthy ageing 41
  refusal to fear death 41
  structure and style 43–4
'The Welcome Guest' (Piccinini) 32–3
Wernick, A. 170
Wilke, Thomas 102
wisdom
  age, connection with 54–5
  ancient models of 55
  Berlin Wisdom Paradigm 64–5
  circumstances needed to flourish 60
  compass 55–8
  as cross-cultural 59
  definition 54
  as embodied and engendered 59
  of fools and sceptics 57–8
  of judges/rulers 56
  as knowledge, type of 58–61
  of magicians and sages 56
  new research interest in 55
  old age, association with 59
  personal response required by 59–60
  practical, of everyday experience 56–7
  as practical knowledge 60
  psychological research on ageing and 61–2
  rediscovery of 63–5
  reshaping 66–7
  return of, reasons for 65–6

as trans-cultural topic in humanities 54–8
types of 55–8
Western culture and 61
women's 58
women
doubled consciousness 126–7
female agency/gender politics, absence of older women from 111–12
invisibility of older 111–12
wisdom 58
Women Are Heroes (JR) 219
Woodward, Kathleen 48, 111, 112
World Health Organization (WHO) 25
Wright, Richard 186n1
Wrinkles of the City (JR) 216, 217

commercial visual culture and *222*, 222–3
eyes, placement and emphasis on 225
Havana project *220*, 220–1
Los Angeles project *222*, 222–3
past/present and private/public 218–22
precarious placement of images 224–5
Shanghai project *224*, 224–5
stories in text accompanying 221–2, 227
universal and particular, ageing as 226–7
witnesses to change, subjects as 225
Women Are Heroes earlier project 219
working-class subjects 226

'The Young Family' (Piccinini) 32